I Think, Therefore I Know

Scientific Thinking for Unscientific Organizations

BRAD NELSON

This book reflects the author's views and experiences. It is provided for informational purposes only and is not intended as legal, medical, financial, or professional advice.

This book is a work of nonfiction. Names, examples, organizations, and scenarios are used for illustrative purposes.

Published by Katafy Press
Printed in the United States of America

ISBN: 979-8-9945321-0-2

Dedicated to my wife, for her patience and encouragement.

And to my kids, who continue to teach me how much there is left to learn.

And to you, for choosing to read this book.

Contents

You don't owe this book your time.
I tried to balance thoroughness with directness, including only what I believed mattered for the argument. I also understand the pressure many of us feel to "complete" books we start.
You don't need my permission, but I encourage you to step away once you feel you've obtained what you need. If it proves useful, the rest will be here when you need it.

Prologue

I learned to distrust management advice on the floor of a contract packaging plant in West Michigan.

I was a line lead on the afternoon shift—the critical window when most orders shipped. When work fell behind, it landed on my line. I had a reputation for meeting impossible timelines, which meant I was regularly handed impossible timelines.

Senior leadership would stay late to "support" these urgent runs. Sometimes the president himself lingered for an hour or two, watching. They were convinced they understood why my line succeeded. The explanation was simple and comforting: I was willing to throw bodies at the problem. More people meant more output. Basic math.

So, I let them have their version.

I fired up multiple lines, removed barriers between stations, and packed 60 workers into a space designed for 20. Leadership nodded approvingly and headed home for the night.

Then I shut it all down.

Once the executives left, I consolidated the work onto a single line with a small core team. The result was always the same. We delivered faster, with fewer defects, and with less frustration than the previous shift's fully staffed operation.

I didn't have language for what was happening. I only knew what I could see. The conventional explanation was wrong—and no one with authority wanted to learn why. They wanted the comfort of having their assumptions validated. When I succeeded in a way that contradicted their assumptions, the reaction wasn't interest. It was discomfort.

Years later, in a different role, in a different industry, I watched the same pattern play out. I was promoted to build a department that didn't exist. I was told the organization was data-driven. I grew the business and nobody noticed. Instead, I received complaints that I wasn't deferring to people who had no experience in the work and whose approaches hadn't worked. When I pointed to the data, it was ignored.

The more I looked, the wider the gap became. It wasn't confined to one leader, company, or industry. I interviewed at a company that sponsored one of the industry's most respected annual research on engineering performance to find out they didn't practice any of it. Another company, whose tool commonly forms the backbone of modern engineering operations, was only beginning its own transformation as a scripted playbook forced upon its teams. One of the most recognized names in technology, a company whose practices other organizations study and attempt to replicate, turned out to be the most plan-driven client my team ever served. When the contract came up for renewal, not a single person on my team wanted to stay on, despite the prestige. Two different companies famous for competing, widely adopted organizational models don't actually use them.

These are just *some* examples I've experienced. The pattern extends well beyond them. These aren't bad organizations. They are ordinary ones.

This book is about that gap.

The gap between what organizations say they want and what they actually reward. Between methods that work and methods that get approved. Between knowing the right answer and being allowed to act on it.

If you want a fantasy of how organizations should operate, there are plenty of books for that. This isn't one of them. What follows is a clear-eyed look at how systems really work, and what becomes possible once you understand them.

Let's start with how we know what we know.

PART ONE

How to Know

CHAPTER 1
What We Think We Know

"It is impossible for a person to learn what he thinks he already knows." – Epictetus

If this were a typical business book, this chapter wouldn't be here. You'd already be reading about synergy or the five habits of someone successful. But before we can talk about performance, leadership, or improvement, we need to be clear about how we decide what is true.

In a world increasingly defined by information, understanding where knowledge comes from matters as much as the knowledge itself. Every belief we hold, every decision we make, and every system we build is shaped by how we determine what is true. Yet we rarely pause to examine the methods we use to justify our conclusions.

While there are many ways humans come to "know" something, four methods dominate: intuition, authority, rationalism, and empiricism. Think of these as lenses you'll apply throughout the book—each reveals something the others miss, and each distorts in predictable ways.

1. **Intuition** – Intuition is knowledge that arises without conscious reasoning or explicit evidence, often shaped by experience, pattern recognition, and emotional response. It can appear as a gut feeling or immediate sense of truth. Intuition is fast and emotionally compelling, which makes it useful in situations where time is limited or precedent is

lacking. Human pattern recognition is arguably the most powerful cognitive tool any species has ever developed—synthesizing sensory data, emotional cues, cultural knowledge, and decades of experience into judgments that are frequently, astonishingly correct. However, it fires with equal confidence whether the pattern is real or imagined. This makes it deeply subjective, highly sensitive to bias, and unreliable as a sole basis for decision-making.

Intuition feels trustworthy because it evolved to keep us alive, not to make us optimal. If we listened to our taste buds, every day would be ice cream and pizza—in that order. Our bodies don't tell us when we've met our nutritional needs; they tell us when our stomachs feel full. Exercise feels uncomfortable in the moment, even though its results feel better over time. Desire and discomfort are signals—often competing ones—not instructions.

The same limitation applies to perception more broadly. Without experimentation, we would never know that mixing every color of paint produces black, while mixing every color of light produces white—or that color itself is not a property of objects, but a reaction created by receptors in our eyes. We did not need this understanding to see for thousands of years, but it has enabled countless modern advancements.

Many empirically supported truths feel unintuitive when first introduced. For that reason, intuition is best used directionally as a signal worth investigating, rather than as a conclusion to be trusted without validation.

2. **Authority** – Authority involves accepting knowledge from a perceived authority, such as a teacher, expert, institution, or body of consensus. This method is unavoidable in modern life; no individual can personally verify every medical guideline, scientific discovery, or historical fact they rely upon. Nor should they try. Trusting credentialed experts whose conclusions are grounded in empirical rigor is the entire basis for humanity's body of knowledge. Without it, many of our modern advancements would not exist today.

   However, authorities can be wrong, outdated, biased, or misaligned with reality. Likewise, not all figures who claim authority have earned it. Without critical evaluation, authoritative knowledge can obstruct reason and progress.

3. **Rationalism** – Rationalism derives knowledge through logic and reasoning. If the premises are true and the reasoning valid, the conclusion must also be true. Mathematics and

formal logic rely heavily on this method.
Rationalism assumes we can think our way to truth through pure logic but suffers from a limitation of perspective. We can only reason from what we know, and what we know is shaped by when and where we lived, who raised us, and which experiences registered as meaningful versus which we overlooked entirely. The Scandinavian executive and the American executive can apply identical logical frameworks to the same business problem and reach opposite conclusions because their context is not the same. They are shaped by different social safety nets, different cultural attitudes toward hierarchy, different historical relationships between corporations and the state, and so on.

4. **Empiricism** – Empiricism asserts that knowledge is obtained through observation, experience, and experimentation. It forms the foundation of the scientific process, relying on evidence that can be tested, replicated, and revised.
What distinguishes empiricism from the other methods is that it is self-correcting. Rather than defending beliefs, empiricism invites them to be challenged. New evidence does not threaten empirical knowledge—it improves it. For this reason, empiricism plays a central role in learning within complex and uncertain environments.

That said, empiricism does not exist in isolation. Its findings are still interpreted, communicated, and acted upon using intuition, authority, and reason. Understanding these interactions—and their limitations—is essential.

Empiricism depends on observation, but observation has inherent limits. We can only measure what we know to look for. And we can only notice patterns our experience has prepared us to recognize.

Your brain processes roughly 11 million bits of sensory information per second, but your conscious awareness can handle only a few dozen bits. To prevent overload, your Reticular Activating System (RAS) filters what reaches conscious attention based on what it's been trained to consider relevant. This is why you suddenly notice a particular car model everywhere after buying one—the cars were always there, but your RAS now tags them as worth noticing.

This filtering creates systematic blindness. Before germ theory, a doctor couldn't observe bacteria. The bacteria were there, but the conceptual framework for seeing them hadn't been built yet. They were literally invisible until someone developed tools and theories that made them observable. Even with modern microscopes, if you don't know what you're looking for, you can stare directly at the slide and see nothing meaningful.

Psychologist Richard Wiseman spent years studying why some people seem consistently lucky while others don't. His research revealed something unexpected: lucky people aren't actually experiencing more fortunate events. They're noticing more opportunities because they're looking for them. In one experiment, Wiseman asked subjects to count photographs in a newspaper. Halfway through, a half-page message appeared in large type: "Stop counting—there are 43 photographs in this newspaper." People who considered themselves unlucky missed it entirely, focused narrowly on their counting task. People who considered themselves lucky spotted it immediately. Same newspaper. Same information. Different outcomes based entirely on attentional breadth.

This has profound implications for empiricism. You can only discover what you're prepared to notice. Organizations optimizing for efficiency train people to ignore anything outside their immediate task—creating the same narrow focus that Wiseman's "unlucky" subjects exhibited. They see what they're measuring and miss everything else, even when it's spelled out in large type directly in front of them.

Imagination operates under similar constraints. We extrapolate from the known, combining and recombining elements we've already encountered. Truly novel concepts—ideas with no precedent in our experience—are nearly impossible to generate deliberately. We discover them by accident or through empirical observation that contradicts our expectations, forcing us to construct new frameworks. The history of science is full of researchers discovering phenomena they weren't looking for because their experiments produced results that made no sense within existing theory. Penicillin, X-rays, the cosmic microwave background—all were accidents noticed by people whose attention wasn't narrowed to the point of blindness.

This book itself relies on multiple methods of knowing. As the author, I am engaging in a form of authoritative knowledge transfer by asking you to consider ideas drawn from research, experience, and synthesis. Those ideas were likely sparked by intuition, refined through reason, and tested empirically over time.

My hope is that you don't accept these ideas on authority alone, but that you validate them for yourself. The notes at the end of this book are there for exactly that reason.

No one has access to absolute truth. Every belief, theory, and model is provisional—subject to revision as new information emerges. What we accept as "true" today may later prove incomplete or wrong.

Maintaining an open mind is not a weakness; it is a recognition of reality's complexity.

One of the most difficult decisions in writing this book was deciding that I had learned enough to begin. There are always more studies to read, more perspectives to consider, and more data to analyze. But learning, like progress, requires action.

A note on the vocabulary throughout this book: I'll introduce concepts, biases, frameworks, and failure modes as if they're distinct categories. They aren't. Reality doesn't arrive pre-sorted into categories with clear boundaries that are just waiting to have labels slapped on. These forces interact, amplify each other, and blur at the edges. A single bad decision might involve three biases operating simultaneously, all invisible to the people experiencing them. The taxonomy exists to make patterns recognizable, to give you handles for noticing what would otherwise remain hidden. But don't mistake the map for the territory. The world is messier than any singular text can capture, including this one.

Modern work—particularly in software development and product-driven organizations—takes place in environments defined by uncertainty, interdependence, and rapid change. In such contexts, intuition, authority, and rationalism alone are insufficient. Practices like Agile, Lean, DevOps, and user-centered design are all rooted—knowingly or not—in empirical learning cycles: experiment, observe, adapt.

Two thousand years ago, Marcus Aurelius articulated the epistemic problem in *Meditations*: everything we hear is an opinion, not a fact, and everything we see is a perspective, not the truth. These practices are not new. The lineage of empirical response stretches from Aristotle's early inquiry, through the Scientific Revolution, to modern operational frameworks. What is new is the scale and speed at which decisions now ripple through complex systems.

The challenge, as we will explore throughout this book, is that humans and organizations often default to the least reliable methods of knowing—especially under pressure. Understanding how we know is the first step toward improving how we work. But understanding how is incomplete without examining why we seek knowledge in the first place—and why organizations so often suppress that drive.

CHAPTER 2
What Drives Us

"The drive to learn is as fundamental as the drive to breathe. Curiosity is the brain's way of ensuring its own survival."
– Dr. Bruce Perry

From the moment we are born, our bodies rapidly grow and our brains start building. We absorb, connect, and problem-solve before we have words for any of it. Learning isn't something we're taught to do. It's what the hardware does by default.

Eventually the body matures into adulthood, and while it continues to change throughout our entire life, for all intents and purposes, it stops growing. Or at least, we hope it does, because if it continues to grow it is generally in unflattering ways.

The mind, on the other hand, remains capable of endless expansion. In fact, research has shown that one's brain maintains a level of plasticity throughout our entire life. Plasticity, or neuroplasticity, is not the amount of microplastics in one's brain, but its ability to physically adapt to the demands put on it.

Scientists noticed that humans and animals who relied heavily on memory for navigation had larger-than-average hippocampi—the brain's memory center. They studied aspiring London cab drivers before they started their rigorous training and after. These drivers would spend years memorizing tens of thousands of streets and landmarks to pass their exam. Through brain imaging, scientists were able to observe this part of the brain increase in mass during this rigorous training.

There have been multiple studies where doctors introduced elderly individuals at risk of dementia to neurobic exercise. Neurobics are brain exercises that stimulate the neuronal systems and increase blood circulation to the brain. After just 4 weeks of these activities, the patients showed significant improvement in overall cognitive function.

Consequently, intellectual stimulation is a fundamental human need. We don't have to motivate infants to learn. They are naturally curious and absorb information at an astounding rate. They engage with their surroundings empirically, constantly testing and refining their understanding.

If I drop this cup, it falls every time. If I move my limbs in a certain way, I might achieve motion. Through relentless experimentation, babies decipher the world around them. As we age, intrinsic curiosity does not disappear, but it is often no longer our default mode. As neural pathways stabilize, the brain increasingly relies on established patterns to navigate the world efficiently. This efficiency enables increasingly complex and coordinated action, but it comes with a side effect: *heuristics* and *biases*—neural shortcuts that conserve cognitive effort by relying on previously learned patterns rather than ongoing exploration.

Over time, exploration gives way to execution. Learning becomes something we must practice deliberately rather than something we do automatically. As neuroplasticity decreases with age, a use-it-or-lose-it dynamic emerges. Social and organizational structures often reinforce this shift by rewarding speed, certainty, and decisive conclusions over inquiry. Practices such as neurobics intentionally reintroduce friction, interrupting automatic pathways and restoring the conditions necessary for learning in complex environments. Beyond performance, this kind of cognitive engagement is also critical for long-term brain health.

However, when we fall out of practice, learning can begin to feel foreign. Neuroplasticity decreases and the brain becomes literally and figuratively more rigid. This compounds when work environments are no longer safe to learn in. Our natural curiosity soon becomes suppressed. It's no longer a question of what is natural, but what we are motivated to do.

Exercising our brains may be healthy for us, but knowing something is good for us has never been enough to make us do it—otherwise there would be no smokers, soda companies wouldn't exist, and we'd never skip the gym. Knowledge, it turns out, is necessary but insufficient. Which should make us suspicious of any approach that treats information transfer as the solution to behavioral problems.

If you are a parent or have spent considerable time around newly born humans (babies, as they are often referred to), it may seem quite apparent that babies are people. And as people, they seem to enter this world with a mind of their own. Their motivations often appear chaotic, sometimes even finding glee from our anguish.

With no sense of reason, cause and effect, or sympathy for the person who has to clean up after their experiments, they are motivated by an innate curiosity of the world around them. And yet, they can often be cajoled by a wave of a cookie or mesmerized by flicking on their favorite program. So, are they motivated by their own whims or the cookie?

The cookie is both an extrinsic motivator and a behavioral response. Behavior is an incredibly complicated thing. We will explore this more in the last chapter of this book, but for now it is important to understand that behavior becomes more automatic when one feels a positive emotion or the relief from a negative one. However, because human beings are complex animals, behaviors and motivation are not the same thing.

When we explore motivators, there are two distinct groups: extrinsic motivators (the expectation of reward or punishment) and intrinsic motivators (things you do because you enjoy it and get personal satisfaction from doing it). Because this is important not only for understanding why we seek knowledge, but also how companies can get the most out of their employees, let's explore these two motivators a bit more.

This distinction doesn't just explain personal behavior. It explains why one of the most common management practices, annual goals, consistently fails to produce the results leaders expect. While it may seem intuitive for leaders to leverage goals as a form of direction and gauge for performance, there is actually no research that validates these assumed benefits.

In fact, research shows that they tend to have the opposite effect on employees. At best, employees and managers just go through the motions to avoid showing up on a compliance list. At worst, it results in artificial ceilings, lack of adaptability, demotivation, and is a distraction from the work at hand.

I certainly remember a time I went back and forth with my manager ad nauseam because he didn't approve of my goals but insisted I write them myself. I think we both left that experience frustrated.

On top of these practices having the opposite effect, they tend to be very costly to perform. Deloitte estimated they were spending close to half a billion on this harmful routine, and Accenture discovered they were spending double, for close to a billion USD, on an activity that at best did nothing.

Just as goals are not effective for motivation, they likewise are not effective for performance review because there is no control group or standard scale for comparing the benefit of achieving each goal. Furthermore, people are often already working on the items that they are capturing as their goals or they will be responding to work requests from the broader organization, regardless of what has been documented.

In a global multi-sector survey, Brightline Initiative found that 90 percent of senior executives reported not attaining their annual goals, emphasizing how rarely these targets are met.

Instead of relying on this archaic process, it is more effective to rely on the intrinsic motivation of purpose or connection, which we will unpack shortly and discuss in further detail in Chapter 10 on leadership.

Extrinsic motivators in the form of financial gain are effective for fulfilling basic physiological and security needs. Beyond that, they lose their effectiveness and may even diminish motivation. The reason positive extrinsic motivators (such as pay raises, promotions, or bonuses) are ineffective in the long term is due to human psychology.

As Shawn Achor explains, we continuously move the goalpost. Achieving a desired outcome only leads to a new ambition: better grades, a higher batting average, a more prestigious job, and so on. This cycle can even lead to dissatisfaction, as individuals realize they are not as happy as they expected, ultimately backfiring on motivation.

Some might assume that keeping people financially insecure could sustain motivation. But research shows financial stress impairs cognitive performance. Individuals under financial strain exhibit a deficit equivalent to a thirteen-point IQ reduction, comparable to losing an entire night's sleep.

To better understand why this approach, as well as extrinsic motivators as a whole, are ineffective, it's best to explore intrinsic motivators.

Self-Determination Theory (SDT)—not to be confused with STD, which research suggests is considerably less motivating—is a macro theory from the mid-1980s developed by psychologists Edward Deci and Richard Ryan. It holds that when external persuasion is removed (the cookie), people are most motivated when three basic psychological needs are met. They called these Autonomy, Competence, and Relatedness. I prefer Control, Competence, and

Connection—the 3C's are easier to remember, and the language maps more directly to workplace dynamics. Also, 'Relatedness' sounds like family therapy, and I'd rather not trigger anyone's Thanksgiving flashbacks.

Control – The ability to act with autonomy, free from excessive external influence.

Competence – The capability to perform tasks successfully and efficiently.

Connection – A sense of belonging and meaningful relationships with others.

Research has shown that a sense of control is the most significant factor in determining an individual's level of fatigue, regardless of the physical demands of their job.

When exploring control or autonomy, I find it is often helpful to reflect on what a lack of control looks like. A lack of control manifests in numerous ways: limited decision-making power, excessive oversight, rigid processes, mandatory tasks and deadlines, and an inability to voice concerns. In general, it's a response to extrinsic motivators.

These stressors activate the body's fight-or-flight response, prompting the adrenal glands to release *cortisol*.

Cortisol prepares the body for immediate threats by shutting down nonessential functions (for the record, it does not survey what it considers nonessential, or perhaps it's lost in my junk mail). One such function is dopamine production. *Dopamine*, a neurotransmitter crucial to motivation, pleasure, and learning, is essential for maintaining focus and reinforcing positive behaviors. When cortisol inhibits dopamine production, individuals experience decreased enjoyment, impaired concentration, and diminished cognitive function.

Cortisol also increases the consumption of *serotonin*, another vital neurotransmitter responsible for mood regulation, alertness, and willpower. Serotonin is the chemical that promotes waking up in the morning, and is a precursor for melatonin, which informs the body when it is time to rest. When serotonin levels are low, individuals may become irritable, anxious, depressed, lose interest, and experience sleep disturbances.

The depletion of dopamine and serotonin explains the cognitive decline linked to stress, reinforcing the idea that happiness precedes success, not the other way around. In the wise words of Stevie Wonder, "You will never feel proud of your work if you find no joy within it; your best work is always joyful work."

This provides biological rationale for avoiding extrinsic motivators that attempt to either entice through reward or coerce through stress. Prolonged elevated cortisol levels are even known to negatively impact all bodily systems. Studies indicate that up to 90 percent of doctor visits stem from stress-related ailments.

The consequences extend beyond waiting rooms. A study of more than ten thousand patients across Ireland found that the most severe type of heart attack—the kind caused by a complete blockage of a coronary artery—occurs at significantly higher rates on Monday mornings than any other time of the week. Researchers reported a 13 percent increase at the start of the working week, consistent with what we know about circadian rhythms, cortisol spikes, and the cardiovascular strain they produce.

The human stress response evolved to help us survive acute threats. It does not differentiate between physical danger and social or performance-related pressure; it simply responds to perceived demand. When the structure of work reliably concentrates stress at predictable moments, biology follows.

Competence, or personal mastery, is the second key intrinsic motivator. In *The Fifth Discipline: The Art & Practice of The Learning Organization*, Peter Senge describes mastery as an ongoing process rather than a fixed achievement:

"People with a high level of personal mastery live in a continual learning mode. They never 'arrive.' Sometimes, language, such as the term 'personal mastery,' creates a misleading sense of definiteness, of black and white. But personal mastery is not something you possess. It is a process. It is a lifelong discipline. People with a high level of personal mastery are acutely aware of their ignorance, their incompetence, their growth areas. And they are deeply self-confident. Paradoxical? Only for those who do not see that 'the journey is the reward.'"

This philosophy underscores the innate human drive for growth. When individuals are encouraged to develop new skills and expand their knowledge, they remain engaged and motivated. As a result, environments that cultivate continuous learning outperform those that rely on rigid processes and fixed mindsets.

In learning environments, a purpose only needs to be provided, and people will naturally seek the means to accomplish it.

The third intrinsic motivator, connection, is fundamental to human well-being. Humans are inherently social creatures, wired to seek community and belonging. Studies demonstrate that positive social interactions reduce pain, anxiety, and stress while boosting mood through increased *oxytocin* production.

Oxytocin interacts with serotonin pathways, making it integral to emotional resilience and overall happiness. In fact, social connection is one of the strongest predictors of life satisfaction and longevity.

In the workplace, strong interpersonal relationships enhance engagement, productivity, reliability, innovation, and collaboration. Employees with close workplace friendships are more likely to be engaged and exhibit higher levels of performance. Companies that foster meaningful connections create resilient, motivated teams capable of overcoming challenges and driving sustainable success.

Another way of creating connection is by providing a purpose. Humans long for purpose—a sense of being part of something greater than oneself, a reason for being. Gallup found that employees are the most engaged and productive when they feel their work contributes to something meaningful beyond just a paycheck.

Employees who are intrinsically motivated are more likely to be engaged than their extrinsically motivated counterparts. Research indicates that highly engaged employees lead to 10 percent higher customer advocacy, 17 percent higher productivity, and 21 percent greater profitability. Conversely, low engagement results in 24 percent more turnover, 28 percent more shrinkage, and 70 percent more workplace accidents.

Given this data, intrinsic motivation is the clear choice for companies seeking to maximize their investment in their employees. Investing in your most valuable asset, and likely most expensive one, benefits everyone. While conventional wisdom might suggest otherwise, empirical data paints a clear and compelling picture.

Humans are motivated by the same forces in both their personal and professional lives because they are, quite simply, the same person in both settings. Even if we could sever work from personal life, like in Apple's sci-fi drama *Severance*, the fundamental drivers of human motivation would remain unchanged.

At our core, humans have an innate desire to learn. What we choose to learn is shaped by three intrinsic motivators: control, competence, and connection. Unlike machines, humans cannot be forced or coerced into true learning. Instead, we thrive when these intrinsic motivators are nurtured, whether in ourselves, our children, our friends, or our colleagues.

So, ask yourself: why are you reading this book right now?

CHAPTER 3

The Science of Good Enough

"Science is a way of thinking much more than it is a body of knowledge." – Carl Sagan

Humans have a romanticized notion that the world is orderly and rational. We build plans, forecasts, and metrics as if uncertainty were a temporary inconvenience rather than a permanent condition. Despite overwhelming evidence to the contrary, we cling to the illusion of control over the uncontrollable. This is the comedy of the human condition. Ironically, part of the reason for this misconception is that humans themselves are not rational creatures to begin with.

The more a person pays for medicine, the more likely they are to report it as effectively treating their symptoms. However, paradoxically, the more people pay for medicine, the less likely they are to take it as directed. Similarly, when bundling a low-value item with a high-value item, consumers are willing to pay less than when purchasing the high-value item alone.

To complicate matters further, humans often believe in things without fully understanding the reasoning behind them. This is fine when it comes to things like gravity, which will inevitably pull you back down every time you jump, regardless of whether you believe in it or not. Amusingly, even scientists do not fully understand gravity, yet they still manage to strap mammals to giant controlled explosions and catapult them into outer space.

In organizations, these tendencies don't stay abstract. Instead, they shape hiring, planning, investment, and what gets defended versus questioned. Where this becomes a problem is when people believe in things without any supporting evidence whatsoever. In fact, studies show that evidence itself is generally not very convincing to most people. The irony is that data shows that data is not effective. Which presents a problem for a book arguing in favor of evidence.

Humans tend to cling to prior beliefs even when confronted with conflicting data, a phenomenon known as *belief perseverance*. In some cases, exposure to contradicting evidence can even strengthen existing beliefs, a cognitive quirk known as the *backfire effect*. Additionally, people selectively search for evidence that aligns with their current beliefs (*confirmation bias*) and employ *motivated reasoning* to justify beliefs when they are emotionally convenient.

The next challenge has to do with how the brain operates. Through a function known as heuristics, humans have adapted mental shortcuts that allow for quick decision-making. This is incredibly useful for habitual tasks like brushing one's teeth or making coffee in the morning, which is critical before the brain is fully caffeinated.

However, heuristics also lead to *cognitive illusions*, such as the *illusion of explanatory depth*, where people overestimate their understanding of a topic, believing they grasp complex concepts more deeply than they actually do. In other words, people rely on assumptions. The true extent of their misunderstanding only becomes evident when they are asked to explain these complex concepts in detail.

This illusion is particularly difficult to overcome because it is often perceived as *confidence*. Confidence is a powerful social signal, shaped by evolutionary pressures that favored decisiveness under uncertainty. Research in evolutionary psychology demonstrates that humans are wired to interpret confidence as evidence of capability, a shortcut that worked well in environments where feedback was immediate and hesitation could be fatal.

The challenge is that these primitive signals remain dominant in modern, knowledge-driven organizations. In systems where learning is slow, feedback is delayed, and outcomes are ambiguous, overt confidence often replaces evidence. This creates what I call the *confidence signal fallacy*—the mistaken belief that confidence is a reliable indicator of competence. In practice, this appears as a *confidence proxy error*, where decisiveness is substituted for evidence in decision-making, evaluation, and leadership selection.

Organizational research studies have found that confidence increases perceived leadership potential regardless of actual competence. Furthermore, groups continue to perceive confident individuals positively even after learning their claimed ability exceeds their actual performance. The confidence signal fallacy persists even when contradicted by evidence.

Social psychologists David Dunning and Justin Kruger noted that as capability increases, self-assessed certainty often decreases. When a person is new to a subject or skill, they are unaware of the depth available to that domain and thus feel more certain of their understanding and abilities. Whereas the person who has deeply studied a domain recognizes how much they do not know. This led to the observation that low performers systematically overestimate their abilities, while high-performers tend to underestimate theirs. This *paradox of confidence* is commonly known as the *Dunning-Kruger Effect*.

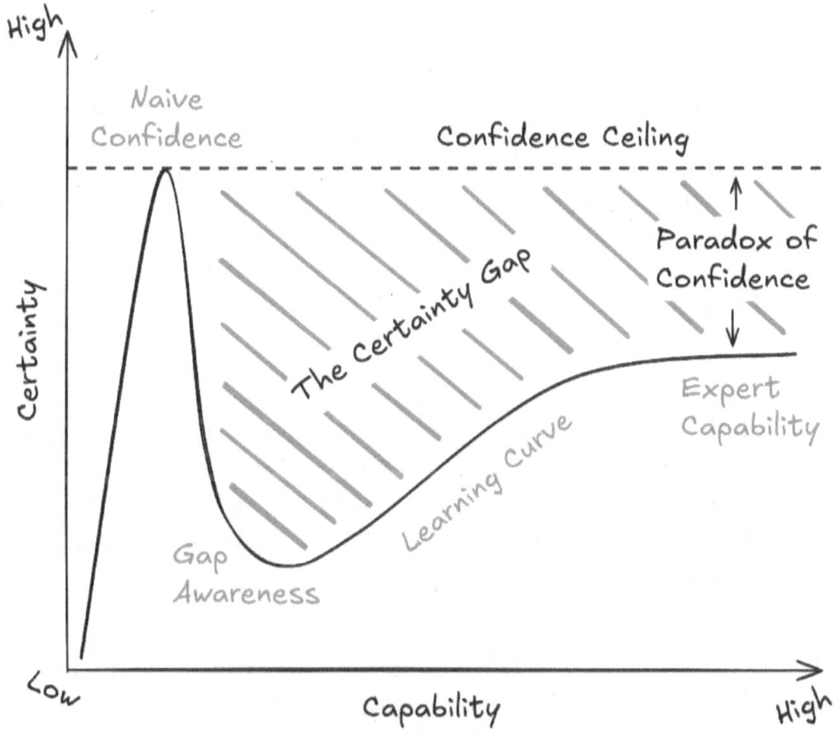

Figure 3.1 - The Dunning-Kruger Curve (adapted)

This creates what I call the *certainty gap*. Organizations calibrate their expectations for confidence based on those who are naïve to the depth of knowledge required—and that becomes the threshold everyone is judged against. And those with that deep capability are often viewed as not confident, resulting in what might be called *the humility trap*—the misperception of lower competency and/or confidence when a person of higher capability and confidence is comfortable acknowledging uncertainty.

This means empirical thinking carries an inherent social disadvantage. It begins with acknowledged uncertainty and earns confidence through action. Ironically, approaches that project confidence often spend the most time trying to guarantee certainty before acting—the opposite of what their presentation suggests. What is often missed is that uncertainty about answers is not the same as a lack of confidence in method. Scientific and empirical thinking do not promise certainty of conclusions; they provide confidence that we have the capability to discover, test, and revise our conclusions over time.

To consistently make effective business decisions, we must accept the inherent irrationality of humans rather than rely on a misplaced belief in their rationality. Humans are, at least, predictably irrational. The challenge then is how to encourage individuals to recognize their biases and engage in a method that counters them.

One approach is to build a foundation for rational analysis that provides clear, repeatable ways to test and refine ideas, helping people see for themselves where their intuition might lead them astray. Great minds before us have devised such a system for testing inductive reasoning against cognitive biases.

Scientific thinking is a set of underlying mental routines of the scientific process. It's a way of reacting to situations. This approach involves using observations, experiments, and reasoning to test ideas and gain knowledge. It applies empiricism to everyday situations (remember: empiricism stresses that knowledge can only be obtained through observation). Scientific thinking is a meta-skill that helps people learn and adapt to new situations, and like any skill, it can be improved through practice.

The term 'scientific thinking' was first used by John Dewey in his *Learning By Doing* philosophy in the 1910s. Nearly a century later, Mike Rother's work on *Toyota Kata* has been instrumental in demonstrating how scientific thinking can be systematically developed and used to good effect in organizations. Rother's contribution was showing how to teach it as a deliberate practice rather than hoping people absorb it through osmosis.

While Aristotle is often credited with formalizing our reasoning system in the 300s BCE, the structured approach to scientific reasoning wouldn't gain prominence until Sir Francis Bacon refined it during the Scientific Revolution of the 16th and 17th centuries. Based on the hypothetico-deductive model, the term 'scientific method' emerged in the 19th century as scientific institutions sought to clarify the boundary between science and non-science.

The scientific method begins with an idea, a thought, a guess, a hypothesis—in other words, a posit that could, in principle, be proven wrong. You gather evidence through tests, evaluate whether results support or refute the idea, and critically, you expect others to reproduce your findings. Science is communal. If only you can produce the result, it's not science. It's a magic trick.

The scientific process was popularized as the scientific method by John Dewey's book *How We Think* in the 1910s and later visualized in the 1920s by physicist Walter Shewhart of Bell Telephone Laboratories. The process can be summarized as hypothesis, experiment, evaluation or plan, do, study.

Dr. Shewhart emphasized that observers should act on their findings, leading to the creation of a cyclical model: plan, do, study, act. Popularized by Shewhart's colleague and protégé, W. Edwards Deming, this would later be referred to as the Shewhart Cycle, Deming Cycle, or Control Circle before being shortened to the now-familiar PDCA (Plan-Do-Check-Act). 'Study' was changed to 'check' for purely preferential reasons by JUSE in 1950 and was something Deming felt lost the nuance required to analyze and understand necessary improvements.

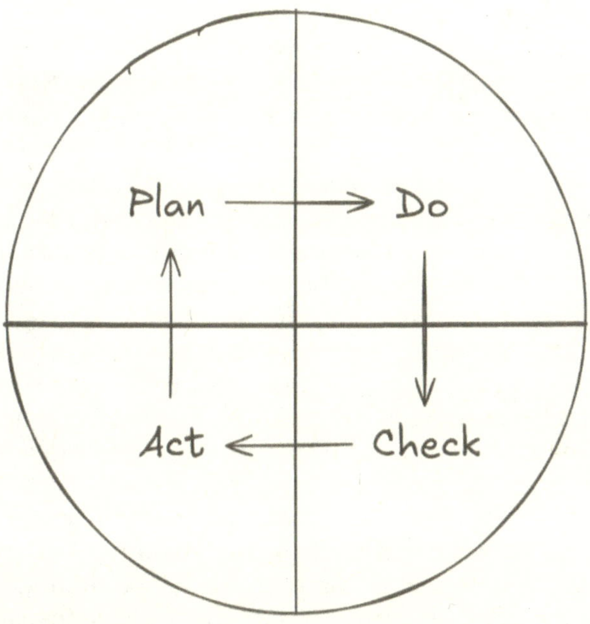

Figure 3.2 - PDCA Cycle

PDCA emphasizes the four cyclic phases of the scientific method as defined by Shewhart:

> **Plan**: Define the desired outcome and hypothesize what actions will achieve the intended results.
>
> **Do**: Implement the plan.
>
> **Check**: Validate the results of the actions. Did they achieve the desired effect?
>
> **Act**: Integrate the findings from the previous step to inform the next Plan phase.

Dr. W. Edwards Deming introduced PDCA to Japan during its post-war reconstruction where it became the foundation of the Toyota Production System and Lean Manufacturing. The Scientific Method and PDCA would go on to inspire numerous business methodologies, including User-Experience Research, Product Management, DevOps, and beyond.

Jeffrey Liker's documentation of the Toyota Production System reveals how Toyota operationalized PDCA beyond manufacturing into organizational culture. What Toyota understood, and what most Western implementations miss, is that PDCA isn't a project management tool. It's a learning system. The cycle forces acknowledgment that plans are hypotheses, that execution generates data, and that adjustment based on evidence is expected rather than treated as failure.

While PDCA provides structure, Mike Rother observed that most organizations struggle to apply it effectively. In *Toyota Kata*, he identified that knowing the steps isn't enough—people need practice developing the mindset and habits of scientific thinking that make PDCA meaningful rather than mechanical. Intellectually, you can teach someone the 4-step cycle in 5 minutes. Teaching them to actually think and react scientifically—to recognize assumptions, design experiments, be open to interpreting results honestly, adjusting based on what they learn—requires sustained practice, usually with coaching (otherwise you just practice your existing mindset). This is why organizations send people to training on Agile or Lean and see minimal lasting change. They're teaching frameworks without building the underlying capability those frameworks assume.

PDCA provides structure but applying it effectively requires recognizing what kind of problem you're facing. Something *complicated* may be difficult to understand, but with enough documentation, it remains comprehensible. Something *complex*, on the other hand, is inherently unpredictable and resistant to rigid control.

Take a watch, for example. It has intricate, moving parts, but those parts fit together the same way every time. The process of assembling a watch can be documented and reliably replicated.

Henry Ford famously applied this principle over a century ago with the Ford Assembly Line. Every automobile component was standardized, processes were optimized to eliminate unnecessary movements, and labor was divided into repetitive, specialized tasks. Standard Operating Procedures (SOPs) were developed (typically by engineers who designed the parts) and served as a starting point. However, it wasn't until skilled laborers applied these procedures repeatedly that inefficiencies were tempered through experience. This refinement process allowed Ford to reduce Model T assembly time to just 90 minutes within its first 5 years.

While the car itself was complicated, this optimization is a classic example of the PDCA cycle in action:

- **Plan:** Design the SOP.
- **Do:** Run the assembly line.
- **Check:** Measure the time and identify bottlenecks.
- **Act:** Adjust the workstations or tools to improve the flow.

IKEA is another example of SOP-driven assembly where the end results are known, except their assembly instructions are designed for customers. Lean Manufacturing emphasizes creating customer-perceived value by eliminating *waste*. Waste is anything the customer isn't willing to pay for. IKEA takes this to another level by treating assembly itself as waste, shifting that responsibility to the customer, and passing the cost savings along. The clarity of their SOPs is critical; any inefficiencies are painfully obvious when you're the one assembling the furniture.

Watches, cars, and furniture share a common trait: the work of assembly, however intricate, remains complicated—not complex. The components, the sequence, and the outcome are all knowable in advance. While it may seem logical to apply the same structured approach to other business decisions, most modern organizations are engaged in work where the "SOP" cannot be written in advance. Any decision reliant on customer behavior is inherently complex because the variables are constantly shifting. Likewise, thought work and creative pursuits fall into the same category, including many facets of software development.

David Epstein offers a useful frame for this distinction: 'kind' versus 'wicked' learning environments. In kind environments, patterns repeat and feedback is immediate, and therefore practice makes perfect. In wicked environments, the patterns shift and feedback misleads. Most business decisions happen in wicked territory, where assuming repeatability becomes a liability.

If complex work resists prediction and control, then the pursuit of certainty becomes not just impractical but counterproductive. This is where a concept called *satisficing* reframes the problem entirely.

Satisficing is a decision-making strategy introduced by Herbert Simon in his 1947 publication *Administrative Behavior*. It is often used in complex, unpredictable environments where perfect solutions are impractical.

In his Nobel Prize acceptance speech for Economics, Simon observed: "Decision-makers can satisfice either by finding optimum solutions for a simplified world, or by finding satisfactory solutions for a more realistic world. Neither approach, in general, dominates the other, and both have continued to co-exist in the world of management science."

This insight highlights a fundamental tension in decision-making: should we optimize within a controlled, theoretical framework, or should we seek "good enough" solutions that align with the messy realities of the world? "Good enough" means recognizing when additional certainty is unavailable rather than undesirable. The standard isn't perfection—it's sufficiency for the decision at hand. Both approaches have their place and understanding when to apply each is key to effective decision-making.

The opposite of satisficing is *maximizing*, the relentless pursuit of the "best possible" outcome rather than a "good enough" solution. On the surface, this may seem like a responsible strategy. After all, why settle for good when you can have the best?

The problem is that maximizing assumes perfection is attainable, or worse, that the cost of pursuing it is always justified. In reality, the pursuit of an optimal solution in an unpredictable world often leads to decision paralysis, diminishing returns, and perfectionism hindering progress. In complex environments where variables shift and outcomes are uncertain, waiting for the perfect solution often means making no decision at all.

Consider a startup that refuses to release its new app because leadership keeps adding features and refining details. They may lose their competitive timing to a competitor who launched an imperfect solution, allowing them to collect feedback and iteratively improve based on real-world usage. These customers may be lost indefinitely. Not only because of the superior refinement of the competitor's product over time, but due to the many cognitive biases that hold users to their initial choices. Anchoring bias, path dependence, status quo bias, first-mover bias, and the endowment effect all contribute to the inertia that makes customers less likely to switch, even if a better product emerges later. Thus, in the oft-attributed words of Voltaire, *Le mieux est l'ennemi du bien* ("The best is the enemy of good.").

This is why modern approaches attempt to mitigate complexity by reducing the scope and duration of both planning and doing, allowing reality to continuously inform and refine the plan. Rooted in the scientific process, this approach promotes iterative learning and adaptation.

This makes rational sense: if complex work is inherently unpredictable and uncontrollable, then the best way to reduce risk is through constant validation. Rother calls this the 'Improvement Kata'—his term for a model for navigating uncertainty. Rother and his colleagues then developed practice routines, which they call 'Starter Kata,' for each phase of the model.

In the Improvement Kata model, you establish where you're trying to go, understand your current condition, experiment toward the target, and reflect on what you learn. Combined with the Starter Kata practice routines, it's PDCA made tangible and teachable. The power isn't in the four-step pattern—that's been known for a century—but in making the thinking process teachable and coachable. You can't teach someone to "think scientifically" through lecture. Likewise, sharing a link to your process documentation won't be any more effective. It's like trying to learn Tae Kwon Do from a book—even with pop-ups. But you can coach them through repeated cycles of articulating target conditions, describing current reality precisely, identifying the next obstacle, designing small experiments, and reflecting on results. Through repetition, the pattern becomes habitual.

Despite this, companies still attempt to compile exhaustive lists of everything required to achieve a desired outcome. These documents are often built on inference rather than rigorous observation, constructed by people removed from the hands-on work. Complex work cannot be controlled or predicted, yet organizations invest excessive time in planning as if an ideal duration exists where all variables can be accounted for. The truth is, the longer we plan, the more outdated our plan becomes—we know the least before starting the work.

Yet teams often reintroduce unreliable techniques that undermine the very benefits of an evidence-based approach. The most insidious examples are methods that look scientific without being empirical.

Nowhere is this more visible than in software development, where teams often adopt estimation rituals that promise predictability but rarely deliver it. Consultants and influencers often appeal to reasoning biases by arguing that humans are better at estimating effort than time. For example, washing dishes requires less effort than changing a car's brakes, and brushing your teeth is easier than brushing a horse. Even if you've never changed brakes or brushed a horse, your brain's inductive reasoning allows you to consistently and accurately compare one task against another.

This idea serves as the foundation for estimation frameworks, often framed as a clever "hack" for improving predictability. However, the boundaries of complex work are inherently opaque, and the uncomfortable reality is that humans are resoundingly bad at estimation altogether. In the end, these methods may produce vaguely accurate results rather than precisely wrong ones, but they remain dependent on flawed data and abstract comparisons that ultimately reinforce the same estimation pitfalls they claim to solve. They also can cost a lot of time to implement.

For example, if you have worked in software development, you have likely encountered the common practice of using the Fibonacci sequence to assign points to work items. These point values are then averaged over time as *velocity*. While it all sounds very *sciencey*, and it certainly may have some redeeming qualities, there is no real evidence of efficacy or overall business impact.

Furthermore, this approach suffers from the *Flaw of Averages*, which can be dangerously misleading. Consider this scenario: The average sale is $1 million. However, in reality, there's a 50 percent chance of a $2 million sale and a 50 percent chance of a $0 sale. If a company invests $900,000, assuming the $1 million average will hold, multiple $0 sales could lead to bankruptcy. The key takeaway is that averages obscure uncertainty and variability. Instead, businesses should always consider the full range of possible outcomes rather than relying on misleading point estimates.

If these common methods fail us, what replaces them? The challenge in applying scientific thinking is finding the right balance of rigor for the risk at hand. Changing a button on a webpage from blue to green carries negligible risk. Completely overhauling your highest-grossing product carries significant risk. The level of validation required should align with the potential consequences of being wrong. And even when you've calibrated the right level of rigor, you're likely not going to be able to set up truly accurate controls due to the complex world we inhabit. Scientists struggle with this too.

Over-reliance on data can lead to decision paralysis, where teams hesitate to act without a perfect dataset. Measuring for the sake of measuring is a waste of resources and can easily lead to *focus bias*, where individuals assign undue importance to certain metrics simply because they are being tracked. Instead, be intentional. Measure what truly matters and ensure that data serves decision-making rather than becoming a distraction.

This brings us to a distinction that separates organizations that learn from organizations that merely collect data. *Data-driven* organizations treat empiricism as the only valid input—which sounds rigorous until you realize they've simply replaced one form of overconfidence with another.

Data must be assessed holistically to ensure that conclusions align with reality. For example, if someone's goal is to lose weight and the scale shows a downward trend, it would be easy to assume that their actions are correct. But context matters. If the weight loss was due to an amputation, most people would agree that this outcome is far less desirable than weight loss itself. This mirrors the medicine pricing paradox from earlier—patients reported better outcomes from expensive placebos not because the treatment worked, but because perception shaped their experience of it. Data without context deceives in both directions. Being *data-informed* means using data as a guiding tool while also considering qualitative factors, human judgment, and contextual knowledge—acknowledging that not all valuable insights can be captured in numbers.

Being data-informed also requires resisting the urge to react to every piece of feedback or new information as if it were a directive. A single complaint, survey response, or anecdote is data, but it is not evidence of a pattern. Treating isolated signals as mandates leads organizations to thrash. It is natural to want to please everyone, but it is not possible to do so. Attempts to satisfy every voice ultimately result in pleasing no one—and in preventing anything meaningful from being completed.

The same failure appears in competitive behavior. When organizations fixate on what competitors are doing, they often respond to visible moves without understanding the system that produced them. Those competitors may themselves be reacting just as blindly, creating chains of imitation rather than learning. Features are copied, processes are mimicked, and priorities are reshuffled—not because the evidence supports the change, but because inaction feels riskier than restraint. This is reaction, not empiricism.

Learning is the ability to recognize patterns and connect signals over time. A single incident is not yet a signal; it is a blip—noise that may never repeat. Novelty rarely appears fully formed or in isolation. It tends to emerge laterally, as ideas intersect across disciplines, domains, and industries, rather than from chasing each new data point as it appears.

Deductive reasoning begins with a premise and tests whether specific conclusions logically follow. When the premise itself goes unexamined or is chosen because it aligns with what we already want to believe, deduction can become a tool for justification rather than understanding. In those cases, conflicting evidence is easy to dismiss while elevating confirming data, a pattern closely tied to motivated reasoning and confirmation bias.

Inductive reasoning works in the opposite direction, forming conclusions from patterns in the evidence rather than imposing them in advance. While we will rely on both throughout this book, the distinction is critical: inductive reasoning encourages learning and adaptation, while deduction, when built on shaky or unquestioned premises, can lock organizations into rigid thinking and selective interpretation of data.

Perfectionism is the antithesis of empiricism—and the enemy of satisficing. It's something I've wrestled with in my own work, and something I've had to consciously resist in writing this. The scientific process understands that the perfect answer cannot be found through excessive refinement. It is uncovered through iterative and incremental refinement based on observable feedback. The faster one can enact these feedback loops, the faster they can learn.

In the end, success doesn't come from making the perfect decision every time. It comes from making good decisions quickly, acting on them, and refining based on what you learn. PDCA provides a simple yet powerful way to operationalize this method, encouraging a deliberate pause to ask: What basis am I using to make this decision? How will I validate it? By continuously refining our understanding through iteration, we move away from intuition-based decision-making and toward a more structured, evidence-informed approach.

These ideas are not independent—they compound. Pattern-seeking, certainty, and narrative construction reinforce each other, creating explanations that feel true long before they are tested. The chapters ahead examine what happens when organizations build entire systems on top of those explanations.

PART TWO

Understanding the System

CHAPTER 4
Incentives Without Intent

"As betting at race ring adds neither strength nor speed to the horse, so the exchange of shares in the stock market adds no capital to business, no increase in the production and no purchasing power to the market." – Henry Ford

As Scottish philosopher David Hume pointed out in *A Treatise of Human Nature*, people often conflate facts and values in debate. We live in a time when individuals increasingly look to corporations for moral mirroring and signaling. Leaders, employees, consultants—everyone, really—are just as guilty of the is-ought fallacy. They take a statement of fact, grounded in reason and observation, and then leap to a statement of value, which introduces ethics and aesthetics.

Our cognitive biases and heuristics fuel this tendency. We see that a company is, and therefore conclude what it ought to do, typically aligning with our own moral judgment. This happens, in part, because we anthropomorphize corporations, assigning them human-like responsibilities and expectations.

Examples of is-ought:

Is: All flamingos stand on one leg.

Ought: Therefore, you ought to stand on one leg at all times.

Is: Telephones ring when they receive a call.

Ought: Therefore, you ought to ring like a telephone when greeting people.

Now, corporate examples:

Is: Corporations exist to generate profit.

Ought: Therefore, corporations should focus on profit maximization at all costs.
Is: Employee salaries align with industry standards.
Ought: Therefore, the compensation package is justified.
Is: Companies provide products and services to people.
Ought: Therefore, companies should always act in their customers' best interest.

It's easy to assume what's best for an organization. So easy, in fact, that we do it instinctively. But what benefits us individually doesn't always align with what benefits the organization, and vice versa. To apply empirical thinking effectively within any system, we must first understand how that system actually operates, not how we wish it would operate.

This chapter diagnoses the modern corporate system. Not to justify or condemn it, but to understand it. Once we identify the underlying why, we can evaluate whether our actions align with our intended outcomes.

Business entities as we know them are relatively young. Early corporations were formed through charters between governing bodies and private investors, often for public infrastructure projects (bridges, canals, roads). These entities were not-for-profit, existing for specific, time-limited purposes.

The British East India Company (1600) marked a turning point. Granted a Royal Charter by Queen Elizabeth I, it established the template for corporate monopolies operating beyond mere commerce, integrating governance, trade, and military power. Free-market theories wouldn't emerge formally until Adam Smith's *Wealth of Nations* in 1776, yet corporations remained largely bound to specific objectives.

As industrialization accelerated in the 19th century, corporations shifted from infrastructure-focused projects to profit-driven ventures. The US Supreme Court began affording corporations legal rights, the Joint Stock Companies Act of 1844 in Britain formalized modern corporate structure, and by 1886, U.S. courts had recognized corporations as legal "persons."

The early 20th century brought massive industrial growth alongside extreme economic disparity. By the 1930s, inequality from concentrated wealth had contributed to the Great Depression, forcing governments to implement regulations aimed at curbing corporate excesses. For several decades, corporations operated under a social contract that balanced shareholder interests with employee welfare, long-term stability, and public benefit. This time period is often referred to as the "Golden Age of Capitalism."

Then, as folk singer Bob Dylan prophesied, *the times were a-changin'*. Though not in the direction Dylan probably hoped.

In the 1970s, economist Milton Friedman, leading the Chicago School of Economics, introduced the doctrine that a corporation's primary—indeed, only—responsibility was to its shareholders. This perspective, embraced by political leaders such as President Ronald Reagan, led to deregulation, tax cuts, and a fundamental shift in corporate priorities. Companies that once valued long-term stability and employee welfare began optimizing for short-term stock performance.

Jack Welch, CEO of General Electric from 1981 to 2001, operationalized Friedman's philosophy. Welch rejected traditional notions of company loyalty, instead prioritizing shareholder value above all else. He popularized mass layoffs (famously implementing "rank and yank" policies that culled the bottom 10 percent of performers annually), aggressive acquisitions, and cost-cutting measures that maximized short-term gains. Welch's approach shifted corporate success metrics from operational excellence to financial engineering.

Simon Sinek's framework of 'finite' versus 'infinite games' reveals a structural mismatch. Finite games, such as sports or board games, have known players, fixed rules, and agreed-upon objectives. You play to win, and when the game ends, someone has won. Infinite games have both known and unknown players, changeable rules, and the objective is to perpetuate the game itself—to keep playing.

Business is an infinite game. Competitors come and go. Technologies evolve. Markets shift. Customer preferences change. There is no finish line where you "win" and the game ends. Yet Friedman and Welch reframed business as a finite game with a clear win condition: maximize shareholder value this quarter.

This reframing had predictable consequences. If the objective is winning quarters, then strategies that win this quarter while undermining next year's capability make perfect sense. Stock buybacks win quarters. Cutting R&D wins quarters. Deferring maintenance wins quarters. Extracting value from acquired companies wins quarters.

Welch's famous achievement—meeting or exceeding analyst estimates for 80 consecutive quarters—illustrates finite game thinking perfectly. It's a scorecard. A streak to maintain. An impressive record of "wins." But business doesn't end after 80 quarters. What matters is whether the organization is positioned to continue competing in quarter 81, 181, and 1,081.

GE's eventual collapse suggests the answer. The tactics that won quarters destroyed the capability required for the infinite game. This pattern repeats across companies that optimized for finite victories: Sears, Kodak, Blockbuster, Nokia. Each dominated their industries. Each treated that dominance as a finish line rather than as a temporary position in an ongoing game. Each lost the capability to adapt when the game continued without them.

The combined effects of deregulation and financialization created the modern corporate landscape—one dominated by shareholder primacy, short-term earnings targets, and financial maneuvering. The structural changes during this era were profound:

Income inequality surged. From 1945 to 1980, incomes grew rapidly and roughly equally across all income levels. Since 1980, the top 1 percent and top wage earners have pulled away dramatically from the middle and bottom of the income distribution.

Retirement risk shifted to workers. The 401(k), introduced in 1978 and popularized by consultant Ted Benna in 1980, replaced traditional pensions. This transferred investment risk and retirement planning responsibility from employers to employees, while reducing corporate long-term obligations.

Finance consumed productive investment. By some estimates, financialization—the increasing dominance of financial motives, markets, and institutions—has cost the U.S. economy over $2 trillion. IBM alone spent $201 billion on stock buybacks between 1995 and 2019. Corporate investment in productive assets fell by half—from 20 percent to 10 percent of revenues—between 2002 and 2015.

Wall Street explicitly strategized around wealth concentration. In 2005 and 2006, Citigroup equity strategists published a series of internal memos analyzing what they termed "plutonomy"—economies where growth is powered by and largely consumed by the wealthy few. The strategists identified the United States, United Kingdom, and Canada as plutonomies, arguing that this concentration created distinct investment opportunities. They recommended positioning portfolios to benefit from luxury goods, high-end services, and financial assets disproportionately held by the top 1 percent.

The framework didn't diagnose inequality as a problem to solve—it identified inequality as an opportunity to exploit. The reports analyzed which sectors would thrive as wealth concentrated further: high-end retail, luxury automotive, private aviation, wealth management services. The strategists weren't making moral claims. They were describing market mechanics and advising clients how to profit from them.

The reports were marked confidential and later leaked, prompting

Citigroup to attempt suppression. The term 'plutonomy' itself dates to the 1850s, when John Malcolm Forbes Ludlow first proposed it as a framework for understanding wealth-driven economies. Victorian critic John Ruskin dismissed it as "base or bastard science"—technically accurate in its mechanics while fundamentally amoral in its application. A century and a half later, Citigroup's strategists proved the label apt. The reports were confidential for a reason. Some strategies sound worse when you say them out loud. Regardless of the controversy, the plutonomy framework influenced institutional investment strategy throughout the 2000s and 2010s. It made explicit what the Friedman-Welch transformation had made structural: optimizing for the wealthy few rather than broad-based prosperity had become not just acceptable but sophisticated financial strategy.

This wasn't a conspiracy. It was a response to incentive structures. It was also authority dressed as expertise.

A consultancy I worked at was acquired by a larger firm. Early on, the acquiring CEO visited our office while evaluating another deal. He was sharp and fluent in acquisitions. He explained that most companies pad their numbers, and accounting for that variance is simply part of the cost of buying a business. In our case, he noted, the opposite was true—we were more profitable than we claimed. He was impressed.

For the first year or two, that mattered. Our practices influenced the larger organization more than it influenced us. The system worked.

Then the incentives changed. The CEO retired. New leadership came in, along with an investor whose model was explicit: increase stock value over a fixed horizon and exit.

Layoffs followed quarterly—not in response to individual performance, but to reduce expense. The most experienced consultants were often the first to go because they were the most expensive, even though expertise was the product being sold. Many of the remaining senior consultants left voluntarily, because they were also the most capable of finding work elsewhere. Capacity that once enabled responsiveness was reframed as waste. What remained looked leaner on a spreadsheet and performed worse in the market.

The people running the company were not less intelligent than the first CEO. As far as I know, they weren't any less moral. They were operating under a different incentive structure. To understand why corporations behave this way, we need to trace the incentive chain.

71 percent of shareholders are institutional investors (pension funds, mutual funds, hedge funds) managing assets on behalf of others. Their primary obligation is delivering returns. These

institutional investors elect board members who prioritize growing stock value. Those board members hire CEOs who promise the greatest return, often through strategies that maximize short-term gains. In turn, those CEOs assemble leadership teams to execute these strategies.

However, stock value does not directly reflect profitability, product quality, strategic direction, employee satisfaction, or customer loyalty. It reflects what investors believe the stock is worth—no more, no less. Why is a rookie baseball card often worth more than one from a player's later career? Why is a Keith Haring painting worth more than your five-year-old's stick figure? Why are diamonds—common carbon crystals that De Beers convinced the world were rare through supply manipulation and a 1947 ad campaign—worth three months' salary?

Because people believe they are.

Economists call this 'fiat value'—worth that exists by collective agreement rather than intrinsic utility. In plain English, it's a high-stakes game of *Let's Pretend*. Corporate stock operates the same way. The product is confidence, and confidence is fungible.

While rising stock prices can create indirect advantages—such as easier access to capital or stronger acquisition currency—a company does not receive cash simply because its stock trades higher in the secondary market after its IPO. Just as a third-party sale of a baseball card above MSRP has no impact on the manufacturer, a company sees no direct return when its stock price soars in secondary markets. As Henry Ford observed, "The stock market never made a business—business makes the stock market." Yet modern markets often treat stock price as a proxy for business health, even though it is, at best, an indirect signal.

The Fortune 500 ranking measures corporations by revenue, not profit. It rewards scale, not sustainability. By 2019, Amazon surpassed Apple on the Fortune 500 (and has held a higher ranking every year since) despite Apple consistently generating profit margins 5-10 times higher. Amazon prioritized volume and market expansion over profitability, operating on razor-thin margins for most of its history. This mindset traces to the dot-com bubble, when companies convinced investors that growth—not business fundamentals—was the ultimate measure of success.

This creates a perverse dynamic: corporations hyper-focus on quarterly earnings. Jack Welch famously met or exceeded analyst estimates for 80 consecutive quarters—a streak that, statistically speaking, should have prompted more suspicion than applause. To ensure quarterly numbers consistently appear positive, executives employ financial maneuvers:

- **Aggressive cost-cutting:** Layoffs, reduced R&D, deferred maintenance
- **Liquidation:** Selling divisions or assets for one-time gains
- **Acquisitions:** Absorbing another company's profits to mask losses
- **Offshoring:** Reducing labor costs by moving operations overseas
- **Revenue manipulation:** Pulling future revenue forward or reclassifying expenses to inflate current-quarter results.

This short-term focus to business is known as *shareholder primacy*. Shareholder primacy rests on a specific set of claims: that markets efficiently allocate resources, that profit signals value creation, that competition weeds out inferior approaches, and that government intervention distorts the natural selection of winners and losers. These beliefs form the theoretical foundation used to justify why maximizing shareholder returns should guide corporate behavior. If markets work as described, then profitable companies deserve their success, and unsuccessful ones should fail.

Yet significant evidence suggests that the practice cannot survive the conditions its theory requires.

Corporations at the top of the Fortune 500 routinely operate business models that depend on public systems to absorb costs they do not internalize. The mechanisms vary, but the pattern is consistent: when costs threaten the model, they are shifted outward. Labor markets are stabilized through taxpayer-funded assistance programs that effectively subsidize wages. Financial institutions receive emergency liquidity support with such regularity that "too big to fail" has become a standing assumption rather than an extraordinary exception. Entire industries rely on foundational research, infrastructure, and risk-taking funded by public institutions like NIH and DARPA, while attributing downstream profits exclusively to private enterprise.

This is not an occasional intervention reserved for rare emergencies. It is structural. Periodic crises require large-scale rescue to prevent systemic collapse, such as the 2008 automotive bailout, which preserved industrial capacity while insulating prior strategic decisions from their full market consequences. And between those crises, ongoing support continues through tax incentives, infrastructure built to corporate specifications, workforce training programs, research grants, and regulatory accommodations. Estimates consistently place federal corporate subsidies in the tens to hundreds of billions of dollars annually, even before accounting for state and local incentives or the enduring economic value derived from publicly funded research.

The companies most committed to free-market rhetoric are often the most dependent on these arrangements. This is not hypocrisy in the sense of individual moral failure; it is rational behavior within a system that rewards the extraction of public resources while allowing success to be framed as purely private. Executives who declined subsidies available to competitors would likely be removed for failing their fiduciary duty to shareholders.

The result is an arrangement that does not align with any coherent economic philosophy. It is not free-market capitalism, because failure is routinely insulated rather than allowed to clear. It is not socialism, because gains remain private while losses are absorbed elsewhere. Whatever we call it, the asymmetry is the point: risk flows downward to taxpayers and workers, while returns flow upward to shareholders.

None of this proves the system is wrong in some absolute sense. But it does demonstrate that the system does not function according to its own stated logic. The theoretical justification for shareholder primacy assumes conditions—market discipline, consequence, and failure—that shareholder primacy itself cannot tolerate. When a model requires continual intervention from the force it claims to oppose, the hypothesis has failed its own test.

Jack Welch's protégés provide a natural experiment: Gary Wendt at Conseco, Paolo Fresco at Fiat, Robert Nardelli at Home Depot, Harry Stonecipher at Boeing, James McNerney at Boeing, David Calhoun at Boeing—a pattern that, in retrospect, explains quite a bit about modern air travel anxiety—and Welch's own successor at GE, Jeff Immelt. Their leadership legacies share a pattern of short-term gains followed by long-term organizational damage.

The tactics that boost quarterly earnings often jeopardize long-term viability. Organizations trim fat, then muscle, until only bone remains. Evidence appears in systemic fragility:

During the COVID-19 pandemic, supply chains optimized for efficiency at the expense of resilience crumbled under pressure. Companies struggled to meet demand, resulting in critical shortages of medical supplies, semiconductors, and basic consumer goods. Now those same fragile supply chains face stress from U.S. tariffs, trade restrictions, and geopolitical tensions (Russia-Ukraine, Red Sea conflicts).

When external shocks hit, companies that sacrificed resilience for efficiency falter first. This is a natural consequence of optimizing for short-term metrics. 90 percent of companies on the Fortune 500 in 1955 no longer exist today. Kodak, Polaroid, Blockbuster, Pan Am,

Compaq—all fell to disruptive forces. The conventional diagnosis is that they failed to innovate.

According to Harvard Business School, innovation refers to the creation of novel and useful products, services, business models, or strategies—not necessarily groundbreaking advancements. But innovation does require investment in uncertain outcomes, a tolerance for failure, and long time horizons. These are incompatible with quarterly earnings targets and 5-year executive tenures.

Even as population, productivity, and capital availability have increased, the number of publicly traded companies in the United States has fallen by more than half since its peak in the mid-1990s. More firms remain private for longer, while growth among large incumbents increasingly comes through acquisition rather than internal capability development. Startups that demonstrate promise are often absorbed before they mature—not always to scale their innovation, but to capture learning that is difficult to obtain at scale and to reduce competitive pressure in ways that support near-term stock performance. Yet learning does not compound automatically after acquisition. In many cases, the conditions that enabled early experimentation are dismantled, and the original capability erodes rather than amplifies.

In fact, research tracking inequality and economic development across two centuries found that the post-1980 rebound of inequality was not followed by faster productivity growth, but by slower instead. Meanwhile, countries that maintained more equal income distributions now exhibit higher hourly output than the United States, despite lower total investment in human capital. The shareholder primacy approach justified as necessary for prosperity produced the opposite results.

This chapter isn't arguing that corporations should behave differently. It's identifying what the current system optimizes for.

If your goals are:

- Long-term sustainability
- Customer value creation
- Employee welfare and development
- Product innovation and quality
- Societal benefit

Then the shareholder primacy approach of short-term stock performance through financial engineering fundamentally misaligns with those goals. Despite this, these behaviors have become conventional. Leaders often act as if it's better to fail through conventional methods than succeed through unconventional ones.

However, not all corporations operate this way. Some prioritize longevity, value creation, and sustainable practices. While they can't entirely escape the system they exist within, employing the same short-term strategies would misalign with their stated goals.

Paul Polman's tenure as Unilever CEO from 2009 to 2019 demonstrated that alternatives exist within the current system. Upon taking the role, Polman announced that quarterly earnings guidance would stop and that shareholder value would no longer be the company's primary focus. Predictably, some investors sold. Others—those aligned with longer-term thinking—bought in to replace them.

The results contradict conventional wisdom about what maximizes shareholder returns. Under Polman's leadership, Unilever proved more resilient through economic downturns than competitors pursuing traditional shareholder primacy. The company remained highly profitable while simultaneously reducing environmental impact, improving supply chain labor conditions, and investing in long-term brand building. Over his tenure, Unilever delivered a total shareholder return of 290%—roughly double the FTSE 100 over the same period. Not despite the shift in priorities but likely because of it.

In 2019, the Business Roundtable—representing 181 CEOs of major American corporations—signed a statement redefining the purpose of a corporation away from pure shareholder primacy toward stakeholder capitalism. Whether this represents genuine strategic shift or merely rhetorical repositioning remains to be seen. But it signals growing recognition that shareholder primacy produces outcomes misaligned with sustainable business and shareholder interests.

The existence proof matters. Organizations can prioritize differently. Some shareholders will leave. Different shareholders will arrive. The sky doesn't fall. Performance doesn't collapse. What changes is timescale—measuring success in years and decades rather than in quarters.

In the end, the question isn't what corporations ought to do. The question is: What does your organization optimize for?

Once you answer that honestly, the strategies that align with your goals become clearer. If your organization exists to maximize short-term gains for shareholders, then short-term tactics make sense. If it exists to create lasting value, those same tactics are destructive.

If this chapter felt heavy, that's appropriate. Understanding the system you're inside is rarely cheerful work. The next chapter examines growth—and finds more physics where corporations hoped to find magic.

CHAPTER 5
The Physics of Growth

"Any intelligent fool can make things bigger, more complex, and more violent. It takes a touch of genius—and a lot of courage—to move in the opposite direction." – E.F. Schumacher

Growth is the unquestioned mandate of modern business. Companies are expected to scale, expand, and dominate. The prevailing wisdom holds that if you're not growing, you're dying.

Yet companies routinely scale the wrong things: headcount instead of capability, revenue instead of profit, bureaucracy instead of efficiency. This results in bloated, inefficient organizations that collapse under their own weight.

In biology, the Square-Cube Law states that as an organism grows, its mass (volume) increases faster than its strength (surface area). An elephant cannot run like a gazelle because its body cannot support the forces involved. This same law limits Godzilla and King Kong to fiction—their legs would snap under their own weight, which is less dramatic than nuclear breath but equally fatal. At a certain size, an animal reaches a physical limit where it cannot consume enough calories to sustain itself.

Businesses are not exempt from the laws of physics.

A company that grows beyond its sustainable size eventually requires more resources than it can generate. Operational complexity, managerial overhead, and communication inefficiencies consume more capital than the company produces. Just as a giant animal would need more food than exists in its environment, a bloated corporation cannot generate enough value to justify its costs.

When I worked at Meijer, we started with a team of over 25 native app engineers developing a mobile app. I began in QA, and my first month I logged 200 bugs. We deployed twice that year. The following year, we changed how work was divided and empowered the teams. By year's end, we were releasing once or twice a month with only 6 engineers—and zero no-go bugs during regression testing. The constraint had shifted from engineering time to finding problems worth solving.

More employees equate to disproportionately more overhead, and some problems cannot be parallelized. A team of one hundred juniors cannot replace the depth of a single experienced expert. As layers of management stack up, decision-making slows. Communication increases, but signal gets lost. More isn't always better—sometimes, it's just more.

Fred Brooks, in *The Mythical Man-Month*, captured this dynamic in software development when he wrote: "Adding manpower to a late software project makes it later." The insight extends far beyond software. Yet companies persist in believing that growth means throwing more bodies at a problem.

Like unregulated cell growth that eventually kills its host, unchecked corporate expansion consumes the resources that sustain it. A healthy organism maintains balance, regulating cell production based on need. When that regulation fails, cells multiply uncontrollably, consuming more resources than they should, which starves healthy tissue. Organizations rarely describe their growth strategies in these terms, preferring words like 'scaling' and 'expansion'—which sound better in press releases.

Companies praised for expanding at all costs follow the same pattern. They pursue headcount increases, acquisitions, and bloated product suites, mistaking unregulated expansion for success. They consume talent, capital, and infrastructure without a plan for long-term survival.

General Electric, which once dominated global markets, ultimately collapsed under its own weight. This is the shareholder primacy playbook from the previous chapter reaching its logical conclusion. Under Jack Welch, GE scaled indiscriminately, acquiring businesses in industries it didn't understand, layering on management and bureaucracy, and eventually reaching a point where sheer size became unsustainable. The same pattern appears in companies that inflate headcount to appear successful, in product teams that ship unnecessary features to justify their budgets, and in corporate strategies that prioritize stock buybacks and acquisitions over value creation.

Each of these behaviors made sense within the incentive structure Chapter 4 described. Welch wasn't irrational—he was optimizing for exactly what the system rewarded. The irrationality was in believing that what the system rewarded would produce sustainable outcomes.

There is no rule that companies must scale headcount to succeed. Some of the most impactful companies have built world-class products with small, highly skilled teams by focusing on quality from the start.

As Henry Ford, who famously doubled the daily wages of his factory workers, once said: "Low wages are the most costly any employer can pay. It is like using low-grade material—the waste makes it very expensive in the end. There is no economy in cheap labor or cheap material."

Ford understood that cutting costs in the wrong places—whether labor or materials—leads to greater expenses in the long run. The same principle applies to building companies: investing in talent and quality from the beginning creates far more value than relying on sheer size or cost-cutting measures.

High-talent small teams deliver faster, produce better solutions, and tackle complex systems that junior teams cannot attempt, while writing scalable, maintainable code that prevents long-term costs. Large, low-talent teams create more communication overhead, higher rework and maintenance burdens, along with band-aid fixes that lead to long-term instability. Teams don't scale linearly—the coordination costs increase drastically.

Valve remains one of the most profitable companies in the world with just 336 employees (at the time of publication). Only 79 people work on Steam, their digital distribution service, which generated roughly $2 billion in commission revenue in 2021 (about $1.3 billion in profit from commissions alone). Craigslist, one of the most successful websites in the world, brought in over a billion dollars annually at its peak with only 50 employees. Before its acquisition by Microsoft, Mojang developed Minecraft—the best-selling video game of all time—with a team of just 25 employees. These examples aren't meant to prove that small is always better. They're meant to disprove that big is always necessary—a distinction that gets lost when headcount becomes a status symbol. "I manage 200 people" sounds more impressive at dinner parties than "I manage 12 people who outperform your 200." But only one of those statements reflects actual capability.

Back when I worked in the digital department at Meijer, we managed native mobile apps for millions of users with a fully staffed product team of fewer than 15 people for both platforms. It remains the most mature product I've had the pleasure of working on, and it led to years of consulting work attempting to teach other companies to replicate similar success.

Robin Dunbar, an anthropologist, proposed that humans can maintain stable, meaningful relationships with about 150 people. This limit arises because our cognitive and social structures cannot handle more than that number in a cohesive, high-trust environment. Beyond this threshold, relationships become more transactional, bureaucratic, and impersonal.

In small companies and teams, trust and alignment occur naturally. A small startup pivots quickly because everyone knows each other, information flows freely, and decisions happen organically. As organizations scale past Dunbar's Number, everything changes: direct knowledge becomes second-hand information, bureaucracy replaces trust, politics emerge as people make assumptions about colleagues they don't know, and coordination slows as hierarchies form.

This explains why small, tight-knit companies often outperform bloated competitors. The moment a company scales past the point where people no longer know each other personally, communication overhead balloons, accountability weakens, and efficiency collapses.

Organizations tend to break at specific thresholds where communication shifts dramatically:

15 people: The size of a tight, high-functioning team. Everyone communicates directly, and decisions happen quickly.

50 people: The beginning of small company dynamics. You still recognize everyone, but you've started forgetting spouses' names, and informal communication starts needing structure.

150 people: The Dunbar Limit. Beyond this, people cannot maintain relationships with everyone, and formal structures become necessary.

500 people: Bureaucracy dominates. Managers manage managers. Communication becomes political. Innovation slows.

5,000 people: The Titanic problem. Changing direction requires massive coordination, and inefficiencies are so deeply embedded that only extreme intervention can prevent decline.

As companies cross these thresholds, they must consciously adapt their structures, communication, and culture—or they risk becoming slow, inefficient, and dysfunctional. When an organization scales beyond the limits of human relationships described by Dunbar, it also grows past its ability to sustain meaningful feedback. Once a critical threshold is crossed, Malcolm Gladwell notes that local feedback no longer governs outcomes and decision-making shifts from lived experience to statistical abstraction.

The math is unforgiving. Metcalfe's Law observes that the number of connections in a network grows proportionally to the square of its nodes. 5 people require 10 connections. Double that to 10 and you don't get 20, you get 45. While connections are shared, each new person must connect to every other—so coordination increases quadratically, not linearly.

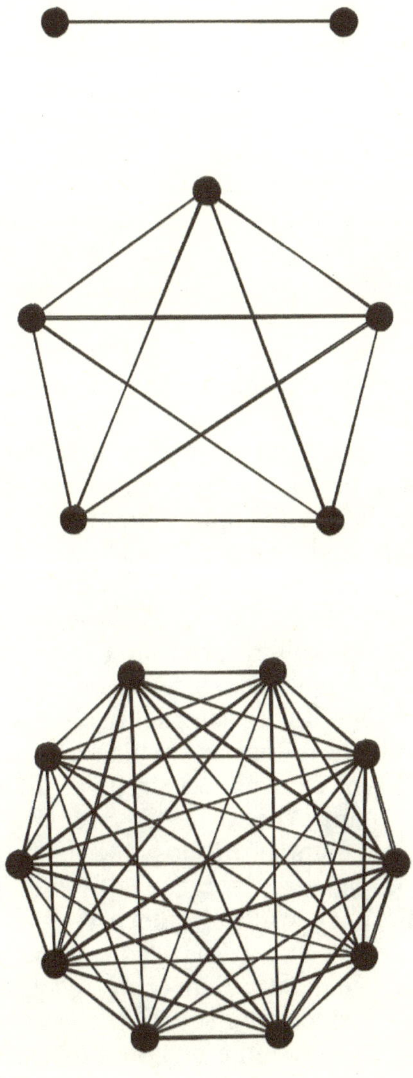

Figure 5.1 - Metcalfe's Law

In organizations, this transition has a subtle but dangerous consequence: failures that would be existential for a small firm become tolerable at scale. Customer dissatisfaction can be absorbed, averaged out, or offset with marketing. A single drop of dye clouds a glass of water but disappears in a swimming pool. Feedback in large-scale organizations suffers from the same dilution effect. Internal friction fades into background noise rather than acting as a catalyst for learning and adjustment.

This is why Jason Fried and David Heinemeier Hansson (DHH) claim in *ReWork* that they limit headcount and project complexity at 37signals, the company behind Basecamp, Hey, and the Once suite. Even Amazon, with over a million employees worldwide, has a "two-pizza rule" limiting teams to the size that can be fed with two pizzas. Spotify, with 9,000 employees, employs a squad model dividing teams into smaller units.

Dunbar's Number forces critical questions: Do we actually need to hire more people, or can we restructure our teams? Are our communication problems due to lack of tools, or are we simply too big? Are we adding bureaucracy that slows us down, or are we optimizing for adaptability?

Many companies don't ask these questions until too late. They hit a Dunbar-like threshold, realize they're no longer nimble, and suddenly find themselves buried under layers of inefficiency. Correcting over-scaling is much more difficult than preventing it—similar to staying in physical shape versus losing weight. This is why 37signals sticks to their philosophy: "hire when it hurts." This sounds harsh until you realize the alternative is hiring when it's convenient. Which is how organizations end up with people whose primary job is to attend meetings about the work other people do. 37signals' approach is something we'll return to in Chapter 11.

Organizations also face trade-offs when scaling through external capacity. Outsourcing—hiring external firms to dynamically increase capability or bandwidth—may seem like a flexible solution, but it introduces the risk of externalizing critical intellectual knowledge, weakening the company's core expertise over time, while jeopardizing the focus of SMEs, leaders, portfolios, and the organization.

While outsourcing can serve legitimate purposes—such as independent audits or specialized expertise—it also operates as a risk-aversion tactic, used by leaders more concerned with appearing busy and having a scapegoat than delivering results. It functions as an expense strategy, since outsourced firms and independent contractors are fully deductible business expenses—not to mention potential cost savings from lower tax rates and cheaper labor internationally.

The fundamental tension is this: if most work produces little value (a pattern we'll explore more in future chapters), then increasing capacity to produce more work simply scales inefficiency. Limited capacity creates healthy tension—forcing teams to be more focused, deliberate, and diligent in prioritizing the right work.

The healthiest organizations understand the difference between sustainable and exploitative growth. Long-term success is not about maximizing expansion—it's about optimizing resilience, adaptability, and value.

Think of an elite athlete: the goal isn't to bulk up, but to build the right balance of muscle for optimal strength, flexibility, speed, and endurance. A company that prioritizes strategic, sustainable growth over sheer size is far better positioned to thrive in the long run. Organizations also need healthy reserves—eliminating all slack makes them weaker, more vulnerable to disruption, and less resilient. Organizations that cut too aggressively in pursuit of efficiency often undermine their own stability and long-term success.

Companies optimizing for short-term gains chase headcount, infrastructure, and bureaucracy without optimizing for real efficiency. When they do focus on efficiency, it's often localized, creating short-term savings at the cost of overall effectiveness. Instead of solving real user problems, they build products based on competitor trends, executive whims, or marketing optics. They intentionally add excess so it can be dramatically cut later to create the illusion of discipline. Rather than earning success through innovation, they exploit financial loopholes, government subsidies, and monopolistic practices to maintain dominance—propping up position through system manipulation rather than value creation.

Companies optimizing for sustainability grow in response to actual demand, not speculative hype. They focus on profitability over revenue, capability over headcount, and efficiency over scale. They reduce waste in both internal processes and product offerings. They understand that success is tied to the long-term well-being of employees, customers, and markets.

At the end of the day, the question isn't whether to grow. The question is: what kind of growth supports your organization's objectives?

The next chapter examines how we analyze success—and why we so often learn the wrong lessons.

CHAPTER 6
Why Outcomes Lie

"Mild success can be explainable by skills and labor. Wild success is attributable to variance." – Nassim Nicholas Taleb

Understanding why organizations fail requires examining how they analyze success. People have a tendency to systematically misinterpret what experience teaches them. They draw confident conclusions from incomplete data, mistake correlation for causation, and construct narratives that obscure rather than illuminate the mechanisms behind outcomes.

This is due to how the human brain evolved to recognize patterns and construct causal explanations, even when none exist. As Morgan Housel observes, "We need to believe we live in a predictable, controllable world, so we turn to authoritative-sounding people who promise to satisfy that need." That need for certainty leads organizations to prefer clear but wrong explanations over accurate but ambiguous ones.

However, humans are exceptionally bad at recognizing randomness. We see patterns where none exist and construct explanations for coincidence. Spotify discovered this when users complained that shuffle wasn't random because they noticed songs from the same artist played consecutively and certain albums appeared multiple times in short periods. Now, to be clear, computers are actually incapable of true randomness. Instead, they rely on deterministic algorithms that produce sequences random enough to pass statistical tests but are entirely predictable if you know the seed value. This “pseudo-randomness” is sufficient for most purposes, and Spotify claimed the algorithm was working correctly. True randomness produces clusters. Flip a coin 100 times and you’ll get streaks of 5 or 6 heads in a row. That’s what randomness looks like.

But it doesn’t always *feel* random. Our brains expect even distribution—one song per artist and albums evenly spaced—which isn’t random at all, it’s carefully orchestrated. Spotify eventually modified their shuffle algorithm to feel more random by being less random, introducing rules that prevented the very clusters that actual randomness produces. They optimized for human perception rather than mathematical accuracy.

This reveals something fundamental about how we process information. Pattern recognition is so deeply embedded in human cognition that we detect patterns even in pure noise. The classic example: if you ask people to write down a random sequence of coin flips, they’ll unconsciously avoid long streaks because streaks feel non-random. Their “random” sequences are more evenly distributed than actual randomness produces. When shown a truly random sequence, they’ll identify it as suspicious.

This matters when analyzing business outcomes. Success that results from random variation looks identical to success that results from superior strategy—until you examine enough cases to distinguish signal from noise. One company succeeds with aggressive expansion. Another fails with the same approach. The temptation is to study what the successful company did differently—better execution, superior culture, visionary leadership. Often, the answer is luck. They expanded during favorable conditions and the competitor didn’t. Or they happened to hire the right person at the right moment. Or their product launched the week before a competitor’s superior offering imploded due to an unrelated scandal.

Nassim Taleb calls this being ‘fooled by randomness’: mistaking luck for skill, seeing causation in correlation, constructing narratives that explain random outcomes as inevitable consequences of decisions. The pharmaceutical industry demonstrates this daily. For every successful drug, hundreds of candidates with similar profiles failed. The difference often has nothing to do with those running the experiments, but random variation in how molecules interact with biological systems we don’t fully understand. We study the successful drug’s development process, extract lessons about what worked, and apply them to the next candidate—which fails anyway because the success was partially random and the pattern we extracted was partially fiction.

The practical implication: when analyzing organizational

outcomes, maintain skepticism about causal claims. Success followed by Intervention X, but that doesn't mean X caused success. Multiple companies tried X. You're studying the one where it worked while ignoring the dozen where it didn't. The pattern you're detecting might be real or might be Spotify's shuffle problem—your brain constructing order from randomness because disorder is intolerable.

The consequences compound over time. Companies that misread their own success stories optimize for the wrong variables, double down on tactics that worked by accident, and ignore the structural factors that actually drive outcomes. Meanwhile, those that fail remain invisible in the analysis. Their lessons go unexamined, and their warnings remain unheard. The result is a distorted map of reality where the path to success appears far clearer than it is.

Success is persuasive precisely because it feels explanatory. Outcomes create the illusion that their causes must have been clear all along. When results are positive, the mind retroactively assigns intent, competence, and inevitability to decisions that were originally made under uncertainty.

This tendency is amplified in organizations. Success validates existing beliefs, reinforces authority, and discourages dissent. When things go well, there is little incentive to question whether the reasons offered actually explain the outcome or merely make it feel intelligible. Success quiets curiosity at the moment it should sharpen it.

A small example shows how easily this happens in everyday work.

I once worked with a consulting manager who kept selling the same approach to clients—and it kept missing the mark. During planning, I raised concerns and pointed to the same risks each time. He'd wave them off: "We're using our A team on this, so it'll be fine."

I'd ask, "Didn't we just sell the A team last week?"

When the project inevitably slipped, the explanation followed a familiar pattern. The people executing were blamed. The plan itself was never reconsidered by the organization. The fact that it had been sold successfully—again and again—was treated as proof that it was sound. Each failure was reframed as an exception. The pattern never counted as evidence.

Survivorship bias occurs when we analyze only those that survived a selection process while ignoring those that did not. The most famous illustration comes from World War II. Statistician Abraham Wald was asked to examine damaged bombers returning from missions to determine where to add armor. The obvious answer was to reinforce the areas showing the most damage, including wings and fuselage riddled with bullet holes.

Wald recognized the flaw. The planes being examined had survived. The bullet holes showed where a plane could be hit and still return. The missing data was the planes that did not come back, which revealed where hits were fatal. Wald recommended armoring the areas showing no damage on returning planes, specifically the engines and cockpit.

Business analysis suffers from the same blind spot. When studying successful companies, we see only those that survived market conditions, competitive pressures, technological shifts, and leadership changes. The companies that failed using similar strategies, possessed similar resources, or operated in similar markets remain out of sight and therefore out of mind. This creates a false narrative in which success appears more predictable and reproducible than reality allows.

Consider the explosion of entrepreneurial advice promising to replicate the success of technology giants. Founders are told to drop out of college like Bill Gates, Steve Jobs, and Michael Dell. I could keep going—Larry Ellison, Jack Dorsey, Jan Koum, Evan Spiegel, Richard Branson, Daniel Ek, Travis Kalanick—and that's precisely the problem. The longer the list gets, the more convincing it *feels*.

But the list quietly ignores the far more common outcome: nearly 25 percent of first-year college students drop out and build nothing at all. Leaving Harvard or Yale with a viable idea is often treated as evidence of courage or insight, but it is not the same risk as dropping out of community college. The difference is not the school; the school itself is incidental to the story. What matters is insulation—access to capital, credible networks, and the ability to fail without permanent consequence. The advice treats these decisions as equivalent when they are anything but.

Likewise, we're told to obsess over product perfection like Apple, to move fast and break things like Facebook, and to prioritize culture like Zappos. Each prescription extracts a pattern from a single success story without accounting for timing, market conditions, initial capital, network effects, or the thousands of companies that tried identical strategies and failed. It turns out, there is more to success than turtlenecks and bowl cuts.

Morgan Housel captures this dynamic in *The Psychology of Money* when he observes that you are more likely to be rich if your brother is rich than you are to be tall because your brother is tall. Wealth correlates with wealth in ways that height does not correlate with height because wealth is heavily influenced by circumstances beyond individual control. These circumstances include the same forms of insulation we conveniently overlook: networks, timing, geography, and access to capital. Yet the narratives constructed around successful people emphasize their unique talents and decisions while minimizing the role of circumstance. We prefer stories about hard work and talent because they imply that we control our outcomes. The alternative—that we're leaves blown by winds we can't see—is less inspiring at commencement speeches.

Bill Gates himself acknowledged this reality. He and his high school friend Paul Allen had access to a computer terminal in 1968. This was a resource available to perhaps one in a million teenagers at the time. Without that access, Microsoft would not exist. Gates was brilliant and hardworking, but so were thousands of other teenagers. The difference was opportunity and timing as much as talent.

Breakthrough innovations feel revolutionary, but they're almost never unprecedented. They're novel combinations of existing elements and opportunities. Henry Ford didn't invent the assembly line, interchangeable parts, or the automobile—he synthesized them into a production system that made cars affordable. Ransom Olds had already pioneered stationary assembly lines for automobiles years earlier. Eli Whitney had already popularized interchangeable parts in firearms manufacturing decades earlier. Ford's contribution was seeing how those components could fit together differently, at greater scale, with systematic attention to reducing unnecessary cost.

Even the lineage of modern manufacturing runs through textiles. Sakichi Toyoda's automatic looms stopped themselves when a thread broke—an early expression of built-in quality—long before Toyota built cars. And the man who brought operational rigor to Ford, Walter E. Flanders, also came from textile manufacturing. Industrial revolutions rarely begin where we think they do.

Steve Jobs didn't invent graphical interfaces, mice, or personal computers. Xerox PARC had demonstrated all of those technologies years before the Macintosh shipped, and Konrad Zuse had designed the Z3 decades before PARC even existed. Jobs's insight was recognizing that combining them in specific ways with obsessive attention to making them accessible rather than impressive could transform computing from specialist tools to consumer products.

This pattern repeats across innovations that retrospectively feel inevitable. The Wright brothers didn't invent wings, propellers, or engines. They combined them with systematic observation of how birds actually achieve controlled flight by paying attention to wing warping and three-axis control that other aviation pioneers had overlooked. Watson and Crick didn't invent X-ray crystallography or biochemistry. They synthesized existing data from Rosalind Franklin's imaging work and Chargaff's base-pairing rules into the double helix structure.

This matters because organizations that expect innovation to emerge fully formed from individual genius systematically undervalue the unglamorous work of synthesis, cross-pollination, and connecting ideas that live in separate domains. They hire for deep specialization and then wonder why breakthrough thinking doesn't happen. They reward expertise within silos while treating people who work across boundaries as dilettantes lacking focus.

The value isn't having the components. Most organizations already possess the pieces scattered across departments, roles, and geographic locations. The value is seeing how they might fit together differently. This requires exposure to multiple domains, permission to experiment with recombination, and tolerance for ideas that don't fit cleanly into existing categories. Innovation is pattern recognition across contexts, not creation *ex nihilo* ('from nothing').

David Epstein's *Range* documents this pattern across fields from sports to music to scientific research: generalists who sample broadly before committing outperform early specialists in domains where the rules aren't fixed and pattern-matching across contexts matters more than depth in any single one. That insight also isn't new, but Epstein's synthesis of the evidence makes the case more rigorously than I will here.

This is why my experience across assembly lines, software development, leadership consulting, and product management provides value beyond what any single domain would offer. The assembly line taught me about flow and waste. Software development taught me about rapid feedback and user behavior. Consulting taught me about organizational dysfunction and incentive misalignment. Product management taught me about validating assumptions before committing resources. None of these insights were novel within their own domains. The synthesis of recognizing that the same principles apply across contexts that rarely speak to each other creates something that didn't exist in any individual piece (to my knowledge).

Organizations that master recombination don't just tolerate generalists. They actively create conditions where cross-domain thinking can happen: rotating people through different functions, rewarding collaboration across silos, protecting time for exploration that doesn't fit annual planning cycles, and celebrating connections between ideas that conventional thinking keeps separated.

Yet organizations rarely build this capability. The level of collaboration required often challenges the leadership-hero complex that equates leadership with having the answers and issuing directives, rather than creating the conditions for decentralized thinking and cross-pollination. Instead, they study successful synthesizers and try to copy their specific outputs—the practices that emerged from synthesis rather than the conditions that enabled it.

This connects to observation's inherent limits from Chapter 1. We can only analyze what we notice, and what we notice depends on what has been made visible and what we've been trained to consider relevant. The companies that failed using similar strategies remain invisible not because the data doesn't exist but because nobody's RAS is tuned to look for them. Success captures attention. We usually hope our failures don't. Conveniently, they usually disappear into statistical aggregates.

Rother distinguishes between practices we observe and the problems they were designed to solve. Organizations tend to see successful practices in action and copy them out of context, mistaking the visible solution for the cause of success. What transfers isn't the practice itself, but the scientific thinking capability that defined the problem and generated the solution in the first place.

Netflix offers unlimited vacation, so we'll implement unlimited vacation. Google famously popularized '20 percent time' (though its practice varied over time and across teams), so we'll block Friday afternoons as innovation time. Tech startups have Nerf guns and ping-pong tables, so we'll buy those too.

But as we've seen, correlation does not equal causation. Toyota's success came not from specific practices but from the systematic approach to improvement that generated those practices. Kanban isn't revolutionary—it's a tool Taiichi Ohno adapted from grocery stores to answer a simple question: *how do we manage inventory based on actual demand?* The andon cord isn't magic—it answered a different question: *how do we surface problems before rework piles up?* The practices are answers to questions. Copying answers without understanding the questions produces cargo cult management.

The danger is not that organizations celebrate success or study successful companies. The danger is that they construct causal explanations from correlational data and then implement those explanations as if they are universal laws. Organizations see ten companies that succeeded with aggressive growth strategies and conclude that aggressive growth drives success, while ignoring the hundred companies that pursued identical strategies and collapsed under debt or operational complexity.

Survivorship bias creates two distinct problems. First, it inflates confidence in strategies and tactics by hiding their failure rate. Second, it leads organizations to ignore the role of randomness, timing, and circumstance in determining outcomes. Both problems undermine empirical learning because they prevent decision-makers from seeing the actual distribution of results. The goal here is to treat experience as ambiguous evidence rather than definitive proof.

A modern example illustrates how easily success stories mislead. In 2011, Ron Johnson, celebrated for building Apple's iconic retail stores, became CEO of JCPenney. Johnson concluded that JCPenney's problems stemmed from irrational pricing games and cluttered customer experiences. He eliminated coupons in favor of "fair and square" everyday pricing, redesigned stores into minimalist shop-within-a-shop layouts, and attempted to reposition the brand for a more affluent, design-oriented customer. The strategy was internally coherent and intellectually persuasive. It also failed catastrophically. Revenue collapsed, loyal customers disappeared, and Johnson was dismissed within 17 months. The mistake was not arrogance or incompetence, but treating a single success as a transferable law. Apple's retail model worked under conditions JCPenney did not share: infrequent purchases, premium margins, and customers motivated by status rather than savings. Thousands of failed attempts to replicate Apple's approach never entered the analysis. A clean narrative replaced a messy reality, and perceived control was mistaken for understanding.

Rory Sutherland has noted that customers routinely claim they would prefer lower prices instead of coupons and sales, yet every serious attempt to remove promotions has failed. At a psychological level, discounts do not merely reduce prices—they create meaning. Organizations mistake stated preferences for actual behavior and confuse rational explanations with causal mechanisms.

Henry Ford provides an even more spectacular example of mistaking one context's success for universal principle. After revolutionizing manufacturing with the assembly line, Ford concluded his methods could solve any problem, including society itself.

In 1928, Ford purchased 2.5 million acres of Brazilian rainforest to build Fordlandia—a utopian company town that would supply rubber for tire production while demonstrating American industrial superiority. The vision was characteristically ambitious: transplant Michigan's efficiency, discipline, and social order to the Amazon. Workers would live in American-style housing, eat American food, follow American schedules, and adopt American values. The rubber trees would grow in neat rows like Michigan assembly lines.

Every assumption proved wrong.

The climate, soil, and ecology of the Amazon bore no resemblance to Michigan. Rubber trees planted in neat rows—optimized for efficiency rather than adapted to local conditions—became vulnerable to leaf blight that decimated entire plantations. Brazilian workers had no interest in American Midwestern lifestyle or labor practices. Ford's managers, selected for their loyalty rather than their knowledge of tropical agriculture or local culture, imposed rules that generated resentment and frequent strikes.

The enterprise failed completely. After burning through tens of millions of dollars (hundreds of millions in current terms), Ford sold the land back to Brazil in 1945 for a fraction of its cost. Not a single ounce of rubber from Fordlandia ever reached a Ford vehicle.

The pattern here mirrors Ron Johnson at JCPenney, but the stakes were higher and the hubris more spectacular. Ford's assembly line succeeded because it matched specific conditions: repetitive manufacturing, standardized components, workers whose primary contribution was physical labor. Those conditions didn't exist in the Amazon rainforest, but Ford never questioned whether his methods would transfer. Success in one domain created confidence that the practices behind that success were universal.

This is survivorship bias in its purest form. We study Ford's assembly line triumph and extract lessons about efficiency, standardization, and systematic management. All accurate observations about what worked in that context. But we don't study Fordlandia with equal rigor, so the lesson that Ford's methods had boundaries goes unlearned. The assembly line's success wasn't evidence of universal principles but it is evidence of practices that worked in specific contexts. Fordlandia revealed the boundaries.

Organizations repeat this pattern constantly. A strategy succeeds in one market, so leadership mandates its expansion to others. A process works for one team, so it becomes policy for everyone. A leader succeeds in one role, so they're promoted to another requiring different capabilities. Each decision treats context-specific success as evidence of context-independent wisdom.

Narrative fallacy is the tendency to construct coherent stories that explain events after they occur. These stories feel true because they align facts into cause-and-effect sequences that make intuitive sense. Intuitive sense, however, is not the same as empirical accuracy. In fact, this is rationalism applied to incomplete data—the exact failure mode we identified in Chapter 1. Sound logic built on flawed premises produces confident but wrong conclusions. The reasoning is valid. The premises are garbage. The outcome is persuasive nonsense. The brain's pattern-recognition capabilities evolved to detect threats and opportunities in immediate environments, not to analyze complex systems with delayed feedback loops and non-linear causality. This fallacy likely exists even in the examples used in this book.

There are signs this constraint can be trained against. Research suggests that modern generations perform better on abstract reasoning tasks, likely because they are required to do so more often. This is promising—but it does not represent an escape from narrative thinking. The capacity for abstraction is growing; the instinct for story still dominates under uncertainty.

This same preference for coherent, straight-line stories is how businesses rewrite their own histories. A company releases a product that succeeds beyond expectations. Early explanations focus on execution, such as strong marketing, superior engineering, or customer-centric design. Years later, when the company's official history is written, those explanations solidify into a narrative in which each decision builds logically on the previous one. Setbacks are framed as learning experiences that informed future success. The outcome appears to be the natural result of talent and strategy.

Ransom E. Olds founded the Olds Motor Vehicle Company between 1897 and 1901. Olds pioneered the first mass-assembled gas-powered automobile, the Curved Dash, using what is now known as a stationary assembly line. Workers lined up around the car, each responsible for a specific task. Production increased fivefold between 1901 and 1902, making Olds the largest automobile manufacturer in the United States by 1903, the same year the Ford Motor Company was founded. Olds also established one of the first automotive supply chains by contracting the Dodge brothers to supply transmissions.

Despite these innovations, Oldsmobile suffered major setbacks when its factory burned to the ground in 1901, and Ransom Olds later left his own company in 1904 due to investor disputes. A decision that prevented him from using his name in future endeavors—something he slyly worked around by using his initials, REO, for his next venture. That company did build automobiles, but the name ultimately became more famous decades later, when an REO truck—the Speed Wagon—lent its name to the band that would pioneer arena rock. The downfall of Oldsmobile likely created conditions that allowed Henry Ford—already on his third attempt—to fill the gap with the Model T.

What gets lost in these narratives is the messiness. Decisions that worked despite being wrong disappear from view. Accidents, external shocks, and structural factors unrelated to internal strategy fade from the story. This is another example of Taleb's fooled by randomness phenomenon. People have the tendency to see skill where luck dominated and inevitability where chance determined outcomes.

The first recorded economic bubble, Dutch Tulip Mania in the 1630s, illustrates this same pattern. After tulip prices collapsed in

February 1637, observers constructed elaborate explanations for why prices had risen so high. They pointed to specific decisions by traders, cultural factors, and prevailing economic conditions. The explanations were satisfying precisely because they made the mania seem rational in retrospect—which is exactly what explanations are for. Understanding why something happened is often just a polite way of pretending it couldn't happen again.

Yet bubbles have recurred across centuries and cultures. The South Sea Bubble, the Roaring Twenties, the Dot-com Bubble, and the Housing Bubble all generated their own culturally specific narratives. In each case, the underlying mechanism was speculative mania driven by the belief that prices would continue to rise. The stories constructed afterward obscure the recurring pattern rather than illuminate it.

Rory Sutherland argues that modern business thinking cares more about reasons than it cares about results. In large organizations, decisions must be justified through business cases, return-on-investment projections, and data-driven narratives before they can be approved. This creates a system in which making a compelling argument becomes more valuable than achieving actual outcomes. Leaders optimize for internal persuasion rather than external validation. A brilliant idea with a bad PowerPoint dies in committee. A mediocre idea with a compelling narrative gets funded. The medium became the message decades ago; we're still pretending otherwise.

This shift from results to reasons has predictable consequences. Analysis paralysis sets in as teams gather more data to justify decisions instead of testing hypotheses through action. Organizations reject ideas that do not fit tidy, data-supported narratives, even when those ideas show promise in small-scale experiments. Innovation is filtered through approval processes designed to prevent missteps, which also eliminate the messy, unpredictable experiments that occasionally produce breakthrough results.

The tyranny of metrics compounds this problem. Sutherland contends that data, particularly averages, can be deeply misleading. A focus on hitting average targets causes organizations to neglect innovation, which typically emerges at the extremes of a distribution rather than the middle. As he notes, the more data an organization has, the easier it becomes to find support for a spurious, self-serving narrative.

This problem is compounded by misunderstandings about what good data actually represents. The Flaw of Averages describes the mistaken belief that a single average value accurately represents a variable situation. Decisions based on averages ignore variability, distribution, and extremes, leading to systematically poor outcomes. This issue will be explored more deeply in the following chapter.

This dynamic helps explain why organizations become paralyzed by their own success. They construct narratives explaining what worked and then codify those narratives into processes and metrics. When market conditions change, organizations double down on the strategies their narratives identified as crucial, even when those strategies are no longer aligned with current reality. The cost of success is not complacency—it is the gradual replacement of learning with justification. And so, they optimize for yesterday's problems using yesterday's solutions.

Workday CEO Carl Eschenbach maintains a rule that he writes in every book he owns: "There is nothing more dangerous than yesterday's success." Jeff Bezos and Doug McMillon have expressed similar views. Success is addictive. Replaying victories provides dopamine hits that feel productive while preventing adaptation. It's the organizational equivalent of watching your own highlight reel. Environments change, competitors evolve, and strategies that succeeded under one set of conditions often fail under another.

Success can result from skill, luck, timing, or some combination of all three. Failure reflects the same mix in reverse. Just as studying failures alone won't explain success, analyzing successful cases alone won't reveal which factor dominated.

Post hoc reasoning is the logical error of assuming that because Event B followed Event A, Event A must have caused Event B. The Latin phrase is *post hoc, ergo propter hoc*, meaning "after this, therefore because of this." The error lies in mistaking temporal sequence for causal relationship.

This mistake is easy to make because sequence sometimes does suggest causality. You flip a light switch and the light turns on. In that case, temporal sequence reflects a real causal mechanism. In complex systems with multiple interacting variables and delayed feedback loops, temporal sequence often obscures causality rather than revealing it.

Consider a company that implements a new product development process and then experiences improved outcomes 6 months later. The natural conclusion is that the new process caused the improvement. During those same 6 months, the company may have hired senior engineers, benefited from a competitor exiting the market, seen interest rates decline, or refined its marketing strategy. Any one of these factors, or some combination of them, might explain the observed improvement. Isolating causation in real organizational environments is rarely possible.

The brain attempts to make reality coherent. When confronted with events, it fabricates correlations and causes through a process known as *confabulation*. This does not feel like fabrication. It feels like memory and reasoning. Neuroscience shows that the brain constructs explanatory narratives after the fact, fitting available information into coherent stories whether or not those stories reflect the actual mechanisms at work.

This tendency leads to what psychologists call the illusion of explanatory depth that was covered in Chapter 3. People believe they understand complex phenomena more deeply than they actually do. Ask someone to explain how a bicycle works, and they will confidently describe pedals, chains, and wheels. Ask them to explain how the force from pedaling becomes forward motion and stability, and most people begin to struggle. People can generally name the parts. Far fewer can explain the forces. The same pattern holds for business strategy, market dynamics, and organizational performance.

The working world is saturated with post hoc reasoning—confident voices promising that if their template is followed, their success will be replicated. What worked for them may have worked because of factors they never recognized and couldn't have controlled. Timing may have been favorable. Markets may have been underserved. Initial capital may have been sufficient to survive the learning period that kills most startups. Networks may have provided early customers or investors. None of these factors appear in simplified success narratives.

Former SEC Chairman Arthur Levitt warned in 1998 that many companies operate in a gray area of legitimacy when reporting earnings. These representations may be legally defensible while still misleading. Through financial engineering, organizations create narratives of steady growth and predictable performance. When those narratives collapse, observers construct post hoc explanations claiming the warning signs were visible all along. If those signs were truly detectable in advance, it raises the question of why markets, analysts, and regulators failed to act. This instinct is not limited to markets. After any unexpected outcome—a collapse, a scandal, a tragedy—observers reconstruct the past into a story that feels inevitable. In real time, it rarely was.

The answer is that patterns often become clear only in retrospect. Determining causation from correlation requires controlled experiments, isolated variables, and replication. These conditions are rarely available when analyzing organizational outcomes. Without them, confident causal claims should be treated with skepticism.

Morgan Housel's discussion of luck and risk emphasizes that these forces are inseparable. Luck occurs when low-probability events work in your favor. Risk occurs when they work against you. Both shape outcomes far more than most narratives allow, yet both are systematically undervalued when analyzing success and failure.

This undervaluation stems from the psychological need for control and predictability. Acknowledging the role of luck in success can feel like diminishing genuine skill and effort. Acknowledging risk can feel like admitting vulnerability. As a result, narratives emphasize controllable factors such as decisions, strategies, and execution while minimizing uncontrollable ones.

Many organizational decisions are not optimized for success at all, but for the *feeling* of control. Predictable metrics, tidy narratives, and defensible justifications reduce anxiety even when they reduce effectiveness. Control feels safer than uncertainty, and safety is often mistaken for competence.

In reality, decisions and execution occur within contexts shaped by timing, market conditions, regulatory environments, technological capabilities, and competitor actions. These contextual factors introduce elements of luck and risk that individuals and organizations cannot control. A decision can be objectively sound and still fail because the context shifts unpredictably. A flawed decision can succeed because favorable conditions mask its weaknesses.

If this chapter feels uncomfortable, it should. Systems that reward success rarely encourage skepticism about the stories used to explain it.

The question is not whether skill and effort matter. They clearly do. The question is whether mental models accurately reflect the balance between controllable and uncontrollable forces. Housel argues for humility by recognizing that understanding is incomplete, that patterns identified from past success may not apply to future conditions, and that confidence should be calibrated to the actual amount of control possessed.

This humility extends to how failure is interpreted. Organizations tend to underestimate the amount of failure that precedes success. They focus on the final breakthrough while minimizing false starts, dead ends, and abandoned approaches. Thomas Edison's observation about discovering thousands of ways that did not work before finding one that did captures this reality. What gets erased is not failure itself, but the density of failure relative to the single success we later mythologize. Learning organizations recognize that failure is part of the learning process, but success cannot be understood through failure alone. Both must be examined with equal rigor.

A commonly cited paraphrase attributed to the Stoic philosopher Seneca suggests that luck is what happens when preparation meets opportunity. Preparation increases the range of opportunities an organization can exploit while reducing exposure to risk. The scientific process remains the most reliable tool for navigating this balance, though it requires discipline, patience, and contextual awareness.

An essential question remains. Who decides what success looks like, and which goals organizations should pursue. These are not empirical questions with objective answers. They are value judgments that determine which outcomes are measured and celebrated.

I was once brought onto a project for one of the most recognized technology companies in the world. The product had been oversold. It passed the demo but failed spectacularly during the main use case. There was nothing we could do though, it was a black box solution that had been prematurely sold, so this tech conglomerate took the project over. The project was mentioned during a keynote watched by millions to highlight the amazing new work they were doing. I guess I received the accolade... years later, there has still been no visible progress.

Another useful illustration of this problem exists on a national scale. Gross Domestic Product is routinely treated as a measure of national success, economic health, and societal progress. It is none of these things. GDP is an accounting metric designed to estimate the total volume of market-mediated economic activity within a country. It answers a narrow question: how much was bought and sold? It does not measure whether that activity improved quality of life, strengthened institutions, or produced durable value.

This limitation was not discovered later. It was stated explicitly at the outset. Simon Kuznets, who led the development of national income accounting in the United States, warned policymakers that "the welfare of a nation can scarcely be inferred from a measurement of national income." He emphasized that GDP excluded distribution, sustainability, unpaid labor, and the qualitative difference between activities that generate revenue and those that generate harm.

Like all proxies, GDP offered something enticing: a single number that could be tracked, compared, and optimized. Growth could be charted. Progress could be declared. Complex social systems could be reduced to a line moving up or down. So, Kuznets's warnings were ignored. Over time, the proxy displaced the purpose. Economic activity became synonymous with success, regardless of what that activity produced.

Once that shift occurred, predictable distortions followed. Natural disasters, environmental degradation, illness, and incarceration all increase GDP by generating spending, while improvements in well-being that occur outside market transactions remain invisible. Costs are counted as gains so long as money changes hands. Fragility, depletion, and inequality disappear from view if transactions continue.

This is the same error organizations make when they confuse utilization with productivity, revenue with value creation, or growth with progress. The metric is not wrong. The inference is. When a proxy becomes a scoreboard, optimization follows the signal rather than the system. And like GDP, proxy metrics are all prone to encouraging undesirable behaviors.

Even if GDP fails to provide a complete view of a nation's wealth, the question remains whether wealth should be the leading indicator of national performance. The United States is one of the wealthiest nations in the world, yet it ranks relatively low in measures of happiness compared to other developed countries. This suggests that optimizing purely for financial outcomes ignores dimensions of human well-being that ultimately contribute to productivity, innovation, and long-term value creation (as discussed in Chapter 2).

Who decides? Should a nation operate the same as a business? If so, is it publicly traded or privately owned? For profit or non-profit? Who are its shareholders, board members, and customers?

The definition of success determines which strategies appear effective and which appear wasteful. It determines which evidence is weighted heavily and which is dismissed. It ultimately determines whether organizations learn from experience or become trapped by their own narratives.

Rory Sutherland suggests three practices for organizations seeking to learn from experience rather than narrative. First, they should embrace lucky accidents instead of rewriting history to create clean, rational explanations. Instinct, experimentation, and chance play substantial roles in innovation, and the most effective solutions often emerge from unexpected directions.

Second, organizations should prioritize understanding human psychology over analyzing what people claim they want. Behavior reveals preferences that surveys and focus groups often obscure. Observed actions provide more reliable insight into how customers, employees, and markets actually behave.

Third, organizations should look beyond their silos. Insights often emerge at the intersection of functions such as marketing and logistics, engineering and customer support, or finance and operations. An excessive focus on internal metrics and departmental goals can inhibit the cross-functional collaboration that generates genuine understanding. It can also introduce inefficiencies through misaligned incentives.

These practices share a common theme. They prioritize learning from observable reality over conforming to predetermined narratives. They accept messiness and uncertainty as features of complex systems rather than defects that can be eliminated. The goal is not to construct satisfying explanations, but to build accurate models of how systems actually behave.

Organizations that master this distinction do not eliminate survivorship bias, narrative fallacy, or post hoc reasoning. These cognitive tendencies are deeply human. Instead, they develop cultural practices that counteract them by seeking conflicting evidence, examining base rates, questioning causal claims, and maintaining humility about what past success predicts about future performance.

The alternative is familiar. Organizations optimize for metrics that do not measure value, scale beyond sustainable limits, extract wealth while claiming to create it, and learn the wrong lessons from their own histories. These outcomes are not failures of intelligence or effort. They are failures of epistemology. They reflect an inability to accurately map reality and adjust behavior based on that map.

PART TWO diagnosed the system: how corporations optimize for extraction, how growth creates fragility, how success teaches the wrong lessons. You now understand why organizations behave the way they do—which is a necessary foundation but insufficient for moving forward.

PART THREE turns to practice. Not best practices, which as we've established, are mostly the scientific process with better marketing. Instead, how to measure without theater, build without waste, and learn without waiting for catastrophe to force it. The tools exist. The question is whether you can wield them inside systems designed to suppress exactly what those tools reveal.

PART THREE

Empiricism in Practice

CHAPTER 7
When Metrics Replace Learning

"It is wrong to suppose that if you can't measure it, you can't manage it—a costly myth." – W. Edwards Deming

The challenge of measurement in organizations is not that leaders lack data. The challenge is that organizations generate enormous volumes of it without the discipline to ensure its accuracy, the infrastructure to make it accessible, or the means to present it in ways that are informative. Everyone is responsible for accurate data, but without commitment to that accuracy, unreliable and often misleading data spreads unchecked through the organization. Once flawed data enters a system, it contaminates related analyses, gets copied into downstream reports, informs decisions that generate more flawed data, and eventually becomes embedded in organizational assumptions about how the world works.

Even accurate data misleads when it measures the wrong thing. Eliyahu M. Goldratt demonstrated in *The Goal* that most organizational dysfunction can be traced to a small number of constraints. When organizations measure and optimize everything *except* those constraints, they generate conflicting signals—high utilization, growing backlogs, and declining throughput—without understanding why. Organizations rarely possess the diagnostic capability to recognize this failure before it becomes institutionalized.

Sometimes the failure is not that organizations measure the wrong things, but that they *present* the right things in ways that distort meaning. A chart can be mathematically accurate and still function as propaganda. Financial news routinely displays single-day stock movements with truncated axes that visually suggest dramatic gains or losses. The data may show a 0.16 percent change, but the representation tells a story of acceleration and momentum. This is not a failure of math; it is a failure of epistemic discipline. When organizations optimize for persuasion instead of understanding, even correct data becomes misleading. These techniques are not new. Darrell Huff documented them decades ago in *How to Lie with Statistics*, showing how scale manipulation, truncated axes, and selective framing can turn technically correct numbers into persuasive falsehoods.

At the same time, truly pure data does not exist. Every measurement involves choices about what to measure, how to measure it, when to measure it, and how to interpret what was measured. Each choice introduces bias. Statistician George Box captured this reality: "all models are wrong, but some are useful."

Probability is one such model. We treat it as a property of events, but it's actually an indicator of uncertainty. Consider a coin flip. We call it 50-50, but that's not because the coin is doing something random. If you had perfect information—exact force applied, angle of release, air resistance, surface friction, initial rotation—you could predict the outcome deterministically. The coin isn't random. Our knowledge is incomplete. Probability is the mathematical framework we use to describe that incompleteness.

This matters when organizations make "data-driven" decisions. A forecast with a confidence interval isn't describing what will happen. It's describing the range of outcomes consistent with current information and the assumptions baked into the model. The forecast might predict 80 percent probability of success, but that doesn't mean reality has an 80 percent chance dial. It means "given what we know and how we modeled it, 8 out of 10 similar situations produced this outcome."

Change the model slightly—different assumptions about customer behavior, different weightings for historical data—and the probability shifts. The underlying reality hasn't changed. The model has. Nassim Taleb emphasizes this distinction relentlessly: models are maps, not territories. The territory remains regardless of what the map claims.

This means we can make educated projections or forecasts based on evidence, and repeated accuracy reinforces confidence in those predictions—much like the *Farmer's Almanac* (which earns trust through historical consistency rather than certainty). However, such forecasts may still fail to capture the full pattern. A nuance or inflection point may exist that has not yet revealed itself in the data.

There is also no guarantee that past behavior will repeat. Recognizing these limitations does not eliminate uncertainty, but it can reduce surprise and unnecessary harm. The alternative is less desirable: decisions based on nothing. When no evidence is present, the decision is not informed—it is an assumption.

This connects to why estimation in complex systems fails so consistently. Teams treat estimates as probabilities—"70 percent confident we'll finish by March"—but the actual work is deterministic. In the end it is either 0 percent or 100 percent delivered based on what happened. The estimate is a "snapshot" that is outdated as soon as work progresses, dependencies respond, and uncertainty resolves. Updated probabilistic forecasts can help navigate towards certainty, but they will fall victim to the same scope and recency limitations.

Recognizing probability as a model rather than a property of reality helps calibrate appropriate responses to forecasts. When someone presents a business case with detailed financial projections, they're not predicting the future. They're describing what would happen if their assumptions hold. Question the assumptions, not the arithmetic.

In the end, this creates a paradox. Organizations need data to make informed decisions in complex environments, but data quality is unreliable, interpretation is subjective, and perfect information remains forever out of reach. The solution is not to abandon measurement. The solution is to develop honest frameworks for evaluating how much confidence a given dataset merits and to calibrate validation effort to the risk exposure of the decision being made.

The real problem emerges when measurement itself becomes corrupted by incentives. Economist Charles Goodhart observed that when a measure becomes a target, it ceases to be a good measure. This principle, known as *Goodhart's Law*, describes how gaming behavior emerges whenever organizations optimize for metrics rather than outcomes. What results is *measurement theater*—graphs and charts that look real pretty, but where actual visibility is lost.

I worked with an organization where finishing early was a failure. Estimation tolerance was symmetrical—miss high or miss low, and you were penalized. The system taught everyone the same lesson: accuracy to the forecast mattered more than outcomes. Efficiency and innovation became risks because they contradicted the plan. Value wasn't rewarded. Predictability of assumptions was. I remember an engineer, visibly frustrated, telling me he had been penalized for completing a project a year early and over a million dollars under budget. When he started working in the code, he discovered an innovative approach that wasn't apparent during the planning phase.

Toyota Motor Corporation is often held up as the archetype of a learning organization, and for good reason. Its production systems were designed to surface problems early, make abnormalities visible, and treat errors as inputs for improvement rather than as failures to punish. Indeed, the Toyota Production System informs much of this book.

Which is why Toyota's certification testing irregularities, disclosed publicly in 2024, are so instructive. They matter because they reveal how learning systems fail when incentives distort behavior, even when they are widely regarded as best in class.

Measurement collapsed, and behavior adapted accordingly. When compliance metrics become performance targets—when passing the test matters more than learning from it—people adapt. The data stops being diagnostic.

This is the same failure mode seen across industries: emissions testing at Volkswagen, safety metrics at Boeing, sales targets at Wells Fargo. The specifics differ. The pattern doesn't. When metrics are used to judge rather than to learn, the system trains people to protect the numbers instead of the underlying outcomes.

Toyota's factory floors were designed so problems could not hide. Their testing systems failed when problems had to hide for people to succeed within the system. The lesson isn't that Toyota abandoned scientific thinking. It's that scientific thinking requires constant vigilance—especially where incentives are strongest and scrutiny is highest.

Much of this confusion stems from a distinction Peter Drucker articulated decades ago about the difference between efficiency and effectiveness. Efficiency is about doing things right—executing work with speed, consistency, and minimal waste. Effectiveness is about doing the right things—choosing work that actually creates value. Organizations are often very good at the former and surprisingly poor at the latter. Metrics tend to reward efficiency because it is easier to observe and quantify, while effectiveness remains contextual, delayed, and harder to measure. When teams are measured locally, they naturally optimize for what they control, even when those optimizations undermine outcomes elsewhere in the system. Over time, what gets measured gets optimized, sometimes at the expense of what actually matters.

At one point, Nokia commanded nearly 50 percent of the global mobile phone market. When the company was later sold to Microsoft for a fraction of its former value, then-CEO Stephen Elop remarked, "We didn't do anything wrong, but somehow, we lost." He wasn't admitting failure—he was revealing a loss of visibility. By the measures that mattered internally, Nokia was executing as expected. But those measures had become disconnected from the environment they were meant to reflect. Outcomes lag reality. By the time results change, the system that produced them has already stopped learning.

This pattern repeats across domains. Call centers optimize for call duration, leading agents to rush customers off the phone whether or not their issues are resolved. Sales teams optimize for closed deals, leading to aggressive tactics that damage long-term customer relationships. Software teams optimize for completion rates, resulting in inflated estimates and fragmented tasks. In each case, measurement drives behavior in ways that undermine the outcomes the measurement was supposed to track.

Then there was the time Hasbro traumatized children across the country. In the 1980s, many Saturday morning cartoons existed for one reason: to sell toys. The shows were essentially thirty-minute commercials. Some invested more in story than others, but the business model was transparent: characters existed to move product. Within that ecosystem, Hasbro's *Transformers* became a phenomenon, and their leader, Optimus Prime, became something nobody at Hasbro anticipated: one of the most beloved fictional characters of his generation.

In 1986, Hasbro released *The Transformers: The Movie* to promote new inventory, in which they killed off Optimus Prime within the first 30 minutes. From a spreadsheet perspective, the decision was sound: retire old SKUs, introduce replacements, capture new revenue.

Story consultant Flint Dille later shared in an interview, "We didn't know that he was an icon. It was a toy show. We just thought we were killing off the old product line to replace it with new products. [...] Kids were crying in the theaters. We heard about people leaving the movie. We were getting a lot of nasty notes about it. There was some kid who locked himself in his bedroom for two weeks."

The replacement toy line underperformed the originals. Within six months, Hasbro reversed course and resurrected the character on television. Forty years later, the company is still apologizing—literally, with a 2026 "Apology Tour" marking the film's anniversary. It turns out there isn't a line item for the emotional attachment of children.

These examples reflect the shareholder primacy framework explored in Chapter 4. When quarterly earnings and revenue growth become the ultimate measure, every metric downstream gets optimized for short-term appearance rather than long-term reality. Measurement theater serves the system's actual goals—looking good to Wall Street—even when it undermines the organization's stated goals of customer value and sustainable performance.

The corruption spreads because organizations treat metrics as objective representations of reality rather than as imperfect proxies constructed through subjective choices. A metric is not truth. It is an abstraction, a simplification, a model. Understanding what a metric reveals requires understanding what it ignores, what assumptions underpin it, and how it might mislead when those assumptions fail to hold.

The failures at Sears under CEO Eddie Lampert illustrate how data-driven decision making can produce catastrophic outcomes when interpretation ignores context. At its peak, Sears was among the most dominant companies in the United States. Its mail-order catalog was widely referred to as the "Consumer's Bible," and by the late twentieth century, roughly 50 percent of U.S. households held a Sears credit card. Lampert implemented a metrics-driven approach that pitted business units against each other, rewarding those that cut costs most aggressively. Units optimized for their individual scorecards by slashing budgets for store maintenance, employee training, and customer service. Stores deteriorated, becoming unattractive and uncompetitive. Employees hit their targets while undermining the company's long-term viability.

Sears declared bankruptcy in 2018, a direct consequence of optimizing for metrics that measured financial efficiency while ignoring customer experience, employee capability, and brand perception. The data was accurate. Costs decreased. Every unit hit its targets. The company declared bankruptcy. The dashboards, presumably, showed green until the day they went dark. The interpretation was fatally flawed because it treated business units as independent rather than as interdependent components of a larger system. This is the difference between being data-driven and being data-informed.

The distinction between data-driven and data-informed decision-making becomes critical in product development, as the next chapter explores. Data-driven approaches optimize for measurable outputs—features shipped, velocity achieved, deployments completed—regardless of whether those outputs create value. Data-informed approaches use metrics as signals while maintaining judgment about what the metrics reveal, what they obscure, and what other factors matter.

Organizations need a practical method for assessing when data quality is sufficient for a decision and when additional validation is warranted. This requires honesty about confidence levels rather than pretending all analyses possess equal rigor. The confidence scale provides a framework for matching validation effort to risk exposure.

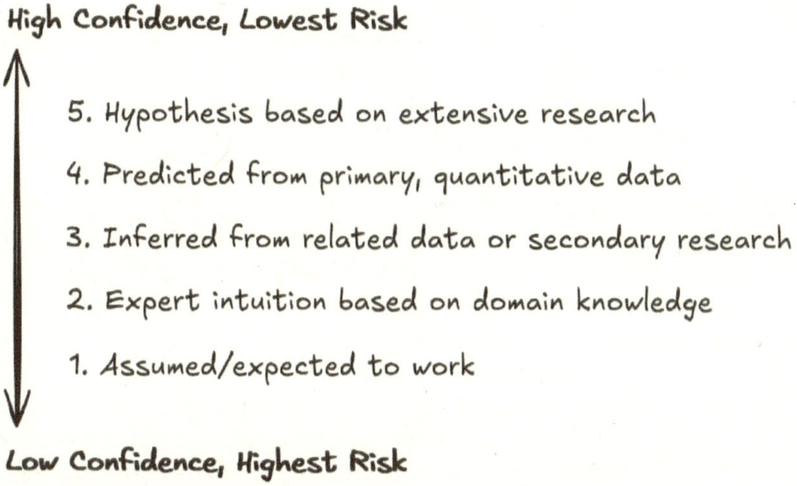

Figure 7.1 - Confidence Scale

The scale distinguishes five levels of confidence, ranging from assumption to extensive research:

Level 1 - Assumption: No data supports the claim. The basis is intuition, pattern matching from loosely analogous situations, or pure speculation. Level 1 decisions happen constantly because not everything merits rigorous validation. The key is recognizing when assumption is driving action and ensuring the risk exposure justifies that approach.

Level 2 - Expert Intuition: Informed judgment from someone with substantial experience in the relevant domain. This draws on pattern recognition developed through years of exposure to similar situations, but remains subjective—influenced by recency bias, availability bias, and the expert's particular history of successes and failures.

Level 3 - Related Data: Conclusions drawn from analogies, industry benchmarks, or findings from adjacent domains rather than direct measurement of the phenomenon in question. Provides more grounding than pure intuition but introduces uncertainty about whether patterns observed elsewhere apply to your specific context.

Level 4 - Primary Data: Direct measurement of relevant variables within the actual context where the decision applies. The data may not be comprehensive, and the analysis may involve simplifications, but the foundation is empirical observation rather than analogy or intuition.

Level 5 - Extensive Research: Controlled experimentation, large sample sizes, statistical modeling, and replication. Monte Carlo simulation exemplifies Level 5 analysis, generating probabilistic forecasts by running thousands of scenarios. This level of research should be weighed against time and cost.

These confidence levels parallel the methods of knowing explored in Chapter 1. Level 1 relies on intuition—pattern recognition without explicit evidence. Level 2 draws on authority, trusting expert judgment developed through experience. Level 3 employs rationalism, inferring conclusions from related data. Levels 4 and 5 embrace empiricism, grounding decisions in direct observation and controlled experimentation. The confidence framework operationalizes those epistemological distinctions, making explicit which way of knowing underpins each decision.

A decision to change the formatting of a README file is low risk—getting it wrong produces negligible consequences. Level 1 or Level 2 confidence (intuition or expert judgment) suffices. Ship the change and observe whether it affects behavior. A decision to overhaul a company's highest-grossing product line carries substantial risk. Getting it wrong can destroy customer relationships, waste months of engineering effort, and undermine revenue. That decision deserves Level 4 or Level 5 confidence. It justifies investment in customer research, prototype testing, phased rollouts, and careful measurement of impact before full commitment.

The mismatch between confidence level and risk exposure creates two distinct failure modes. Organizations demand Level 5 confidence for Level 2 decisions, creating analysis paralysis where teams hesitate to act without perfect data. Or organizations proceed with Level 1 confidence on Level 5 decisions, treating critical strategic choices as if intuition alone provides an adequate basis.

This connects directly to work-in-progress constraints. Organizations that attempt to validate everything equally spread analytical resources so thin that nothing receives adequate scrutiny. Doing less work enables deeper validation of what remains. When a team focuses on 3 initiatives instead of 15, each initiative can receive the level of validation its risk exposure deserves.

A director of user experience research that I used to work with observed that teams often need less data than they think they do. The instinct to gather more information stems from discomfort with uncertainty, not from rational assessment of decision quality. At some point, additional research produces diminishing returns. The question becomes whether the marginal increase in confidence justifies the time and resources required to obtain it.

The confidence framework guides not only how to interpret existing data but also when to gather new data through experimentation. The framework for responsible experimentation emerges from combining confidence level with risk exposure. Low confidence combined with low risk suggests shipping changes and observing results due to the cost of being wrong is negligible. Low confidence combined with high risk demands validation before commitment, because getting the decision wrong carries severe consequences.

Consider a product team deciding whether to remove a feature that appears unused based on analytics. If analytics show zero usage over six months and the feature is obscure, confidence that removal will not harm users is reasonably high. But analytics reveal frequency, not criticality. A feature can be unused most of the year and indispensable during a narrow window.

A responsible approach involves incremental validation rather than immediate deletion. The team might hide the feature from the interface while leaving the underlying functionality intact and proactively notify customers of the planned change. If no one objects across a full usage cycle, confidence increases that removal is safe. The team can then fully deprecate the feature, monitoring for any indication that the decision was premature. This staged approach costs little more than immediate deletion while providing multiple opportunities to detect problems before they escalate.

This principle extends to any change with uncertain outcomes. When possible, structure interventions to allow reversal if early indicators suggest problems. Run experiments on small populations before scaling to everyone. Deploy changes gradually, monitoring impact at each stage. Build escape hatches that allow retreat to previous states if assumptions prove incorrect. These practices do not eliminate risk, but they minimize it.

Understanding confidence levels requires tools for evaluating the reliability of data and the validity of interpretations drawn from it. Librarians developed the CRAAP test as a framework for evaluating information sources. The name is intentionally crude. The framework is not. CRAAP stands for Currency, Relevance, Authority, Accuracy, and Purpose.

In practice, this means asking a few disciplined questions: Is the data current enough for your decision? Does it actually address the question you're asking, or just adjacent information that feels related? Who generated it and do they have legitimate expertise? Can you verify it through other sources? Does the source have incentives to present data in misleading ways?

Applying these criteria filters out obviously unreliable sources while maintaining appropriate skepticism toward even seemingly credible ones. A study funded by an industry trade group may be methodologically sound but might emphasize findings favorable to industry interests, as seen historically in nutrition research on sugar and heart disease. Academic research may be rigorous but may also reflect publication bias toward novel findings rather than replication of existing work, as evidenced by the replication crisis that emerged across large portions of psychology and biomedical science.

Beyond source evaluation, interpreting data requires understanding how analysis can go wrong even when underlying measurements are sound. The distinction between correlation and causation represents the most fundamental pitfall. Two variables that move together are correlated—that does not mean one causes the other. Ice cream sales and murder rates both increase during the summer months. At first glance, the data appears to suggest a relationship—until you realize no one has ever been killed by a double scoop of mint chip. Weather influences both independently.

Yet organizations routinely mistake correlation for causation when analyzing performance. A company implements a new training program, and productivity increases over the following quarter. Leadership concludes the training caused the improvement. During that same quarter, the company hired experienced talent, a competitor exited the market, and economic conditions improved. Any of these factors might explain the observed change. Isolating causation requires controlling for confounding variables, which organizational environments rarely permit.

These biases corrupting data interpretation—mistaking correlation for causation, survivorship bias obscuring failures, narrative fallacy creating false coherence—are the same forces explored in the previous chapter that lead organizations to mislearn from their own histories. When measurement lacks rigor, it amplifies rather than corrects these cognitive distortions.

The Flaw of Averages compounds this by obscuring variability. Consider a company deciding whether to invest in expanding server capacity based on average load. If the average load is 60 percent of capacity, expansion seems unnecessary. But if load varies between 20 percent and 95 percent, with brief spikes reaching capacity limits, customers experience degraded service during peak periods despite comfortable average utilization. The average obscures the distribution, leading to decisions that optimize for conditions that rarely exist.

Sample bias represents another common corruption vector. Data collected from volunteers differs systematically from data that would be collected from randomly selected participants. Surveys sent to customers who recently made purchases miss those who considered purchasing but decided against it. Performance metrics from teams that adopted a new process voluntarily differ from metrics that would emerge if the process were mandated universally. The convenience of gathering data from willing participants introduces systematic distortion that undermines the validity of conclusions drawn from it.

Avoiding measurement theater requires recognizing when precision adds value and when it creates the illusion of rigor without improving decisions. Not every initiative needs detailed metrics. Not every question deserves A/B testing. The goal is not comprehensive measurement. The goal is sufficient confidence for the decision being made.

Measurement theater represents a specific type of waste—activity that masquerades as rigor while consuming resources without generating insight. Chapter 9 explores how such waste accumulates across organizations and how to eliminate it systematically.

Designer Douglas Bowman famously left Google in 2009, citing the company's obsessive testing culture. Google tested forty-one shades of blue to determine which performed best in click-through rates, paralyzed by the need to justify every design decision with data. Bowman argued this approach optimized away delight, intuition, and the qualities that make products compelling rather than merely functional. The deeper problem is that the experiment was technically invalid because Google had no control over how colors displayed on different monitors. The same blue appears differently across devices, making the results unreliable from a measurement validity standpoint. This is data theater—the appearance of rigor without actual validity.

Distinguishing valuable measurement from theater requires asking what decision hangs on the answer. If the answer is clear regardless of what data reveals, measurement is theater. If the data might genuinely change the course of action, measurement is justified. If the decision must be made regardless and data merely provides political cover, measurement is theater masquerading as rigor.

George Box's observation that all models are wrong but some are useful provides a frame for resolving the tension between imperfect data and the need to act. The standard for data quality is not perfection. The standard is usefulness relative to available alternatives.

Monte Carlo simulation exemplifies this principle. It generates probabilistic forecasts by randomly sampling from historical throughput data thousands of times, producing a distribution of possible outcomes rather than a single point estimate. This provides far more realistic planning than traditional estimation methods that pretend the future can be predicted precisely. Monte Carlo acknowledges uncertainty explicitly, quantifying the range of likely outcomes and the confidence level associated with each.

Daniel Vacanti's work on probabilistic forecasting using Monte Carlo methods demonstrated that flow metrics (throughput, cycle time, work item age) provide more reliable planning inputs than traditional estimation. The simulation doesn't eliminate uncertainty—it quantifies it, showing the range of likely outcomes and the probability of each. This is empiricism about uncertainty itself: measuring what you can observe (historical completion rates) to generate realistic forecasts rather than making confident predictions based on intuition.

But Monte Carlo does not eliminate uncertainty. It models historical patterns forward, assuming those patterns will continue. If team composition changes, if the nature of work shifts, if external dependencies introduce new variability, historical data may provide poor guidance for the future. The model is wrong in the sense that it simplifies reality, makes assumptions that may not hold, and cannot account for unknowns. It is useful in the sense that it produces better forecasts than intuition or arbitrary deadlines.

Monte Carlo also carries a subtler limitation: it forecasts capacity, not focus. Knowing that a team can likely complete fifteen items by March says nothing about whether those fifteen items are the right fifteen. That requires a different discipline entirely.

DORA metrics—which share DNA with Vacanti's flow metrics—provide another example of useful wrongness. They measure lead time for changes, deployment frequency, mean time to recovery, and change failure rate. These metrics have been found through rigorous research by Dr. Nicole Forsgren to actually correlate with organizational performance (unlike other commonly leveraged performance metrics such as effort, utilization, or lines of code), but they measure delivery capability, not impact. A team can achieve elite scores across all four metrics while shipping features nobody uses. Forsgren herself has emphasized that the four metrics are incomplete on their own—they do not capture developer productivity or the value delivered to the business. They remain useful because they identify patterns that distinguish high-performing delivery organizations from low-performing ones, but they cannot tell you whether what gets delivered matters.

Throughput, measuring completed work per unit of time, offers an empirical alternative to estimation that acknowledges rather than pretends away uncertainty. If a team historically completes 30 tasks per month, future throughput will likely cluster around that rate. This does not account for holidays, changing priorities, unexpected technical challenges, or learning curves on unfamiliar work. It provides a reasonable baseline that can be adjusted based on contextual knowledge.

The uncertainty of projected completion dates is unavoidable, yet deadlines are routinely treated as certainty. In creative work, the tension is explicit: no amount of planning can guarantee when the next good idea will arrive. As Andre "Dr. Dre" Young said in *The Defiant Ones*, Episode 4:

"I think release dates are the enemy of creativity. You know? You never know when you're gonna be inspired—what's going to inspire you. You can't put a time limit on creativity. You know? I don't know if the idea I have today is a good idea. You don't know. You know what I mean? We're artists. We're just being creative. So, it's like man, just shut the fuck up and let us do our job. And then we'll give it to you, and you can make your money."

This is not romantic resistance to accountability. It is operational insight from someone whose judgment has proven repeatable. Dre went on to help build three successful studios in succession; each associated with artists who would define their era, before declaring himself hip-hop's first billionaire following Apple's $3 billion acquisition of Beats Electronics. At that point, the reasonable conclusion is not luck, but a working model: creativity produces disproportionate returns when it is protected from premature certainty imposed by people who bear none of the creative risk.

While Dre is speaking about music, the underlying dynamic applies to all forms of creative problem-solving. Programming, design, and product development are creative work in the same sense: the quality of the outcome cannot be scheduled into existence, only discovered through iteration.

There is a tendency to treat a release date, a forecast, or an estimate as a promise. Each of these tools is wrong in ways that become obvious under scrutiny. Each is directionally useful when applied with awareness of their limitations. The skill isn't finding perfect models—those don't exist. The skill is selecting models useful enough for decisions that must be made anyway, then noticing when they stop being useful.

Organizations fail not because they lack perfect data but because they misinterpret imperfect data, demand precision where approximation suffices, accept ambiguity where rigor is warranted, and confuse measurement with understanding. The antidote is not more data. The antidote is better judgment about when data is good enough, what it actually reveals, and how to act despite inevitable imperfection.

What confidence level does your most important pending decision actually possess? Does that level align with the risk you are taking?

Nowhere do these questions matter more than in product development—where organizations routinely build features nobody uses, follow assumptions nobody tested, and ship solutions to problems nobody has. The measurement discipline this chapter established becomes the foundation for deciding what to build.

CHAPTER 8
What Gets Used

"The value is in what gets used, not in what gets built." – Kris Gale

I built my first website when I was eleven years old. The tool I used was a free no-code editor called HotDog by Sausage Software, hosted on my America Online account. It was objectively terrible—capable of displaying only one item per line, with zero design standards, stolen clipart, and what I'm certain was profound storytelling from a millennial tween. It didn't matter. I was hooked.

Over the years I built dozens of sites for my own whimsical purposes, teaching myself programming through trial and error, stealing code from other websites, and innovating experiences that mixed graphics and scripting in ways that would have made MacGyver proud. I even interned as the head web designer for a local studio during my senior year of high school. Head designer because I was the only web designer there.

Everyone maintained page view counters back then, those primitive tickers showing how many times your site had loaded. The counter was the epitome of a vanity metric—I remember refreshing the page repeatedly just so it wouldn't look like nobody had visited my website.

As my skills improved, I created increasingly intricate designs. One favorite technique involved saving buttons as images, then using hover effects to swap them for animated GIFs that simulated the Flash-based interfaces popular at the time, with significantly reduced loading times. The technical challenge delighted me. Making something work through clever problem-solving gave me genuine pride. It still does.

The frustration started when I began building sites for others. Suddenly I faced requests that contradicted my carefully cultivated aesthetic judgment. As designers have observed cynically for generations, everyone thinks they're a designer. I found myself fixing bugs in poorly constructed code someone else had written, making buttons blue when I knew they should be red, and avidly debating why we should build my feature (that I intuitively knew was needed), instead of someone else's idea that was also likely just someone's opinion. I was building the thing, surely, I understood what worked best.

Here was the problem I couldn't see at the time: I had taught myself to code empirically, through observation and experimentation. I reverse-engineered other sites, modified values to see what happened, ran tests until I could reliably reproduce desired results. The scientific approach came naturally when working with code.

But it never occurred to me to apply that same methodology to content or audience. I built what I thought people wanted based on my preferences, my aesthetic sense, and my technical interests. I extrinsically knew that everyone has different preferences, but intrinsically I still thought I had the best judgement of what was valuable. As Don Norman, *the Father of User Experience*, likes to remind us, "You are not the user."

This cognitive bias is known as the *False-Consensus Effect*. People assume their preferences represent the majority opinion. Executives who enjoy a particular interface pattern believe customers will share that enthusiasm. Product managers who find a feature intuitive assume users will too. Designers who appreciate minimalist aesthetics expect that sensibility to resonate universally.

This bias operates below conscious awareness, making it particularly insidious. Nobody believes they're designing for themselves while ignoring users. They genuinely think their judgment reflects a broader truth.

The False-Consensus Effect is compounded by survivor bias, which we examined in Chapter 6. Teams remember the features that shipped and succeeded while forgetting the ones that failed or were quietly abandoned. This selective memory reinforces the illusion that intuition reliably predicts success.

Sunk-cost fallacy adds yet another layer: people attribute value based on the amount of time, effort, or funding invested. A feature that consumed six months of development must be valuable, otherwise the investment was wasted. This reasoning inverts causality. Investment doesn't create value; customer adoption does.

Solution-first thinking only further adds to these biases. People often arrive at what they want to build first, then construct reasoning to justify it afterward. The hypothesis doesn't precede the solution; it gets retrofitted to defend it. This inverts the empirical process entirely. Instead of "we believe customers have problem X, so let's test whether solution Y addresses it," teams operate as "we want to build Y, so let's find a problem it might solve." Confirmation bias then filters incoming evidence to support the predetermined conclusion. Contradictory data becomes "edge cases." Lukewarm user feedback becomes "they just need more time with it." Failed pilots become "we didn't explain the value proposition clearly enough." The solution was never really a hypothesis. It was a destination dressed up as an experiment.

My first project as a business analyst was a textbook case. A retired executive from a vendor had invested in a startup, then sold our VP on their solution because they were old friends. The product was vaporware and solved no problem statement. I was told to make up a use case.

Stakeholders eager to please this VP jumped in with their own use cases. We piloted it in five locations, before I was able to accumulate enough evidence to kill the project and its funding. Every failure mode described above was present.

These biases operate at the individual level. They explain why smart, well-intentioned people consistently build things nobody uses. But individual misjudgment alone doesn't explain the scale of the problem.

To be clear, not all speculative investment is waste. Sometimes organizations invest in emerging technology without a defined use case because they want to understand its capabilities before they need them. The difference is intent. Exploration is structured around learning. It is bounded, timeboxed, and tied to explicit outcomes. Success is defined as insight, not adoption. Meijer frequently approached this through dedicated research roles, proof of concepts, and hackathons to ensure we stayed current on the art of the possible.

This solution-first pattern repeats at scale across the software industry. Companies fall victim to their own ingenuity, assuming that if they build something technically impressive, users will materialize to justify it. I call this the *Field of Dreams* strategy: *if I build it, they will come*. Classic movie, poor product strategy.

Research from Pendo reveals that 80 percent of features in production software are rarely if ever used. The Standish Group determined that in some packaged applications, fewer than 5 percent of features see regular adoption. Google and Microsoft Bing found that 80-90 percent of their features tested neutral or negative when subjected to controlled experiments. 70 percent of features created by Slack's monetization team failed to demonstrate positive impact.

This is not primarily a failure of execution, though execution failures and misjudged demand can coexist. The features may work as specified. The waste lies in building them at all. And yet, software remains one of the highest margin industries in history—even while wasting most of what it produces. Imagine if even half of the features built were moderately used.

If something lacks demand, it possesses no value regardless of the effort or cost invested. Many organizations are so focused on how long something will take to build, they forget to ask if they should.

Melissa Perri distinguishes between being *product-led* (focused on solving customer problems) versus being a *feature factory* (focused on shipping new features). The difference isn't semantic. Product-led organizations start with desired outcomes and work backward. Feature factories start with stakeholder requests and work forward, never validating whether those features create the outcomes anyone actually wants.

If most shipped features go unused, then a substantial portion of development capacity is funding work that produces no measurable return. Inventory that degrades rather than appreciates. Infrastructure that must be maintained despite serving no one. Complexity that makes everything else harder to change. Organizations measure what they build: features shipped, tasks completed, releases deployed. They rarely measure what gets used, which is the only metric that correlates with value creation. If you paid for a meal and 80 percent of it arrived cold and untouched, you'd complain. Software gets a pass, somehow.

Goodhart's Law, which we examined in the previous chapter, predicts exactly what happens next. Teams optimize for metrics rather than outcomes, creating the appearance of progress while undermining actual value creation.

The dynamic plays out predictably. Leadership declares that completion rates, feature count, or deployment frequency will determine success. Teams respond rationally by maximizing those numbers. Completion rates climb through scope reduction or estimation inflation. Feature counts rise as complex work gets subdivided into superficial increments. Deployment frequency increases by shipping trivial changes.

The metrics improve. The product doesn't.

Most engineering output fails to create measurable value, and most engineers don't work for free. Any investment that meaningfully reduces that failure rate—through product management, research, experimentation, or analytics—pays for itself as long as it costs less than the waste it prevents. To channel Goldratt: delivery is not the constraint, certainty is. The question isn't whether you can afford discovery; it's whether you can afford to continue funding blind execution in a system optimized for shipping rather than learning.

Perri calls this the 'build trap.' A trap easy to fall into because it is easier to optimize for outputs than outcomes.

Individual biases explain misjudgment. But they don't explain why organizations systematically perpetuate waste even when individuals within them recognize the problem. The answer lies in structural forces that reward the wrong behaviors at multiple levels.

Things like planned obsolescence and microtransactions exist because the people making those decisions are rewarded for doing so. And a good product requires saying no—a lot. However, saying no rarely makes friends, and even more rarely does the number of times bad features were turned down appear on annual performance reviews.

Financial engineering determines product architecture. I once worked for a client in a regulated industry where rates were set by a governing agency, and the company was permitted to earn roughly a 10 percent return on approved capital expenditures. That single constraint shaped everything. Operational spending was heavily scrutinized, while new builds were encouraged—even when existing systems already did most of the job. Building something new counted as CapEx: capital expenditure that could be justified, depreciated, and framed as investment. Improving what already existed counted as OpEx: operational cost.

Over time, this logic narrowed what solutions were even considered. The definition of "CapEx" became rigid, and proposals that didn't clearly fit that box rarely survived review. Rather than asking how to improve the system, teams asked how to structure work so it would be approved. Predictably, the answer was almost always another new build.

The result was dozens of overlapping systems, each created to satisfy a capital requirement rather than an operational need. Project management overhead ballooned alongside them: separate plans, reviews, status reports, and approval cycles for work that often differed only in name. As a consultant supporting multiple teams, I was frequently spread across a dozen projects at once. Each week ended with an hour or more of time reporting just to reconcile that fragmentation—work the organization paid for, but never traced back to the decisions that created it. Repeat that across thousands of people, week after week, and the cost becomes substantial. As long as funding flowed to projects instead of teams, that overhead wasn't a bug. It was a feature of the system.

A counterexample I've seen illustrates how much leverage those constraints actually have. Years ago, I worked with a CTO who had previously come from a CFO background. He applied an explicit economic constraint to product decisions: every project or feature had to have the *potential* to return at least six percent. If it didn't, the capital was better invested elsewhere. The requirement wasn't proof—it was plausibility under uncertainty. That single constraint eliminated most debates before they started.

During a large ERP implementation, he applied an even stricter rule. Any customization required a business case made directly to him. Customization wasn't forbidden—it was treated as a liability that needed justification. In the end, only three conflicts remained between company policy and the tool, and those policies were changed to accommodate the system. The implementation finished on schedule. It's the only ERP implementation I've seen do so.

Conway's Law introduces another organizational constraint that affects product structure. When teams are organized around solutions, technologies, or components, each team represents funded capacity tied to maintaining and extending that domain. Even in environments with strong psychological safety—where a team could admit the original problem has been solved—that capacity will not remain idle. Roadmaps will be filled. Improvements will be identified. New initiatives will emerge.

When boundaries are defined by technology rather than customer outcomes or value streams, the existence of the team begins to shape the product. Work does not disappear when value has been delivered; it shifts to sustain the structure that funds it. The UI is redesigned. The code is refactored. Again. And again.

Goodhart's Law ensures the rest. The unglamorous work that makes products objectively valuable doesn't move the metrics leadership watches. So, it doesn't happen.

I witnessed the interaction between individual bias and structural forces firsthand at many places. Leadership requests that a team builds a specific feature. When executives whose judgment commands up to seven-figure salaries weigh in on product decisions, their input carries disproportionate weight regardless of its merit. Teams operating under that dynamic face a choice. They can validate ideas empirically, accept findings that contradict executive preferences, and then attempt to change minds backed by evidence.

Or they can treat executive opinions as requirements, build what leadership wants, and avoid the career risk of appearing insubordinate.

Many choose the safer path. The organization optimizes for executive satisfaction rather than customer value. Products ship with features that make internal stakeholders happy while confusing or frustrating actual users.

Consider the lifecycle of a focused startup. They solve one problem well. The product is sharp, coherent, and valuable precisely because it doesn't try to be everything to everyone. Then they are acquired. The acquiring company usually doesn't just want the product. They want "strategic synergies," which translates to bolting features onto their existing platform while systematically buying out any potential disrupters. What was once a focused tool becomes a menu item in someone else's product suite. And companies know it's easier to buy someone else's customers than to try to grow their own. The problem is that they rarely invest adequately to serve these new users well.

This pattern repeats until products become Swiss army knives—attempting dozens of functions, none particularly well.

This is where strategy is supposed to do its job. Strategy connects why the organization exists to what it chooses to build—and more importantly, what it chooses not to. A good strategy constrains. It gives teams a reason to say no that doesn't require a career-risking confrontation with an executive who wants their pet feature prioritized.

Most organizations don't have that. They have a vision statement, maybe a set of objectives, and a gap where strategy should be. The vision says something aspirational about transforming an industry or delighting customers. The objectives say "grow the business," "increase user adoption," or "decrease costs." And between them, nothing. No articulation of *how*—which customers, which problems, which bets, and critically, which things we will stop doing.

That vacuum gets filled by whatever has the most political momentum. Every initiative sounds reasonable when evaluated against "grow revenue" because almost anything could theoretically contribute to growth. The strategy constrains nothing, so it permits everything. Roadmaps become a collection of stakeholder requests ranked by seniority rather than evidence.

Startups rarely have this problem because the product *is* the strategy. There's no distance between what the company does and why it exists. Once the product and the business become separate concepts—through growth, acquisition, or organizational complexity—the product starts serving the organization's needs instead of the customers'. Strategy is the bridge that's supposed to prevent that drift. When it's missing, or when it amounts to "make money," the Swiss army knife outcome is inevitable.

This accumulation of features is often justified in the language of iteration. We tell ourselves we're evolving the product step by step. Consider the iterative development diagram everyone loves to reference: start with a skateboard, evolve to a scooter, then a bike, then a motorcycle, then a car. The point is that each stage delivers usable value while incorporating learning toward the final vision.

Figure 8.1 - Adapted from Henrik Kniberg, *Making Sense of MVP*, published by Crisp, licensed under CC BY-SA 3.0.

Here's what actually happens: they build a skateboard. It works. Then they bolt handlebars onto it and call it a scooter. Next come pedals and a gearbox to turn it into a bicycle. The product becomes a Frankenstein assembly of bolted-on features, each adding fragility because the foundation was never rebuilt to support it. Just wait until we strap a motor to it.

This isn't iterative development. It's what I call *prototype permanence*, treating prototypes as finished products and essentially shipping demos as production software. The proof of concept demonstrates feasibility, gets shipped as a "feature," and never receives the investment required to make it actually good. Teams move on to the next POC while the previous one remains in production, half-baked and unloved.

The result is *design by committee* that generates those Swiss army knife-like products. Features are funded by various stakeholders with their own agendas. The original purpose gets buried under accumulated features that serve organizational needs rather than customer needs.

This is the dark side of "ship fast and iterate." It becomes "ship fast and move on." The iteration never comes because the team is already three features down the roadmap, bolting motors onto skateboards that should have been rebuilt as motorcycles.

Google's history illustrates this dysfunction clearly. Google+ created a social network that struggled with adoption. Google Wave developed a futuristic collaboration tool that confused users. Google Stadia launched a gaming platform that ignored market realities. Google's product graveyard is extensive enough to have its own Wikipedia page. This is what happens when the ability to build exceeds the discipline to determine demand.

Breaking this pattern requires changing what gets rewarded. Measure usage and impact, not features. Celebrate enhancement of existing capabilities, not just addition of new ones. Create teams around customer outcomes, not technical components. Allow teams to declare victory when outcomes are achieved and redefine their focus rather than manufacturing new work to sustain their structure.

Most importantly, resist the temptation to bolt one more thing onto the skateboard. Sometimes you need to rebuild from scratch with everything you've learned. That's not waste—that's how learning converts into capability.

But rebuilding isn't always the answer either. Greenfield rewrites that promise to replace decades of accumulated software rarely go to plan. They lose focus through scope creep, recreate the same problems by copying the existing product, and often carry forward the same unused functionality that justified the rewrite.

And if you find yourself in this sort of situation, it's unfortunate, but you're going to have to pay the piper for the transgressions of your predecessors. There is no "easy button" solution for legacy monolithic systems, but I would challenge you to think carefully about why it needs to be replaced, what things are actually being used, and where the most benefit lies. And most importantly, how can you iteratively release this new solution for continuous validation and rolling ROI.

The discipline required is knowing when bolting on degrades the foundation beyond repair versus when enhancement is the right approach. Both decisions require empirical thinking: what are users willing to pay for, what technical debt is genuinely blocking progress, and what's the actual cost of each path forward? The answer is rarely "always rebuild" or "never rebuild." It's "measure the trade-offs honestly and choose based on evidence rather than executive impatience or engineering preference." On the latter, I have experienced more than once where we invested in refactoring a system because our engineer lead or architect said it was imperative, only to have them replaced upon completion with another that demands we refactor the freshly refactored code. Be careful of preferential biases.

The alternative—building less but building better—seems obvious in retrospect yet proves difficult in practice. Apple's products feel clean, intentional, and effortless to use because the company adheres religiously to a philosophy of fewer features with higher impact. Where other manufacturers cram functionality into every available screen and menu, Apple kills features that don't demonstrably add value. This restraint is disciplined empiricism applied to product development.

Innovation without validation is expensive guesswork dressed as strategy. Google can afford this expensive validation strategy, whether they should or not, but can your company?

The correction for individual bias requires external validation. Observing what users actually do when confronted with working implementations. Behavior reveals truth that self-reported preferences obscure, as David Ogilvy has noted, people don't think what they feel, don't say what they think, and don't do what they say. Therefore, asking a customer what they want produces unreliable data. The only time it is considered acceptable to ask your user is when it is something that cannot be inherently observed, e.g., what was your reason for coming here today?

Markets often reveal preferences through behavior that contradicts predictions. The resurgence of vinyl records, manual transmission cars, and board games wasn't rejection of technology—it was customers seeking qualities that over-digitization had eliminated: tangibility, permanence, intentionality. Products built on assumptions of linear "progress" toward more digital, more features, more convenience missed what customers actually wanted. The trend appeared obvious only after behavior made it undeniable.

It *is* tempting to "upgrade" automotive infotainment systems to replace tactile volume knobs with deep-nested touchscreen menus, make appliances "smart" so that they require a Wi-Fi connection just to toast a bagel, and digitize restaurant menus that force diners to navigate to a glitchy PDF via a QR-code just to see the price of a burger.

Many of these features and products are validated by vanity metrics. Consider a search feature released with all the conventional markers of success: on schedule, within budget, meeting technical specifications. Monitoring reveals high usage: customers searching repeatedly, page views climbing steadily. A manager might celebrate this engagement, interpreting high search volume as validation that the feature delivers value.

But observation may tell a different story. Users search again and again because the first results failed them. They're not engaged; they're frustrated. Forced to reformulate queries because the system doesn't surface what they need. What appears as adoption is actually dysfunction made visible. The metric succeeded while the product failed. *Success theater*: the art of presenting dysfunction as engagement.

This distinction between apparent and actual success explains why organizations need to be careful when choosing what metric defines success. And likely, multiple metrics may need to be employed.

Little Caesar's Pizza demonstrates this concept well. They don't make gourmet pizza. They don't compete on quality metrics that pizza enthusiasts care about. Their Hot-N-Ready pizza is cheap, fast, and available immediately without calling ahead or waiting.

That's what their customers actually value. Not artisanal ingredients or perfect crust texture, but the ability to feed a family for five dollars with zero friction. Little Caesar's built their entire business model around delivering that specific value proposition reliably and at massive scale.

Attempting to compete on "best pizza" would misalign their operations, pricing, supply chain, and brand positioning with what their customers pay for. They'd invest resources in improvements customers don't value enough to pay extra for, while potentially compromising the speed and price that customers do value.

Understanding what customers value—not what you assume they should value, not what you'd prefer they value, but what they demonstrably do value through their purchasing behavior—determines whether product development creates or destroys value. This requires empiricism, because assumptions don't survive contact with reality.

Therefore, before committing resources to building anything substantial, three questions deserve honest answers:

The first concerns *desirability*: do customers want this? Not whether they might use it if it existed, which invites speculation, but whether they have demonstrated the problem this solves and whether it matters enough to change their behavior.

The second concerns *feasibility*: can we build this reliably with current capabilities? This isn't asking whether something is theoretically possible—most things are, given unlimited time and resources—but whether the organization possesses the skills, systems, and knowledge required to execute without unacceptable risk.

The third concerns *viability*: will there be a worthwhile return on this investment? Should we build this given strategic priorities and resource constraints? Even desirable, feasible products may not deserve investment if other opportunities promise greater return.

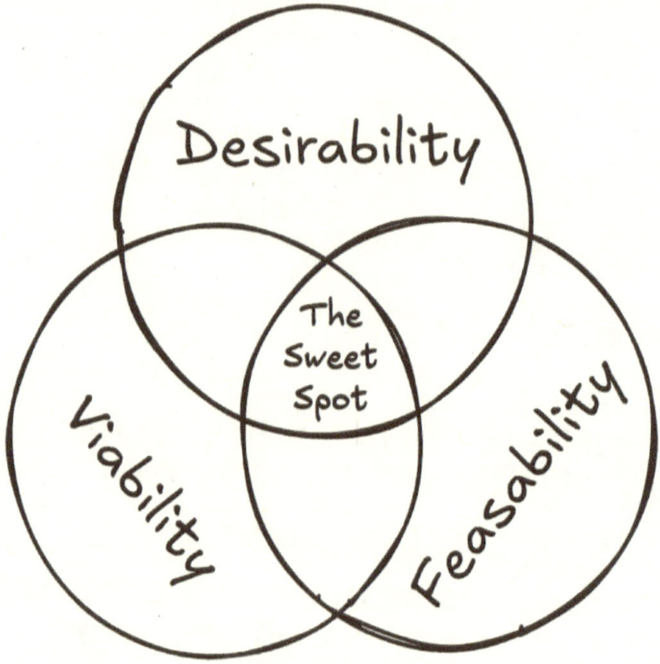

Figure 8.2 - The Innovation Sweet Spot

These three dimensions create what's known as the *Innovation Sweet Spot*—the intersection where all three conditions align. Most product ideas fail to reach this intersection. That's its purpose. The sweet spot amplifies the likelihood that what gets built matters. And I assure you there is plenty of work that falls within this intersection.

The sweet spot functions as a filter, not a formula. Ideas that satisfy only one or two dimensions rarely succeed. A desirable, feasible product that lacks viability consumes resources better spent elsewhere. A viable, desirable product that exceeds current feasibility creates commitments teams can't deliver on. A feasible, viable product nobody wants becomes another entry in the graveyard of features nobody uses.

This validation framework operationalizes the scientific thinking explored in Chapter 2 and reflects what Rother identifies as the core discipline: making your thinking process visible and falsifiable rather than hidden and assumptive. When teams say, “we should build feature X because customers want it,” they’re asserting a belief. When they say, “we hypothesize that customers who experience problem Y will adopt feature X, and we’ll test this by releasing a prototype to 100 users by measuring adoption rate,” they’ve made their thinking falsifiable. The difference is whether you’re defending a position or testing an assumption. Organizations that build accountability around defending positions punish course correction. Ones that build accountability around testing assumptions reward learning.

While the sweet spot establishes what questions to ask before building, the often-harder challenge is defining what success looks like after the solution is built—measuring outcomes rather than outputs.

Most organizations approach this backwards. They begin with organizational goals: increase revenue, reduce churn, improve engagement. These objectives cascade into initiatives, which decompose into features, which get assigned to teams. Somewhere in that cascade, the customer disappears. Teams optimize for shipping what leadership requested rather than validating whether customers benefited.

Impact mapping, a technique developed by Gojko Adzic, attempts to connect deliverables back to business goals through a structured hierarchy. But the standard approach carries a subtle flaw: it anchors on organizational objectives first. The starting point determines what gets optimized.

The inversion that makes this framework genuinely useful starts with the actor being served rather than the outcome being sought.

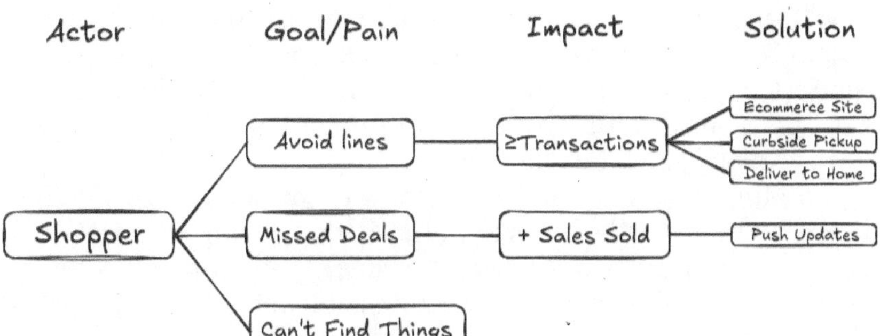

Figure 8.3 - Actor-First Impact Mapping Example

Consider how this changes the conversation. Instead of asking “how do we increase mobile app engagement?” (an organizational goal that could be achieved through dark patterns, notification spam, or genuinely valuable features), the question becomes "who are we serving, and what do they actually want?"

This first became apparent to me when I worked at Meijer. I remember thinking to myself, "if I made this feature, and users actually used it, we'd make so much money." I quickly realized user adoption does not work that way. The thing I loved about working for their loyalty program is that users generally appreciated it. It was super profitable for Meijer, leaning on behavior design to encourage shoppers to be more exclusive with where they shopped and to spend more each trip, but customers enjoyed the savings too (some perceived, some actual). I further remember talking to some ladies at a wedding reception who were enthusiastically professing their love for *my* digital progeny, when I decided to ask them about a feature I had been unsuccessfully championing for weeks. One lady said, "Oh, I don't care about that, what I really want is..." That was the moment that solidified this understanding.

Thus, I developed the actor-first impact mapping approach which flows from this insight: Actor, then Goal or Pain, then Impact, then Deliverable.

The Actor identifies who we're observing and serving. Not a demographic abstraction but a person with context, constraints, and competing priorities. It doesn't have to be a robust persona, but shoppers at this retailer weren't a homogeneous mass. Some optimized ruthlessly for price. Others valued convenience over savings. Still others wanted specific products unavailable elsewhere. Each actor type suggested different goals worth addressing.

The Goal or Pain captures what that actor is trying to achieve or avoid—in their terms, not ours. "Doesn't want to miss out on a good deal" reflects how customers actually think. "Increase promotional response rate" reflects how the organization thinks. The distinction matters because it determines what we observe to validate success. Customer goals can be confirmed through behavior. Organizational goals can be gamed through metrics.

The Impact defines how we'll know we moved the needle. Ideally, it's something that benefits both the actor and the organization. This is where the framework earns its value. Finding metrics that align customer benefit with business benefit forces genuine product thinking rather than extraction thinking.

For the deal-seeking shopper, the impact metric was discounted item sales. When customers bought more items on promotion, they saved money (their goal), and the company moved inventory (our goal). The metric couldn't be gamed without actually serving the customer. Contrast this with "push notification click-through rate," which could be inflated through misleading copy or manufactured urgency without delivering any value to the shopper.

Only after establishing actor, goal, and impact does the framework turn to Solution aka the features, products, or services that might create the desired impact. This ordering matters. These deliverables become hypotheses rather than requirements. Push notifications are one possible way to help deal-seekers. So is a personalized deals page, a price-match guarantee, or a browser extension that tracks price history.

This connects directly to the validation questions explored earlier. Desirability asks whether customers want what we're building, which requires knowing what customers actually want, not what we assume they want. The actor-first approach surfaces that knowledge before solutions are proposed. Feasibility asks whether we can build it, which only matters for deliverables worth building. Viability asks whether we should build it, which depends on whether the impact metric justifies the investment of feasibility.

This approach also provides natural checkpoints for empirical validation. After launch, and accounting for trends, did the impact metric move? If discounted item sales increased after introducing deal-focused push notifications, the hypothesis held. If the metric didn't move, something in the chain broke: either we misunderstood the actor's goal, chose the wrong impact metric, or built a solution that failed to create the expected impact. Each possibility suggests different next steps.

Most importantly, this approach makes outcome measurement concrete rather than abstract. "Did we create value?" becomes "did deal-focused shoppers buy more discounted items?" The question has an answer discoverable through observation. Instead of speculating whether a feature was successful, we can start examining whether the impact occurred. This is the PDCA cycle from Chapter 2 in action.

This doesn't eliminate judgment or guarantee success. Impact metrics can still be poorly chosen. Actor goals can be misunderstood. Solutions can fail despite sound reasoning. But the framework creates conditions where failure teaches something useful rather than disappearing into vanity metrics that always trend upward.

The discipline required is refusing to skip steps. Organizations perpetually want to jump from vague business objectives directly to feature lists, treating the messy work of understanding customers as unnecessary delay. Impact mapping insists on that work precisely because skipping it produces the 80 percent of features that go unused, which makes impact mapping a great way to introduce empiricism into product development. Although it's certainly not the only way.

This continuous validation operates in the same tension as a refinement workflow should. Refinement is the process of documenting the who, why, and what so the new feature can be built. The challenge is reducing uncertainty just in time rather than too early or too late. Requirements don't arrive fully formed. They emerge through an iterative process of experimentation and learning.

Therefore, product development is applied empiricism: forming theories about what will create value, testing those theories as cheaply as possible, incorporating what you learn into the next iteration.

Rother uses the Improvement Kata Model to describe this: Consider the challenge or direction, grasp the current situation, establish your next, closer-in target condition, define the next step (hypothesis), and run the experiment(s) to learn. Product teams practicing this approach treat every release as a hypothesis test rather than a commitment to defend. The target condition is clear: what outcome are we trying to achieve for which customers? The current condition is observable: what's actually happening now? The next step is small enough to learn from quickly: what's the smallest experiment that tests our riskiest assumption? And the reflection is honest: did results match expectations, and what does that tell us about our next step?

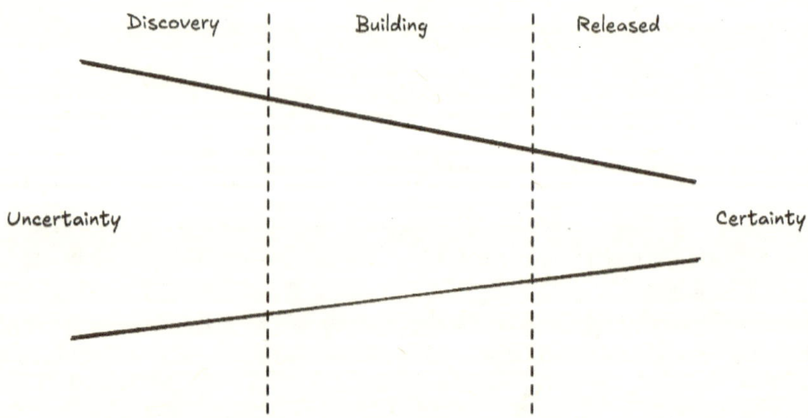

Figure 8.4 - Cone of Uncertainty

The Cone of Uncertainty illustrates why this iterative approach produces better outcomes than attempting to define everything up front. At idea inception, estimates can vary drastically in either direction. As work progresses—designs become concrete, prototypes get tested, actual usage provides feedback—the cone narrows.

Maximum certainty arrives only after release to production, when customer behavior reveals what the requirements should have been in the first place. It's worth mentioning, though, that certainty may never be fully realized, and is unlikely to arrive after a single release.

Marty Cagan observes that it typically takes several iterations to get implementation of an idea to the point where it actually delivers expected business value. Released software isn't the end of validation—it's the beginning. Only production use generates the data that reveals whether your hypotheses were correct. Organizations that celebrate shipping as completion are confusing the start of learning with its conclusion.

Kent Beck summarizes this perfectly in his 1999 publication *Extreme Programming Explained*, "The development of a piece of software changes its own requirements. As soon as the customers see the first release, they learn what they want in the second release... or what they really wanted in the first. And it's valuable learning, because it couldn't have possibly taken place based on speculation. It is learning that can only come from experience. But customers can't get there alone. They need people who can program, not as guides, but as companions."

The released product generates data unavailable through any amount of pre-launch testing. Which features do users actually adopt? Which workflows create friction? Which assumptions about usage patterns hold under real conditions? Which value hypotheses prove correct and which don't? This feedback can only come from production use.

Organizations uncomfortable with this reality invest heavily in upfront planning, attempting to narrow the cone before work begins. This rarely succeeds. Planning can't eliminate the uncertainty inherent in building novel systems for complex domains. What it can do is create the illusion of certainty, which proves more dangerous than acknowledged uncertainty.

Mike Cohn observed that initial planning provides significant value. Shared understanding emerges. Major risks surface. The team aligns on a direction. But continued refinement past that optimal point produces minimal additional clarity while consuming more time. The value curve flattens even as the cost curve rises.

This is because comprehensive upfront planning refines details that will change once development begins. It attempts to resolve uncertainty that can only be narrowed through execution. It transforms informed guesses into false precision, creating confidence unwarranted by actual knowledge. There is no amount of planning that will result in absolute certainty, only absolute waste.

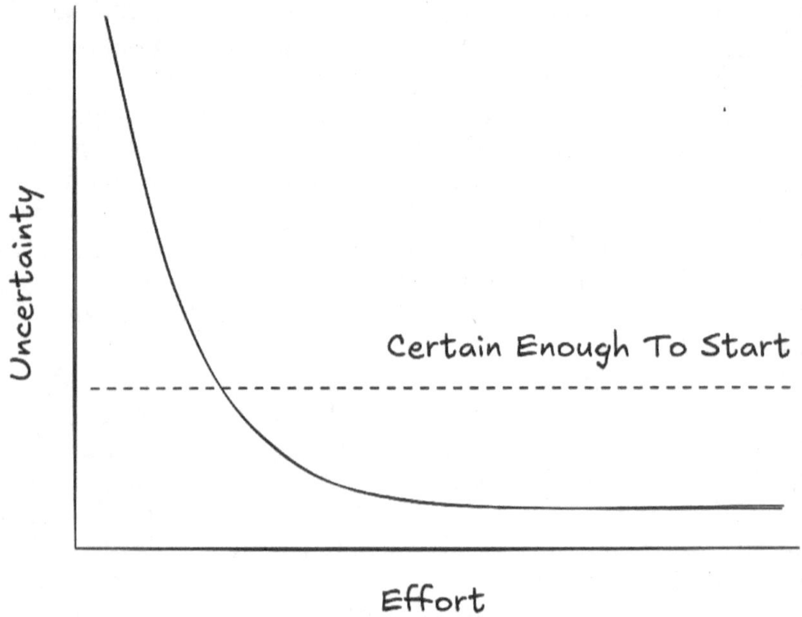

Figure 8.5 - Diminishing Returns of Planning

The alternative, just-in-time (JIT) planning, treats requirements as inventory. Work planned but not yet developed degrades over time. Markets shift. Technology evolves. Assumptions break. Just-in-time refinement is a pragmatic approach that emphasizes refining work as close to it being developed as is reasonable. This balances the waste from over-planning against the waste from under-planning.

This requires judgment specific to the work's risk profile and the team's experience. The confidence scale from Chapter 7 applies here directly: a routine interface change might justify Level 2 validation (expert intuition), while a fundamental product pivot demands Level 4 or 5 (primary research or controlled experiments). Calibrate the investment in validation to the cost of being wrong.

To be clear, there is a vast chasm between comprehensive documentation and completely eliminating planning altogether. JIT planning is not the practice of no planning. It spreads it out and thus looks different. Instead of exhaustive specifications assuming stable requirements, planning should identify critical uncertainties and design experiments to resolve them. Instead of committing to scope, timelines, and budgets before validation, planning establishes hypotheses about value and outlines how to test them.

This is also why limiting work in progress matters as much for products as for operations. A product development team working on five features simultaneously delivers all of them late. More critically, the team forgoes the learning that early release of the first feature would provide. Learning that should inform whether features two, three, four, and five deserve investment at all.

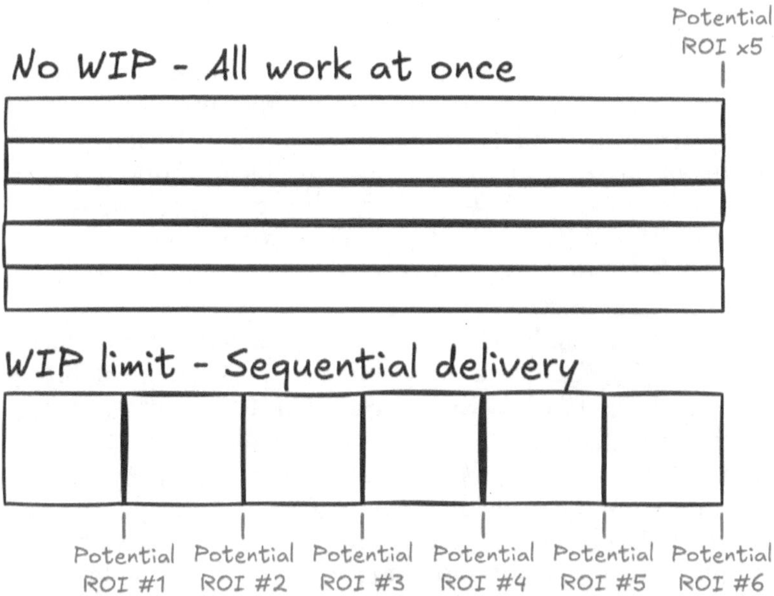

Figure 8.6 - WIP Limit Value Potential (Faster to Market)

Sequential delivery not only enables learning as we go, but it results in faster overall delivery. It also allows each release to generate revenue or savings that fund subsequent work, capture market position before competitors, and validate or invalidate assumptions before doubling down. Whereas the parallel approach delays all value until everything completes while creating the illusion of progress through visible activity on multiple fronts.

This pattern creates a self-fulfilling prophecy—Chapter 9 examines the mechanism in detail. The very actions taken to show progress across multiple efforts prevent anything from finishing.

Furthermore, instead of treating plans as commitments, organizations should treat them as forecasts. Predictions subject to revision as evidence accumulates. Plans can be managed to time or scope, but not both. While we certainly can, and should, limit our time investment, value realization is rarely considerate of our arbitrary dates and timelines. Therefore, like meteorologists can't guarantee the weather, teams are only capable of forecasting when work will be complete (with high certainty through disciplined practice).

Vacanti posits that commitments assume certainty that doesn't exist in complex work, creating incentives for sandbagging, scope negotiation, and unsustainable hours. Forecasts acknowledge uncertainty explicitly: "Based on historical throughput, we have an 85 percent confidence that these items will be completed within 2 weeks." The number might be wrong, but it's honest about being provisional.

Everything covered in this chapter is accessible. It doesn't require special tools or advanced training, although those things can help. It is simply treating product development as applied science.

Some of the things may feel wasteful. The question to ask is what are we optimizing for? Are we optimizing for easy delivery or for learning? Reworking a small code change because we learned that users didn't respond how we expected is less waste than delivering an entire suite that misses the mark.

The question isn't whether your organization will waste effort building things nobody uses. It will. The question is whether you've created conditions where teams can identify that waste early, learn from it honestly, and apply those lessons to the next decision. Or whether you have optimized for appearing productive while systematically ignoring what actually creates value.

Product development is one domain where waste accumulates. But the unused features, the validation skipped, the prototypes shipped as production—these are symptoms of patterns that extend far beyond product teams. Waste hides in processes, meetings, handoffs, and organizational structures that exist through inertia rather than intent. Naming it is the first step toward eliminating it. Chapter 9 provides the taxonomy.

CHAPTER 9
The Cost of Not Knowing

"The most dangerous kind of waste is the waste we do not recognize."
– Shigeo Shingo

In 1944, the Office of Strategic Services (precursor to the Central Intelligence Agency) distributed a classified field manual to operatives working behind enemy lines in occupied Europe. *The Simple Sabotage Field Manual* contained instructions for crippling organizations from the inside without raising suspicion or risking detection. Its genius lay not in recommending explosives or violence, but in recognizing the natural dysfunctions that organizations accumulate over time and teaching agents how to amplify them.

The recommended tactics read like a parody of corporate culture: make speeches of great length, illustrating points with extended anecdotes and personal experiences; refer all matters to committees as large as possible for further study and consideration; bring up irrelevant issues as frequently as possible; haggle over precise wordings of communications, minutes, and resolutions; insist on doing everything through channels, never permitting shortcuts to expedite decisions; demand perfect work in relatively unimportant products, sending back for refinement any flawed work where possible.

What makes the manual unsettling is its contemporary relevance. These behaviors haven't disappeared with the dissolution of the OSS or the end of the Second World War. They persist as standard operating procedures in most large organizations, normalized through decades of institutional momentum and unexamined tradition. The manual's effectiveness derived from understanding that organizations don't need external enemies when they've already internalized the mechanisms of their own decline.

Waste, in this light, isn't simply inefficiency. It's normalized self-sabotage through patterns of behavior that consume resources without creating value. Patterns we've learned to accept as inevitable rather than interrogate as choices.

Interestingly, for most of human history, waste didn't exist as a concept. Before the Industrial Revolution, nothing was disposable. Clothes were mended until the fabric disintegrated, then repurposed as rags or stuffing. Tools were repaired and passed down through generations. Food scraps fed livestock or enriched soil. When something broke, you fixed it—not out of virtue, but out of necessity.

The shift came with mass production. Suddenly, corporations could manufacture goods more cheaply (and conveniently) than individuals could repair them. The economics had inverted: buying new became less expensive than maintaining old. But consumers still operated with pre-industrial instincts. They valued durability, craftsmanship, and longevity. A product that lasted a lifetime represented better value than one that lasted a year, regardless of the math.

So, companies had to teach people to throw things away.

They introduced disposable packaging (cellophane, Saran Wrap), engineered obsolescence into product design (GM's annual model changes, Phoebus Cartel limited lightbulb lifespans), and championed single-use convenience (Crown Bottle Cap, Dixie Cup). Marketing campaigns celebrated novelty and stigmatized age. By the 1950s, LIFE magazine could publish a feature titled "Throwaway Living" without irony, depicting a family gleefully tossing disposable plates and utensils into the air like confetti (a practice that typically doesn't go over well at birthday parties). Within a generation, disposability had become the default orientation toward material goods. People no longer wait for items to break or become obsolete before replacing them. Automotive and mobile phone manufacturers, in particular, count on customers buying new every few years.

Yet organizations developed a paradox: embracing disposability in practice while lacking the discipline to actually dispose of anything internally. Projects that should have been killed years ago persist as zombie initiatives, consuming resources without delivering value. Processes implemented to solve long-forgotten problems remain mandatory decades later. Systems multiply rather than replace, each new tool layered atop the last, creating a surplus of abandoned technologies still humming away on forgotten servers. If your organization has never killed a project, it's not because every project succeeded. It's because nobody wants to admit failure—so the undead keep shambling forward, consuming resources in its search for brains.

The antidote to this dysfunction has existed for over a century, though it took decades to mature and cross from manufacturing to knowledge work.

In 1906, production manager Walter E. Flanders began reorganizing Henry Ford's factory floor. Flanders realigned machines to minimize the distance parts traveled between operations. He created specialized roles like runners who ensured components arrived before workers needed them and stockers who ensured parts never ran out. Flanders was eliminating waste or inefficiencies from the system. He was designing work around flow rather than around departmental boundaries or equipment categories.

Seven years later, Ford's engineers applied these principles at scale when they introduced the moving assembly line at the Highland Park Plant. The innovation wasn't the conveyor belt itself (that technology had existed for decades), but the systematic elimination of unnecessary movement, waiting, and inventory. Workers stood in fixed positions while work came to them. Parts arrived exactly when needed, neither early (creating inventory) nor late (creating waiting). Each station performed a single operation, repeated thousands of times, allowing workers to develop mastery and identify improvements imperceptible to those rotating between tasks.

It's worth noting that Ford challenged the norms of his day by replacing artisanal craftsmanship of individual parts with standardized, interchangeable components, but he didn't eliminate the need for mastery. That depth of skill simply shifted. Mastery moved away from shaping each part in isolation toward understanding how parts fit together within a system. This pattern repeats throughout history. Technology rarely destroys mastery; it displaces it. Yesterday's expertise becomes less valuable, while new domains emerge where expertise matters more.

The results proved transformative. Assembly time for a Model T dropped from over 12 hours to 90 minutes at under half the cost within the first 5 years. Manufacturing sectors worldwide scrambled to imitate these principles: flow, standardization, minimal inventory, rapid feedback, continuous improvement.

In the 1920s and 1930s, Walter A. Shewhart at Bell Telephone Laboratories developed statistical process control and the PDCA cycle we explored in earlier chapters—plan, do, check, act—creating a scientific framework for iterative improvement. When American companies showed little interest, at the behest of General MacArthur, his colleague W. Edwards Deming brought these ideas to Japanese manufacturers in the 1950s as a part of the postwar reconstruction.

At the same time, Toyota had narrowly avoided bankruptcy through a bank-led reconstruction mediated by the Bank of Japan. As part of that restructuring, new leadership was tasked with securing a technical tie-up or capital partnership to ensure the company's survival. In response, Toyota sent senior leaders to Ford Motor Company's headquarters in Dearborn.

When geopolitical restrictions during the Korean War prevented Ford from investing, the financial rescue came instead through U.S. military procurement. But Ford agreed to host Toyota executives as trainees. During six weeks at Ford's River Rouge plant, Eiji Toyoda observed both the power and the limitations of Ford's production system.

Taiichi Ohno and Sakichi Toyoda synthesized these influences into the Toyota Production System. They took Ford's insight about flow and made it more rigorous. They took Deming's emphasis on empirical learning and embedded it in daily operations. Most critically, they articulated a philosophy of waste that transformed manufacturing and eventually rippled across industries. Rother describes the difference as going from a contiguous to a continuous flow model.

Quality is the ability of a system to produce consistent results when it is operating normally. When a system produces uneven results under normal operating conditions, it generates byproducts customers are unwilling to pay for—waste. In the short term, an organization can borrow speed or cost by allowing greater variation in how work is done. That variation generates waste, and if the debt isn't repaid, it compounds disproportionately. As quality degrades, the system spends more and more of its capacity producing and fighting that waste, slowing delivery while total cost rises.

This challenges the familiar "pick two" framing of the project manager's iron triangle. Time and cost are often treated as variables to be balanced against quality, but they are not independent constraints. In the end, there is only one constraint. That constraint is quality—and it isn't binary; it exists within a tolerance.

On paper, this definition of waste proves deceptively simple. In reality, it forces an uncomfortable question: what portion of organizational activity actually creates value customers recognize? The answer is typically far less than leadership assumes. Most work serves internal processes, bureaucratic requirements, or historical precedent rather than customer needs. Identifying this waste, however, requires first naming it by creating a taxonomy specific enough to be actionable but general enough to apply broadly. We'll get to that taxonomy shortly. First, it's worth understanding why so many organizations fail to eliminate waste even when they claim to be trying to.

Jeffrey Liker's comprehensive study of Toyota's principles identified that the Toyota Way rests on two pillars: continuous improvement and respect for people. The first pillar gets plenty of attention with Lean practitioners obsessing over waste elimination, kaizen events, and process optimization. The second pillar often gets ignored, despite being the foundation that makes the first pillar possible.

Respect for people, in Toyota's implementation, means trusting workers closest to the work to identify problems and propose solutions. It means Psychological Safety to stop production when something's wrong. It means investing in developing people's capabilities rather than treating them as interchangeable resources. This wasn't a humanitarian philosophy, but a competitive strategy. Organizations that develop people's problem-solving capability outperform those that merely tell people what to do.

In many organizations, Psychological Safety tends to thin the higher one moves in the hierarchy. When advancement depends on an empty seat appearing above you, leadership environments become zero-sum. Risk becomes personal. In these conditions, many leaders default to preservation over improvement. Doing nothing feels safer than doing the wrong thing—especially in large organizations designed to absorb waste without immediate consequence.

The opposite dynamic emerges when new leaders arrive. With something to prove and limited time to prove it, they reach for familiar solutions: a tool, framework, or initiative that worked—or appeared to work—elsewhere. The organization funds and adopts the new program, but before its impact can be meaningfully validated, the executive moves on, leaving behind another layer of unfinished change. Delivery is celebrated. Learning is deferred.

This tension explains why Western organizations so often struggle to implement the Toyota Production System. They import the tools—kanban, 5 Whys, A3s—while retaining Taylorist assumptions about management. They optimize for extraction (how much output can we get from each person?) rather than development (how capable can we grow each person?). The tools fail because the culture rejects them, and leadership concludes that "Lean doesn't work here." What doesn't work is attempting to implement empirical tools inside authoritative systems.

Six Sigma's rise reveals exactly this dynamic. Developed at Motorola in the 1980s and popularized by Jack Welch at GE in the 1990s, Six Sigma appealed to Western management because it looked like Lean while preserving Taylorist control. Where Lean trusted workers closest to the work to identify and solve problems, Six Sigma created a hierarchy of experts—Yellow Belts, Green Belts, Black Belts, Master Black Belts—whose specialized statistical training gave them authority over improvement initiatives.

The DMAIC methodology (Define, Measure, Analyze, Improve, Control) operationalizes this expert-driven approach. A problem is identified (usually by management), assigned to a certified expert, studied extensively through statistical analysis, solved through expert-designed intervention, and then locked down through control mechanisms to prevent deviation. This is a rigid, linear, and control-based approach applied to process improvement—big upfront analysis, single implementation, rigid enforcement.

Notice what's absent: the people doing the work. They're subjects of study, not participants in problem-solving. They provide data during the Measure phase, get observed during Analyze, have changes imposed during Improve, and get monitored for compliance during Control. Their expertise about the work itself—the kind of tacit knowledge that only comes from daily repetition—is treated as irrelevant compared to statistical rigor.

This made Six Sigma wildly successful in corporate America, not despite being authoritarian but because it was authoritarian. It let executives maintain the illusion that improvement flowed downward from management expertise rather than upward from worker observation. It preserved existing power structures while appearing to pursue improvement. Most critically, it provided a certification hierarchy that could be used for performance management that enabled employees to "level up" through training and projects, creating measurable career progression that had nothing to do with whether the initiatives actually improved anything.

Welch made Six Sigma mandatory at GE, requiring Black Belt certification for promotion to executive levels. Other companies copied it because it looked systematic and rigorous. That rigor came at a cost: projects took months, consumed significant resources, and often optimized local metrics while degrading overall system performance. Yet the methodology's formality, credentialing, and statistical framing made outcomes difficult for non-experts to question.

The irony is that Six Sigma's statistical tools aren't useless. Understanding variation, identifying root causes through data, and designing controlled experiments are all valuable. Toyota uses statistical process control extensively. The difference is that Toyota puts those tools in workers' hands rather than creating a priesthood of experts who do improvement to workers rather than with them. This is not to shame the practitioners of Six Sigma. The ones I've met are generally thoughtful and genuinely care about improving things. The critique here is structural, not personal.

Esther Derby distinguishes in her work between change done to people versus change done with people. Leaders attempting the former get compliance at best, active resistance at worst. Leaders practicing the latter involve people in diagnosing problems, designing solutions, and implementing changes. The involvement itself builds commitment so people support what they help create. This is a core tenet of Lean Change, which we will expand upon in the final chapter.

When companies claim they're implementing "Lean Six Sigma," what they usually mean is they're doing Six Sigma (expert-driven, statistically rigorous, management-controlled) while borrowing Lean vocabulary (waste, flow, value stream). The tools look similar enough that leaders can claim they're being empirical while maintaining the authoritarian structures that empiricism actually requires them to dismantle.

The tells are in the implementation. If improvement requires certification and formal project charters, it's Six Sigma wearing Lean clothing. If improvement happens through daily experimentation by teams working the process, with statistical tools used as needed rather than as mandatory methodology, it's actually Lean. If "continuous improvement" means waiting for expert-led projects rather than everyone improving every day, you've optimized for control over learning.

This explains why so many Lean transformations fail. Leadership hears "eliminate waste" and "optimize flow" and think they can achieve this through top-down analysis and expert-driven change. They can't. Waste is most visible to people doing the work. Flow is most obvious to people navigating the process. Improvement that ignores their knowledge optimizes away the wrong things while missing what actually matters.

Improvement, then, has to begin where the work actually happens. To assist with this, the Toyota Production System published a taxonomy that includes 7 categories of waste, later expanded to 8 and captured in the acronym **DOWNTIME**: Defects, Overproduction, Waiting, Non-utilized Talent, Transportation, Inventory, Motion, Extra Processing. The acronym is easy to remember, especially if you're a manufacturer whose biggest nightmare is excessive downtime, and that memorability keeps it fresh on the mind.

While originally developed for manufacturing, the framework doesn't prescribe solutions—that would be antithetical to empirical thinking—instead it provides language for diagnosis, allowing teams to recognize patterns previously invisible. This proves especially valuable in knowledge work industries like software development, product management, and organizational operations, where waste is less tangible than in manufacturing. As Henry Ford observed a century ago, "Time waste differs from material waste in that there can be no salvage. The easiest of all wastes and the hardest to correct is the waste of time, because wasted time does not litter the floor like wasted material."

Defects represent work that must be reprocessed. In manufacturing, a defect might be a misaligned part requiring rework. In knowledge work, it manifests as production incidents requiring emergency fixes, customer complaints necessitating rushed patches, or strategic plans requiring revision when underlying assumptions prove false. The concept extends to include any unplanned work—shoulder taps, production fire drills, executive escalations, urgent "SWAT" calls—that interrupts planned flow and force reactive effort.

The waste isn't merely the time spent fixing the defect. The true cost compounds. A bug caught during coding takes minutes to fix when the developer still has full context. The same bug discovered in QA testing takes hours because context must be rebuilt, reproduction steps documented, and coordination with testers is required. That's roughly ten times the cost. If the bug reaches production, the cost multiplies again by ten or more due to emergency response, customer impact, rushed patches, post-mortems, and potentially brand damage. What could have been fixed in minutes now consumes days or weeks.

This compounding cost curve explains why quality isn't negotiable, and why "good enough" from Chapter 3 never means "sloppy." Satisficing applies to scope and features, not to the integrity of what you actually build. Shipping less, done well, beats shipping more, done poorly. Organizations that optimize for speed while neglecting quality don't move faster. They're just borrowing against future speed at ruinous interest rates. Each defect that escapes creates surface area for more defects. Each workaround for poor architecture makes the next change harder. Quality problems multiply faster than quality improvements, creating a downward spiral that accelerates until the system becomes unmaintainable.

The inverse is also true. Higher quality enables faster delivery and lower total cost of ownership. High-quality systems can be modified quickly, allowing rapid iteration. Teams spend time building new value rather than maintaining old mistakes. More iteration cycles means more learning, which produces better decisions, which captures revenue faster than competitors stuck debugging last quarter's technical debt.

Overproduction occurs when work creates outputs nobody needs or uses. As we explored in the previous chapter, research consistently shows that 80 percent of features in production software go unused. This isn't a matter of poor execution. These features work as specified. The waste lies in building them at all.

Every unused feature carries hidden costs: infrastructure to host it, security vulnerabilities to monitor, documentation to maintain, support staff to field questions about it, and complexity that makes everything else harder to change.

Time, budgets, and headcount function as structures in the same way. Cyril Northcote Parkinson famously observed that work expands to fill the time available, but the principle extends further. Once a team exists, work will be found for it. Budgets are spent because they exist. Timelines are consumed because they are granted. Projects are almost never early—they are either on time or late. Work is created to justify the team, budget, or timeline, regardless of the actual value created.

Waiting manifests whenever work sits idle. In manufacturing, waiting might mean an assembly line halted because parts haven't arrived or it might mean parts sitting in inventory overflow due to overproduction. In knowledge work, it appears as peer reviews languishing unreviewed for days, work items dependent on an external force to be finished, or critical decisions waiting for executives who attend meetings perpetually—their calendars a monument to their importance and a bottleneck for everyone else.

The visible waste is the idle time. The hidden waste is larger: incomplete work accumulates as inventory, team members context-switch to other tasks and struggle to regain context when the blockage clears (increasing the likelihood of defects), and delivery schedules slip because waiting compounds across multiple handoffs.

Non-utilized talent occurs when organizations fail to leverage the expertise, creativity, and judgment of people closest to the work (just as we identified with Six Sigma's approach). This was Taylorism's fundamental flaw: the assumption that workers should execute decisions made by distant managers rather than participate in improving the work itself. Toyota inverted this through practices like the andon cord, which allowed any worker to stop production when they identified a problem, triggering immediate collaborative problem-solving.

In knowledge work, non-utilized talent appears when developers implement requirements without understanding customer problems, when product managers dictate solutions rather than defining outcomes, when designers execute stakeholder preferences rather than apply their expertise about user needs. This waste produces worse outcomes while demotivating people by treating them as interchangeable resources executing others' decisions. The fastest way to demotivate an expert is to treat them like a vending machine: insert requirements, receive output, repeat.

Transportation waste emerges from moving work, information, or materials beyond what's necessary. In manufacturing, this might mean inefficient factory layouts requiring parts to travel excessive distances between operations. In knowledge work, it manifests as handoffs between teams or silos, requirements passed from product to design to engineering, or work passed between component teams. Each transition introduces delays, misunderstandings, and the need for re-explanation. Every handoff creates opportunities for information to degrade, context to disappear, and priorities to shift.

Organizations amplify this waste when they distribute work geographically primarily to reduce labor costs rather than to access specific capabilities. The promised cost savings from offshore labor arbitrage rarely materialize once hidden costs accumulate: additional coordination meetings, duplicated work from miscommunication, security incidents, quality issues requiring rework, and the productivity tax of asynchronous collaboration far exceed the reduced labor costs.

Remote and distributed teams can thrive when built around capability rather than cost. The dysfunction emerges when geographic distribution is treated as a simple cost-reduction strategy, often attracting vendors competing primarily on price—those for whom being cheapest on paper represents their most compelling differentiator.

Inventory in manufacturing means materials or products sitting unused—components awaiting assembly and finished goods awaiting shipment. In knowledge work, inventory appears as partially completed work: features specified but not developed, code written but not tested, designs created but not implemented, strategies documented but not executed. This work in progress represents invested effort that hasn't yet created value. Like physical inventory, it degrades over time—especially when it consists of decisions made long before they can be tested. Requirements become stale as market conditions shift, code falls behind current architecture standards, and designs age as competitor offerings evolve.

In knowledge work, over-planning creates a subtler kind of inventory: decisions made too early. Research consistently shows that people with a plan are more successful than those without one—regardless of how good the plan is. The advantage comes from planning itself, not from the plan. As Dwight D. Eisenhower observed, "Plans are worthless, but planning is everything."

The failure mode is treating plans as finished goods. When teams plan too far ahead, they stockpile assumptions—requirements, designs, roadmaps, commitments—that may never be used or may need to change due to future information. What once looked certain becomes stale as conditions change, forcing rework or, worse, continued execution against a now-flawed plan.

This is why purpose matters and why just-in-time (JIT) planning matters. A living plan keeps a wide field of view but a near focal plane. Goals set direction. JIT planning constrains attention to the next best decision while preserving the ability to learn and adapt with minimal rework.

Big outcomes are built from many small ones. Progress emerges through the accumulation of small, correct decisions made over time. But accumulation only works under focus—and focus is defined by what you choose not to do. Large, upfront plans fail not because people lack intelligence or effort, but because they attempt to decide everything at once, when the least is known, resulting in too many assumptions before any can be validated.

Work in progress accumulates silently, like carbon dioxide in a sealed room, slowly suffocating productivity. Organizations often justify starting multiple efforts simultaneously through familiar psychological patterns (which we'll explore in the final chapter): when progress feels slow, the response is to start more work rather than finish existing work. This reaction compounds the problem. The waste of increased inventory then further hinders delivery capabilities, reinforcing that nothing ever gets accomplished and perpetuating the cycle.

The hidden cost of this inventory buildup is not just time but attention. Thought work requires uninterrupted spans long enough for context to stabilize, yet excess WIP fragments focus and imposes recovery costs each time work is resumed. Humans can overlap physical tasks, but reasoning is sequential. When organizations load teams with too much concurrent work, they do not increase throughput—they prevent thinking from occurring. The result is degraded quality, increased errors, and rework that surfaces later as defects, delays, and missed commitments. Limiting work in progress is therefore not about personal productivity; it is a system design choice that determines whether understanding, judgment, and learning can occur at all.

Motion (or *unnecessary motion*) waste represents effort spent by workers moving, searching, or performing actions that don't directly contribute to the product. In manufacturing, this might be walking to retrieve tools or bending awkwardly to access components. In knowledge work, it appears as context switching between projects, meetings that could be an email, relearning systems after periods away from them, searching for information that should be readily accessible, or performing repetitive manual tasks that could be automated. Surveys show that the average developer spends only 32 percent of available time writing code and 35 percent managing it (the rest is spent in meetings, responding to that urgent request from the manager, the ever-stimulating annual compliance training, updating one's password, and so on). After presenting this data at conferences, multiple organizations have told me their internal measurements were even lower—sometimes dramatically so.

Motion can be a deceptive trap for organizations, requiring careful consideration and a systems view. This is prevalent in teams that forego direct communication (and ultimately understanding) for a standardized intake form. The latter can be a useful tool, but not when it substitutes the former. Reflect on the last time you needed support but instead were directed to a generalized FAQ.

Extra processing occurs when work exceeds what customers value. Gold-plating features with functionality nobody requested, over-engineering solutions to simple problems, building components for future consumption, refining deliverables beyond the point where additional effort yields meaningful improvement are all forms of extra processing. This often stems from perfectionism or fear of judgment, driven by the belief that mediocre work reflects poorly on competence. In practice, extra processing delays value delivery, increases inventory, risks rework, and misallocates effort from higher-priority work.

The principle of *YAGNI—You Aren't Gonna Need It*—addresses this waste directly: build what's required now, not what might be required later. This is satisficing applied to architecture by accepting that future requirements are unknowable rather than building for every contingency the imagination can conjure. There will always be things you would have done different in hindsight.

Extra processing also appears as comprehensive documentation created before learning occurs, robust feature sets implemented before basic needs are validated, and overly intricate designs where simpler ones would suffice. Requirements are not instructions; they are placeholders for conversation. Iterative, incremental validation of customer needs prevents delivering more than is necessary—and avoids overwhelming users with complexity they didn't ask for. Before designing a unique experience, introducing a third button type, or building a new API endpoint, ask a simple question: *what value does this add over what already exists?*

These 8 categories aren't rules to be followed, but a diagnostic lens for seeing what's normally invisible. Their manifestations will differ across industries, organizations, and teams. The real question isn't whether you exhibit every form of waste listed here, but which patterns of resource consumption fail to create value customers recognize.

Observing waste is the first step. Developing people's capability to identify and address it themselves is what makes improvement sustainable. Mike Rother developed a starter practice routine for this in what he calls the 'coaching kata'—a repeatable practice pattern for developing scientific thinking in others, at the point where work happens.

My own experience with waste came from the factory floor in West Michigan, at a company in Ford's supply chain. At a young age, and without fully understanding all the concepts as defined in this book, I improved throughput by 67 percent while reducing team size by 25 percent, simply by focusing on unnecessary motion and waiting. At the time, I thought of it as ergonomics. I optimized flow by rearranging tasks based on timing constraints, preparing for the next step immediately before it was needed, while machinery processed the current step. Through this rigor and experimentation, I shifted the bottleneck from the operators to the machinery.

What was odd about this experience is that this factory was my first introduction to Lean and Six Sigma. They had dedicated Job Instruction (JI) Trainers, trained in the Training Within Industry (TWI) method. Engineers had documented comprehensive SOPs. But it took a computer nerd trying to avoid dabbing grease on faulty plugs for eight-plus hours a day to realize these gains.

Later, when I ran that packaging line with 6 workers instead of 60, I didn't convince anyone with an argument. I simply changed the environment.

I reduced unnecessary movement by rearranging stations. I eliminated handoffs that created confusion about responsibility. I adjusted workflow so materials arrived when needed rather than accumulating as inventory. Nothing about the people changed. The work changed.

More workers didn't increase throughput because labor wasn't the constraint. Coordination was. Each additional person introduced delays, waiting, rework, and communication overhead. The system was perfectly designed to slow itself down.

At the time, I still didn't understand this fully. I trusted what I observed because it kept producing the same result. Over time, the pattern became impossible to ignore: effort and motivation were rarely the limiting factors. Structure typically was.

This is why leadership strategies focused on "getting people to work harder" so often fail. Performance doesn't emerge from individual heroics. It emerges from the systems people operate within. People on truly high-performing teams rarely describe working harder. They describe the friction disappearing. Change the system, and behavior follows. Leave the system untouched, and no amount of motivation will compensate.

What enabled these improvements wasn't a framework or a mandate, but proximity to the work itself. I spent time where the work happened. I watched how materials moved, where people waited, where coordination broke down, and where small changes produced larger effects. But most importantly, it wasn't what *I* saw; it was what my team saw. I reduced the waste of non-utilized talent by listening to my team who identified improvements and tested changes. I used to laugh watching other leaders wear themselves out trying to personally manage every inch of their line. I still remember the incredulous looks when I told them it was easy—that my team made me look good. People liked working on my line too, which didn't go unnoticed. Other leaders would try to poach my "best" workers, convinced I had somehow assembled a stacked roster—sometimes reaching for the very people they had previously passed over. Many understood the basics of waste in materials. They struggled to recognize it in motion and in people.

I repeated this pattern across multiple orders, different teams, and various product types. The variables changed; the result held. Some of those teams defied what were considered obvious constraints at the time. Yet the work still flowed. Years later I finally realized I had rediscovered principles articulated more than a century before me by Walter E. Flanders: reduce unnecessary motion, take advantage of idle time, and design work in a way that supports mastery. The frameworks—Lean, the Toyota Production System, DOWNTIME—gave me language to explain what I had learned empirically. But the learning itself came from watching what actually happened, not from applying theory.

While manufacturing waste produces tangible piles of inventory, workers standing idle, and defective parts accumulating in bins; knowledge work waste hides in plain sight. It looks like meetings, email threads, status updates, and planning sessions. It feels like work because it consumes time and demands effort. Distinguishing productive activity from waste requires observation that most organizations never perform.

The practice that enabled my assembly line discoveries operationalizes Toyota's principle of *Genchi Genbutsu* ('go and see for yourself'). Liker identifies this as one of Toyota's foundational practices: decisions cannot be based on reports, dashboards, or second-hand information. You must go to the *gemba* ('the actual place where work happens') and observe directly.

In manufacturing, the gemba is the factory floor. In knowledge work, it is wherever people are thinking, writing, designing, coding, or deciding. The principle remains constant: observe what actually occurs rather than what reports claim occurs.

Leaders in knowledge work organizations rarely do this. They attend meetings where work is discussed, review dashboards where work is measured, and read status reports where work is summarized. Each layer of abstraction filters out the friction, the waiting, the false starts, the rework, etc. By the time information reaches decision-makers, it has been sanitized into a narrative of progress that obscures the waste embedded in how that progress was achieved.

Genchi Genbutsu inverts this pattern. The observer goes to where work happens and watches. The intent is not to evaluate performance or catch people slacking (that surveillance mindset poisons the practice before it begins), but to understand. What does work *actually* look like? Where does it flow smoothly? Where does it stall?

In software development, this might mean sitting with a developer for a morning—not to review their code or assess their productivity, but to understand the texture of their day. The question isn't how fast they type; it's everything that happens when coding *isn't* happening. How long does it take to get a development environment running? How often do they context-switch? How much time is spent waiting—for builds, deployments, or code reviews? How much attention leaks into Slack, email, or meetings that could have been messages?

The questions that surface waste follow from observation. Why did that take so long? What were you waiting for? How many times did you have to ask the same question? These aren't interrogations, they're invitations to share what's normally invisible. People closest to the work usually know where waste lives. They've simply learned that nobody with authority wants to hear about it.

Trust determines whether these conversations reveal truth or theater. Workers who fear judgment will describe their days as productive and efficient regardless of reality. Workers who believe their observations will be heard point directly at the dysfunction they navigate daily. Building that trust requires demonstrating, repeatedly, that surfacing problems leads to solving problems rather than to blame.

Discovering waste is only useful if that discovery reaches people with authority to act on it. This presents a political challenge that technical frameworks ignore. Waste often exists because it serves someone's interests or because acknowledging it would embarrass someone with power. Making waste visible means navigating these political realities.

The first challenge is language. Waste is a loaded term. Telling a vice president that their weekly status meeting is waste doesn't invite reflection; it invites defensiveness. Reframing waste as opportunity cost sidesteps this reaction. The question isn't whether the status meeting is worthless. It exists for a reason: to create shared understanding, surface risks, and maintain confidence that work is progressing. The real question is whether that purpose requires the time and structure it currently consumes.

Quantification makes invisible costs concrete. If ten people spend two hours preparing and one hour attending, that's thirty person-hours each week—nearly a full-time employee. What value could that person-equivalent create if the same clarity, alignment, or assurance were achieved with less effort? If developers spend 30 percent of their time in meetings, and the average developer costs the company $200,000 annually in salary and benefits, then meetings cost $60,000 per developer per year. For a team of ten, that's $600,000. Is the organization getting $600,000 of value from those meetings? Maybe. But asking the question in those terms forces a different kind of evaluation.

The second challenge is that waste often spans organizational boundaries. The deployment process is slow because security review takes two weeks, but security review takes two weeks because requests arrive without required documentation, and documentation is incomplete because product requirements keep changing, and requirements change because executives revise priorities after planning is complete. Who owns this waste? Everyone and no one. Cross-functional waste requires cross-functional visibility through value stream mapping—a process of tracing work from customer request to delivered value, noting every step and every delay.

The third challenge is safety. Surfacing waste can feel like exposing incompetence. Organizations that punish messengers train people to hide problems rather than reveal them. Psychological Safety determines whether waste stays hidden or becomes addressable. Building that safety requires consistent demonstration that identifying problems is valued, not penalized. Psychological Safety is closely coupled to waste identification, and we'll go into more detail on it in the next chapter.

Toyota's andon cord institutionalized this principle. Any worker could stop the entire production line by pulling a cord when they identified a problem. Stopping the line was expensive, but the alternative was allowing defects to propagate, which cost more. The system worked because workers trusted that pulling the cord was expected and appreciated, not punished.

Liker documents that early Western observers visiting Toyota facilities couldn't believe the andon cord was real—surely it was theater, staged for visitors. The idea that a line worker could stop a billion-dollar production system seemed absurd. But Toyota understood what Western management didn't: the cost of stopping the line briefly to fix a problem is trivial compared to the cost of shipping defective products or building entire batches before discovering a systemic issue.

The commitment to learning went further than merely allowing pulls. Toyota actively monitored pull frequency and treated it as a leading indicator of cultural health. Rother tells a story at one plant where the typical baseline was around 1,000 andon cord pulls per shift. When that number dropped to 700, Western-trained managers might have celebrated—fewer problems, right?

As Rother notes, the plant president saw it differently. The plant president called an all-employee meeting and presented two possibilities: either workers weren't calling for help when problems occurred (meaning learning opportunities were being lost), or problems had genuinely decreased—but since the system was designed to handle 1,000 learning opportunities per shift, they should reduce inventory buffers to surface more problems. In either case, they wanted pulls back up to 1,000. Each pull represented a chance to improve.

This reveals something most organizations miss: Psychological Safety isn't a state you achieve and then maintain passively. It requires active cultivation. Toyota didn't assume that because workers could pull the cord, they would pull it. They monitored behavior and investigated when it changed. A decrease in problem reporting wasn't evidence of success. It was evidence that something had broken in the culture that made speaking up feel safe.

The andon cord is waste prevention, not production interruption.

Western factories optimize for keeping the line running, accepting a defect rate as inevitable cost of speed. Toyota optimized for zero defects, accepting that achieving zero defects requires stopping to learn whenever a defect occurs. The first approach looks more productive on a daily basis. The second approach produces better products, faster, and at lower total cost.

This is not a theoretical claim. Studies from the mid-2000s showed that the main Japanese manufacturers all outperformed the domestic Big Three with 25% faster overall build hours, despite line speeds being relatively comparable. Furthermore, studies from the 2010s found that Toyota earned nearly triple the profit per vehicle compared to the domestic Big Three. DORA's research in software development confirms the same relationship holds across domains: quality isn't a trade off against speed and cost, it produces them. Ron Harbour called this *qualitivity*, because the correlation was that consistent.

Even after waste becomes visible, organizations face a prioritization problem. Waste exists everywhere. Resources to address it are finite. Which waste matters most?

Some principles help distinguish high-value targets:

Waste that compounds deserves attention first. A defect introduced early propagates through every subsequent stage. Catching that defect earlier saves not just the immediate rework but all the downstream effort it would have generated.

Waste that affects many people deserves attention before waste that affects few. A ten-minute friction in a process that everyone performs daily costs more than an hour of friction in a process that one person performs monthly.

Waste that blocks flow deserves attention before waste that merely slows it. Eliyahu Goldratt's Theory of Constraints identified that systems are limited by their bottlenecks. Improving capacity anywhere except the bottleneck creates no additional throughput. Finding the constraint requires tracing where work accumulates. The queue reveals the bottleneck.

Waste that's easy to address deserves attention before waste that's hard, other factors being roughly equal. Early wins demonstrate that improvement is possible, create political capital for tackling harder challenges, and teach the organization how to identify and address waste.

Lastly, for items that require investment, weigh the cost against the other prioritized work. Despite the colloquialism, saving money is not the same as making money. However, you might be surprised to find that some optimizations net higher returns.

One anti-pattern deserves explicit mention: don't start with tools.

The instinct when facing process problems is to search for software that will solve them. Sometimes tools help. But tools encode assumptions about how work should flow. If those assumptions don't match your actual situation, the tool creates new waste while failing to address the original problem.

Begin by understanding the waste. Make it visible by mapping the value stream, visualizing the team's workflow, or standardizing procedures. These visualizations are often enough to make both work and waste unmistakable. Only then does it make sense to determine whether the right response is behavioral, structural, or technological.

But the hardest part of addressing waste isn't identifying it or making it visible. It's maintaining discipline when pressure mounts. Organizations under delivery pressure have a tendency to default to their old behaviors. Behaviors that increase waste. The more leaders feel a lack of control, the more control they try to impose on the system. They start more work to show progress, add people to struggling projects, and schedule more meetings to improve coordination. Each response feels logical in the moment. Each makes the underlying problem worse.

Work in progress provides the clearest example. When deadlines approach and deliverables aren't ready, the instinct is to start additional work streams by hedging bets, creating options, and demonstrating activity. This instinct is nearly universal. It's also nearly always wrong.

This instinct is rooted in an assumption that capacity is the constraint. But in most organizations, it isn't. As discussed earlier, roughly 80 percent of features in production are rarely or never used. That isn't a capacity problem; it's a selection problem. The constraint isn't how much work teams can do—it's how much unnecessary work enters the system in the first place.

Treating work in progress as the constraint puts pressure where it belongs. Limiting WIP forces organizations to choose more carefully, reducing the cost of being wrong, and preventing effort from being consumed by building things that don't matter.

Politically, starting work signals responsiveness. Explaining that work must wait until current work completes sounds like obstruction. Psychologically, starting work provides a sense of control. Doing something—anything—alleviates anxiety temporarily, even when the something doesn't improve the situation.

Holding the line against these pressures requires conviction that the counterintuitive approach actually works. That conviction develops only through experience. Small demonstrations matter—finding one team willing to limit work in progress, protecting them from political pressure long enough to produce results, and making those results visible to skeptics.

Building organizational muscle for limiting WIP starts with explicit agreement on WIP limits or how many things can be in progress simultaneously. The number matters less than the existence of a number and should be determined through experimentation. Then comes the discipline of honoring the limit.

Here's what honoring the limit looks like in practice. A stakeholder arrives with an urgent request. The team's WIP limit is three, and three items are in progress. The response isn't "we'll squeeze it in" or "we'll work overtime." The response is: "We can take that on. Which of these three should we stop?" That question asked out loud and requiring an explicit answer is where prioritization actually happens. Most organizations never ask it because parallel work lets them pretend everything is equally important, but there can only be one priority (the word itself comes from 'prior,' meaning first). It is also common for people to assume all requests are urgent, when a simple clarifying question, "When is this needed?" can help to optimize flow and ease tension.

When new work matters more than something already in progress, stop the old work explicitly. When it doesn't, queue the new work. The discomfort of that conversation is the point, because it surfaces conflict that parallel work buries under the illusion that everything is moving forward. It also forces prioritization conversations that parallel work avoids.

The pressure to break discipline will be constant. Holding the line requires treating the WIP limit as a constraint rather than a guideline. This protection takes concrete forms: leaders attending prioritization meetings and supporting difficult tradeoffs, making WIP limits visible at organizational levels, celebrating throughput rather than activity, changing incentives so that people are rewarded for finishing.

Value doesn't accumulate through maximizing activity. It emerges from minimizing waste to create space for work that matters.

This behavior is most appealing at the turning of the calendar. Most organizations treat January (or whatever month begins their fiscal year) as a reset button—retiring last year's objectives and unveiling new ones, regardless of whether the previous objectives were achieved, invalidated, or still mid-stride. The annual strategy cycle operates on the assumption that objectives have a twelve-month shelf life. But why would they? Business models don't change every year. Customer needs don't reset on a fiscal calendar. The problems worth solving rarely arrive and resolve themselves within tidy annual boundaries.

An objective to reduce customer churn by improving onboarding might take fourteen months to validate. An initiative to shift from project-based to product-based funding might require two years of organizational learning before results stabilize. A strategic bet on a new market segment might need eight months of experimentation before the data even becomes legible. None of these care what month it is.

Yet organizations routinely abandon objectives in December that were sound in March—not because evidence invalidated them, but because the calendar did. Teams that finally achieved traction in Q3 watch their momentum dissolve in Q1 when leadership announces a "refreshed strategy" that is often last year's priorities rearranged with new vocabulary. The waste isn't just the lost progress. It's the institutional message: nothing you're working on will survive long enough to matter, so why invest deeply in any of it?

If objectives were treated empirically—pursued until evidence suggested they'd been achieved, proven wrong, or overtaken by changed conditions—they would naturally conclude at different times. Some would wrap in six months. Others might persist for three years. The portfolio of active objectives would stagger like a healthy product roadmap rather than marching in lockstep to an arbitrary drumbeat. This is what continuous planning actually looks like: not the absence of direction, but direction that responds to evidence rather than to the calendar.

The annual strategy cycle persists for the same reason most organizational rituals persist: it serves institutional needs that have nothing to do with effectiveness. It aligns neatly with annual financial reporting, giving executives a stage to narrate the future while accounting for the past. The strategy offsite, the consultant engagement, the cascading OKR workshops—these generate enormous activity that feels like strategic thinking without requiring the ongoing discipline of actually thinking strategically. It is, in the language of this chapter, motion waste dressed in a suit.

Organizations don't just waste effort in operations. They notoriously waste capital on "strategic" activities that create no value for customers. This strategic waste operates at the boardroom level rather than the factory floor, but it follows the same Lean logic: waste is capital spent on activities that customers won't pay for (at least not knowingly).

The difference is that strategic waste often looks like decisive leadership. Stock buybacks demonstrate financial discipline. Acquisitions signal growth ambition. Restructuring shows willingness to make hard choices. Each decision has a compelling narrative. Each can destroy more value than it creates.

Stock buybacks exemplify this dynamic. As we examined in Chapter 4, IBM spent billions repurchasing its own shares rather than investing in productive capability. The buybacks boosted stock prices and enriched executives whose compensation tied to stock value. What they didn't do is create products, serve customers, or build sustainable business capability.

Vanity acquisitions serve similar purposes. Companies acquire startups or competitors to perform innovation for investors and analysts. The acquisition announcement generates headlines and justifies executive bonuses tied to deal-making. What happens afterward matters less. The acquired company's talent often leaves, its technology languishes unintegrated, and the purchasing organization gains nothing but a line item on quarterly earnings. This results in a reduction of value for customers in the end.

Failed mergers follow the same pattern. When due diligence focuses on financial metrics while ignoring cultural fit or operational integration, billions get destroyed through layoffs, duplicated systems, and organizational chaos. But the merger announcement already served its purpose: demonstrating scale or creating the appearance of strategic vision. The subsequent value destruction is someone else's problem, often after the executives who championed the deal have collected their bonuses and moved on.

In general, mass or frequent layoffs are a common strategy employed by short-term leadership that research has shown no tangible long-term benefits, only the steady erosion of trust, learning, and the very capacity required to improve.

Excessive executive compensation also divorces pay from value creation. CEOs earning 300-500x their median employee's salary aren't creating 300-500x the value. But the compensation serves narrative purposes: signaling executive "quality" to the market and reinforcing the cultural mythology that extreme inequality reflects merit (another echo of shareholder primacy).

Consultant dependency represents institutional outsourcing of thinking. Organizations pay premium rates for advice they don't implement or insights they could generate internally if they trusted their own people. The waste isn't merely the fees; it's the foregone development of capability and the political cover consultants provide. Executives can implement layoffs or restructuring while deflecting accountability: "McKinsey recommended it." The consultants leave. The strategy remains. When it fails, the consultants are conveniently unavailable for accountability—but very available for the next engagement.

Ironically, despite how quantitative strategic discussions often sound, many organizations struggle to explain what their money is actually being spent on. Not because the information is unavailable, but because it's fragmented across cost centers, allocation models, and project budgets that were never designed to reflect how work unfolds over time.

Project-based budgeting, in particular, creates distance from reality. Funds are often allocated a year in advance, before vendors are selected, before scope is understood, and before it's clear how much attention a team can realistically provide. Budgets assume full utilization, stable priorities, and linear progress—conditions that rarely exist. As a result, reported spend reflects planned intent more than actual behavior. This budget complexity obscures waste.

The antidote is embarrassingly simple: start with operating costs.

Utilities: Power, water, HVAC, internet connectivity. These are largely fixed and predictable. When they're not, that's worth investigating. An unexpected spike often signals waste like servers running unused workloads or inefficient space utilization.

Licenses: Software licenses, professional memberships, subscriptions. For many companies they're usually renewed on a yearly or multi-yearly basis. Pull the list and you'll have your number. You could also use this as an opportunity to review how many are actively used. Do any duplicate functionality? Do any exist because someone left three years ago but nobody cancelled the renewal? This is low-hanging fruit that most organizations ignore because licenses live in different budget lines owned by different managers, and nobody has incentive to look across the whole.

Salaries and benefits: This is typically the largest operating expense, and if you have built an organization based on the lessons in this book, it'll be fairly stable. Even so, if you have a team of 6 engineers to develop a product all year, then you know their salary for that year. Salaries are something that should be reviewed proactively anyway, to ensure talent is properly compensated.

Contracts and services: Cleaning services, security, maintenance, consulting retainers, cloud infrastructure. These often auto-renew indefinitely. Pull the list. Which ones are essential? Which exist through inertia? Which could be renegotiated or eliminated?

This exercise doesn't require sophisticated financial analysis. It's additive for budgetary purposes, and saves substantial time wasted on comprehensive project charters, budget plans, and any other procedural steps that serve the illusion of control but only obfuscate actual spend instead of value delivery. I have worked with companies where software project budgets combined vastly dwarfed the combined salaries of the engineering teams responsible for the work. These were projects where the cost was solely engineering time. This allocated money could be invested elsewhere. The bonus is that then it's easy to ask "what are we actually paying for?" and then demand answers in plain language rather than accepting spreadsheet complexity as proof of rigor.

Just be prepared for leaders to deflect because it can't be that simple and it's generally considered a boring topic for executives. Yet, operating costs are where waste accumulates silently, compounding year after year. A strategic acquisition that fails spectacularly at least gets noticed. A portfolio of unused licenses renewed automatically for a decade never does.

The political dynamic matters here. Budget owners defend their budgets for two reasons: first, because organizations typically make it difficult to increase budgets in following years, and, second, because budget size correlates with organizational importance. Reducing spend feels like losing status. This explains why cost-cutting initiatives often target headcount—the most visible expense—while ignoring the infrastructure waste that survives because it's distributed across cost centers nobody examines holistically.

Start with your own budget, whatever portion you control. List every recurring cost. Ask whether each one creates value proportional to its expense. Act on what you learn. Then expand the scope. The practice compounds—each waste source eliminated creates capacity to examine the next one.

This is boring management work. It also matters more than most of what gets celebrated in the business press.

In the end, waste elimination isn't a project with an endpoint. It's a continuous practice of ongoing interrogation of what creates value versus what merely creates activity. The question isn't whether your organization has waste. It does. The question is whether you've created conditions where people can identify it, speak about it honestly, and collaborate on eliminating it—or whether it's been normalized so thoroughly that attempting to name it feels like sabotage.

Creating those conditions is leadership work in the form of system design where the right behaviors emerge naturally. What that kind of leadership requires, and why it differs so fundamentally from what most organizations reward or what Hollywood glamorizes in shows like Mad Men, is the subject of the next chapter.

CHAPTER 10
Systems, Not People

"Every system is perfectly designed to get the results it gets."
– Paul Batalden

Traditional organizational change management teaches that organizations don't change, people do. Yet Management 3.0 insists we shouldn't try to change people but should change the system instead. This appears to be a fundamental contradiction at face value, but a deeper understanding reveals the truth: You change people by changing the systems they inhabit.

By systems, I don't mean abstractions or org charts. I mean the physical layout of work, the incentives people respond to, the information they receive, and the consequences attached to their choices.

When I ran that assembly line with 6 workers instead of 60+, I didn't convince anyone that fewer people meant better throughput. I changed the physical environment. I rearranged stations to minimize unnecessary motion. I adjusted workflow so materials arrived exactly when needed. I eliminated handoffs that created confusion about who was responsible for what. The workers didn't need to adopt a new mindset or embrace a new philosophy. The system stopped fighting them, and they performed.

Long before modern debates about culture, motivation, or accountability, W. Edwards Deming spent decades demonstrating a counterintuitive truth: most performance problems are attributable to the system, not the people working within it.

When outcomes disappoint, the instinct to correct individual behavior is understandable, but it is usually misplaced. People operate within constraints they did not design, respond to incentives they did not choose, and act on information that is often incomplete or distorted by the system itself.

A small example appears in grocery store parking lots. At Meijer, cart corrals are placed close enough that customers routinely return their carts without being asked, reminded, or monitored. The system makes the right behavior easy.

When a second cart size was introduced, returning a cart now included a sorting task. Rather than relying on instruction or enforcement, Meijer labeled the corral: one side for large carts, the other for small. With the structure made visible, people generally comply without friction.

Nothing about motivation changes. The environment clarifies the choice. And notably, the people making that choice aren't employees—they're customers with no obligation to comply.

A colleague of mine would often quote his grandmother: "You can lead a horse to water, but you can't make it drink—but you can salt the oats." That's what leadership is: designing systems where success becomes easier than failure.

This principle scaled dramatically at NUMMI, the joint venture between Toyota and General Motors in Fremont, California. When Toyota reopened what had been GM's worst-performing plant, they called back the same supposedly dysfunctional workers everyone had written off. But they didn't call back a single leader. Every manager was replaced. The leadership system was broken, and the workers performed exactly as it trained them to. Within months, the plant went from producing the lowest-quality cars in America to matching Toyota's Japanese facilities in both quality and productivity. Same workers. Different system.

Remember the CFO-turned-CTO from Chapter 8? I watched that same leader apply the same logic to leadership itself. He adopted agile ways of working for a simple reason: risk reduction. Agile, at its core, is scientific thinking applied to work—short feedback loops, smaller bets, and faster learning. Assumptions surfaced earlier. Problems became visible sooner. Failure, when it happened, was cheaper. It made financial sense.

To support this, everyone in the organization went through the same baseline agile training, followed by role-specific training—leaders included. Parts of the hierarchy were flattened to shorten communication paths and enable decentralized decision-making. He held open forums where he would sit with a room of people, talk through what was on his mind, and take questions directly.

He didn't worry about appearing to have all the answers. He designed conditions where good work was more likely—and then got out of the way.

Yet many modern leaders are still living in the shadow of Frederick Winslow Taylor's *Scientific Management*—a theory from the early twentieth century arguing that work could be optimized by studying individual motions, timing them precisely, and enforcing standardized procedures. Workers became interchangeable components, their value measured by conformity to prescribed methods. Management's role was to design those methods and ensure compliance. It looked like empiricism, but it functioned like authority.

Taylor's time studies at Bethlehem Steel did increase productivity, and his emphasis on systematic observation over intuition aligned with empirical thinking. But his approach contained a fatal flaw: it treated humans as machines that could be programmed through sufficient measurement and control.

As we explored in Chapter 7, measurement serves learning when applied appropriately. Taylor measured to *confirm* his predefined methods, not to learn how those methods should change. He measured individual output to enforce compliance with predetermined methods, optimizing for extraction (maximum work from each body) rather than for learning or adaptation.

Furthermore, Taylor failed to account for a phenomenon that would later become well established across multiple sciences: the act of observation itself alters behavior. The moment behavior is watched, measured, or ranked, it changes. People stop performing and start acting for the observer. They optimize for visibility rather than value, and compliance rather than learning. Systems designed to observe work inevitably begin to shape it—and rarely in the direction intended. This has been shown to hold whether the observer is human or machine.

This logic has evolved into something even more extreme: organizations that replace managerial judgment with algorithmic control. At Amazon, delivery and warehouse work has been widely reported as being directed and evaluated by software systems that assign routes or quotas, track performance continuously, and in some cases generate disciplinary actions when targets aren't met. When the model is wrong—when traffic deviates, weather turns, gates are locked, scanners fail, or reality simply refuses to cooperate—the worker bears the cost. The organization calls it objectivity. It isn't. It is a choice to embed judgment inside a model, then treat the model as if it cannot be questioned.

A system optimized for throughput will interpret context as noncompliance. And once discipline can be generated automatically, accountability can be outsourced automatically too.

This reflects a confusion of methods of knowing we established in Chapter 1. Taylor conflated authority with truth, believing that positional power confers superior understanding of how work should be done. He treated management intuition as more reliable than worker observation, despite workers being closest to the actual work. The method of knowing most likely to produce accurate understanding (empiricism—direct observation by those doing the work) was systematically suppressed in favor of the method least likely to be self-correcting (authority—decisions made by distant managers).

This assumption persists today. Managers still believe their job is knowing the answer and ensuring everyone follows it. Leaders still treat expertise as a signal of authority rather than as one input among many. Organizations still promote people based on technical excellence, assuming that being good at work qualifies someone to manage others doing that work.

Similar to Hume's is-ought fallacy from Chapter 4, the *halo effect* neatly explains this pattern. When someone excels in one domain, we assume they excel in others. An engineer who writes elegant code must be capable of leading a team. A sales representative who closes deals must understand what customers need from the product. An executive who maximized short-term earnings must know how to build sustainable organizations. None of these inferences necessarily hold, yet they shape promotion decisions constantly.

This creates what Laurence J. Peter identified as the Peter Principle: people rise to their level of incompetence. An excellent individual contributor becomes a mediocre manager. A competent middle manager becomes an ineffective executive. Organizations often select for the wrong capabilities at each level, promoting based on performance in the previous role rather than aptitude for the next one. The system is perfectly designed to elevate people into jobs they can't do, and those people are incentivized to take it because it is often the only career path available.

But as we established in Chapter 3, organizations systematically mistake confidence for competence—treating decisiveness as evidence of understanding. Those most certain of their answers rise fastest, regardless of whether that certainty was earned through learning or manufactured through ignorance.

This creates a compounding dysfunction. The confidence signal fallacy ensures that those who project certainty get promoted. The

Peter Principle ensures they get promoted into roles requiring different skills. And the authority that comes with those roles further insulates them from the feedback that might reveal their limitations. Each promotion reinforces the signal that got them there: confidence works. Uncertainty doesn't.

The leaders who reach the top are disproportionately those who never learned to say "I don't know"—or who learned early that saying it carried costs. This isn't because humble people lack ambition. It's because organizations interpret humility as weakness, scientific thinking as indecision, and appropriate uncertainty as evidence of insufficient capability.

The irony is that the most reliable way to become capable—empiricism, experimentation, learning from failure—requires precisely the stance that organizations punish. The confidence ceiling described in Chapter 3 becomes a filter: those who operate below it (because they've learned enough to recognize complexity) are systematically overshadowed by those who haven't yet discovered what they don't know.

The pattern is consistent across industries and decades. Organizations design systems that reward visibility over effectiveness, compliance over learning, and short-term outputs over long-term capability. People respond rationally to those incentives. When outcomes deteriorate, leadership blames individuals rather than interrogating the system that shaped their behavior. The mistake isn't moral. It's architectural.

Organizations aren't ignorant of this pattern. The majority invest in leadership development programs, with some estimates from the early 2010s suggesting annual spending approached $14 billion. The timing reveals part of the dysfunction: organizations typically train leaders years after they've already been thrust into leadership roles, attempting to retrofit capabilities they needed when they were first promoted. And even when the training is sound, leaders return to systems that punish the very behaviors they just learned. The message is clear, "these lessons are nice and all, but they're just not practical in the real world."

The consequences compound at executive levels. Research consistently shows that 30 percent or more of new CEOs fail within their first 18 months. These aren't necessarily incompetent people. They rose through multiple organizational layers to reach the C-suite. But the capabilities that made them successful as individual contributors, middle managers, or even senior vice presidents don't automatically transfer to enterprise leadership. The system promotes people based on what they've done, not on what they'll need to do next, then acts surprised when they struggle.

The problem compounds when people learn to game the system. Individuals optimize for appearing promotable rather than for being effective. They claim credit for team successes, cultivate relationships with decision-makers, master the language of leadership without developing its substance. The Gervais Principle, derived from the television show *The Office*, satirizes this dynamic: the sociopaths (who understand the game) rise to power, the clueless (who believe the stated rules) occupy middle management, and the losers (who see through the charade but opt out) remain at the bottom by choice.

This creates a leadership deficit—not a shortage of people in leadership positions, but a scarcity of people capable of actually leading. Organizations filled with managers who reached their positions through technical competence, political maneuvering, or simple longevity rather than through demonstrated ability to design systems, develop people, or make good decisions under uncertainty.

Authority itself becomes both an advantage and a handicap. Consider a scenario from an individual contributor's perspective: persuading someone requires intricate negotiation, influence, and convincing arguments. Contrast this with a leader's experience, where a directive often suffices and questions tend to be clarifying rather than challenging. Authority, as Robert Cialdini identified, is one of the six principles of influence that can turn opinions into "facts," and it narrows the feedback leaders receive.

This privilege atrophies essential leadership qualities. Communication skills erode when you can rely on position to hold your audience's attention rather than on skilled oration. Networking becomes passive when people seek connections with you rather than requiring you to build relationships actively. Emotional intelligence (EQ) declines when nobody challenges you or provides honest feedback about how your decisions affect them. Research observes that EQ measurably decreases as leaders advance in authority. This creates a paradox where those with the most power to affect others' lives become least capable of understanding their experience. The corner office comes with a complementary empathy lobotomy.

This leadership deficit collides with a workforce that increasingly recognizes it. By the 2020s, Millennials and Gen Z represented the majority of workers. Recent research reveals that only 6 percent prioritize reaching formal leadership positions as their main career goal—a dramatic departure from previous generations' ambitions. What they do prioritize is meaning, development, financial security, and well-being. 63 percent report they don't receive adequate leadership training, and 67 percent say they'll leave within 3 years if development opportunities are lacking.

This creates a compounding problem. A generation shaped by different expectations isn't rejecting leadership, they're rejecting the command-and-control hierarchies that organizations keep trying to train them into. They want control, competence, and connection: the intrinsic motivators we explored in Chapter 2. Organizations optimizing for traditional authority structures are systematically misaligned with what actually motivates their workforce. The gap between what organizations claim to value and what they actually reward becomes increasingly visible to people who've grown up questioning whether title and control constitute real leadership at all.

The cost of ignoring this gap is measurable. When employees leave organizations, replacing them typically costs between 90–200 percent of their annual salary. SHRM research from the early 2010s documented replacement costs of $102,000 for a journeyman machinist, $133,000 for an HR manager, and $150,000 for an accounting professional—figures that have only increased as labor markets tightened. Half of workers who quit cite their direct manager as the primary reason, not the work itself, the company, or the compensation.

The dysfunction is worsening. U.S. employee engagement hit a ten-year low in 2024, hovering around 31 percent. Globally, engagement remains below 25 percent. Organizations that get leadership right see dramatic differences: companies with high employee engagement experience revenue growth 2.5 times higher than their peers, while high-trust organizations outperform market averages by a factor of three. Leadership isn't a soft skill that makes people feel good. It's a direct lever on organizational performance, and many organizations are getting it catastrophically wrong.

The term 'soft skills' was coined by the U.S. Army in the 1960s to describe human-centric abilities (communication, judgment, collaboration) because they were harder to quantify than technical tasks. The name stuck, and with it a quiet insult. These skills aren't *soft*. They're often the hardest to develop, the hardest to evaluate, and the most predictive of whether a team can function under pressure. Yet organizations still hire and promote based on what's easiest to measure.

Harvard Business School's Raffaella Sadun spent years studying what actually predicts organizational performance across thousands of companies. Her conclusion challenges everything most leadership advice teaches: "The evidence is clear that boring management matters."

Not vision. Not charisma. Not inspirational speeches. The

practices that correlate most strongly with performance are mundane: regular one-on-ones, documented processes, structured feedback, and consistent communication. What makes these practices work isn't their execution—it's the foundation they require: Psychological Safety. Without it, one-on-ones become performance theater, feedback becomes filtered, and communication optimizes for what leaders want to hear rather than what they need to know.

This isn't what gets celebrated in business press profiles or leadership books. Nobody writes admiring features about executives who hold weekly staff meetings and maintain clear documentation. But Sadun's research reveals that these "boring" practices—the systematic discipline of good management—matter more than the charismatic qualities we've been taught to celebrate.

The implication is uncomfortable: most leadership development focuses on the wrong capabilities. It trains people to be compelling speakers and strategic thinkers while neglecting the unglamorous work of building systems, maintaining structure, and ensuring information flows. Organizations promote based on visibility and charisma while the actual predictors of performance go unmeasured and unrewarded.

This disconnect between what gets measured and what matters points to a deeper confusion about what leadership actually is. Leadership, understood properly, is not about being the smartest person in the room. It's not about having the answer before anyone else does. It's not about heroically solving problems others couldn't. Those behaviors reflect individual contribution, which matters but doesn't constitute leadership. Leadership is creating conditions where everyone can contribute effectively—where problems surface early, where solutions emerge from those closest to the work, and where learning happens continuously rather than requiring crises to force adaptation.

As we established in Chapter 2, humans possess three fundamental psychological needs: control, competence, and connection. When these needs are met, people thrive. When they're suppressed, the cortisol response we examined in that chapter kicks in to impair exactly the cognitive function that knowledge work requires.

Research demonstrates that a sense of control is the most significant factor determining an individual's level of fatigue, regardless of physical demands. Organizations that micromanage, that require excessive approvals, that mandate rigid processes without input from those doing the work systematically induce stress in their workforce. The biological response is predictable: decreased cognitive function, impaired decision-making, reduced creativity, higher error rates, and eventually burnout.

Control directly feeds into the second motivating factor: competence. Competence is often misunderstood as raw skill or intelligence. In organizations, it's something more fragile: the ability to apply judgment, learn from feedback, and improve over time. Systems that suppress information, punish mistakes, overload attention, or reward appearance over understanding don't just frustrate people; they prevent competence from developing. When learning is risky, when feedback is delayed or distorted, and when success depends on navigating politics rather than solving problems, people stop getting better at the work itself. The organization doesn't just underperform; it becomes incapable of improvement.

Connection is the third need, and it's the one organizations treat as optional because it's harder to measure and easier to dismiss. But when systems systematically erode connection through constant churn, shallow coordination replaces real collaboration. When work rhythms prevent relationships from forming, the downstream effects aren't just cultural. They show up as disengagement, anxiety, and burnout, then get misdiagnosed as individual fragility instead of predictable outcomes of a social system designed without regard for human social needs.

Leaders who understand this design systems differently. They create conditions that address these fundamental needs rather than suppressing them. DORA is the largest and longest running research program designed to understand the capabilities that drive software delivery and operations performance, founded by Dr. Nicole Forsgren over a decade ago, and acquired by Google in 2018. Their research identifies five characteristics that distinguish leaders who enable high-performance: vision, inspirational communication, intellectual stimulation, supportive leadership, and personal recognition.

Each characteristic maps directly to intrinsic motivators. Vision addresses connection by helping people see how their work contributes to meaningful outcomes. Communication maintains that connection during uncertainty. Intellectual stimulation develops competence by encouraging experimentation and framing setbacks as learning. Supportive leadership builds Psychological Safety, enabling the autonomy required for control. Personal recognition validates progress and signals that growth is valued.

DORA's research found significant differences in these characteristics among high-, medium-, and low-performing teams. High-performing teams reported leaders with the strongest behaviors across all five areas. Teams with leadership in the bottom third were only half as likely to be high-performers.

The research identifies what leaders should do. The harder question is whether organizational systems—particularly compensation—support or undermine those behaviors.

Concrete examples exist of organizations that align compensation, purpose, and intrinsic motivation successfully. Costco has maintained wages significantly above retail industry standards for decades while achieving employee retention rates dramatically higher than competitors. Where typical retail turnover exceeds 50 percent annually, Costco's turnover for employees past the first year remains in the single digits. This isn't charity. It's recognition that higher wages offset costs elsewhere: lower recruiting expenses, reduced training overhead, less shrinkage, and institutional knowledge that creates competitive advantage. Compensation also functions as a signal. It tells people whether their role is viewed as essential or interchangeable, respected or merely tolerated. Something Henry Ford even acknowledged with his $5 workday (more than double the prevailing wage at the time).

Trader Joe's demonstrates similar principles in frontline retail. Above-average wages combined with genuine autonomy where employees can make decisions without manager approval has transformed the customer experience. Customers report that Trader Joe's employees seem to actually enjoy their work, which translates directly into service quality that competitors with transactional wage models struggle to replicate.

The common pattern across these cases isn't that higher pay creates motivation. It's that removing financial stress changes constraints. As we established in Chapter 2, cortisol suppression from financial insecurity impairs cognitive function akin to a 13-point IQ drop. When that suppression lifts, people can focus on the work itself rather than on survival anxiety. Pay doesn't motivate—it removes barriers to the intrinsic motivators that actually drive performance: control, competence, and connection.

This also explains why pay increases alone often fail. When Whole Foods was acquired by Amazon, existing compensation remained competitive, but autonomy eroded, metrics intensified, and the systems contradicted stated values. Engagement declined despite wages. When organizations neglect or abuse how work is actually structured, measured, and controlled, raising salaries merely makes the contradiction more expensive.

As we discussed in Chapter 2, once physiological and security needs are met, extrinsic motivators like additional salary increases provide diminishing returns. What matters more are the intrinsic motivators. Organizations and leaders that get this right create conditions where those motivators can operate without being suppressed by financial anxiety or contradicted by dysfunctional systems.

But—and this matters critically—leaders are a part of a larger system. They need leadership above them offering the same kind of support. Just like a leader with perfect interpersonal skills presiding over a dysfunctional deployment pipeline won't produce high-performance through inspiration alone, a leader within a larger, organizational context will have a limited circle of influence heavily impacted by their leaders.

There is also a real danger in having a rigid worldview on what leadership looks like. As is the case in evolutionary survival, so is in organizational survival: diversity strengthens odds. Organizations need technical leaders who understand the work deeply enough to identify what's possible and what's waste. Delivery leaders who can design processes that enable flow rather than create friction. And people leaders who can build Psychological Safety and develop capability. Rarely does one person possess all three in equal measure. Organizations that recognize this distribute leadership across multiple people with complementary strengths rather than expecting every leader to excel at everything. The key is to ensure that all leaders are focused on unlocking the potential of the organization's most valuable asset, its employees. This requires a strong aversion to autocratic leadership approaches.

Jeffrey Liker's research revealed an apparent contradiction in Toyota's leadership: leaders were simultaneously expected to develop people's capability and to maintain high standards through rigorous problem-solving processes. Western observers saw authoritarianism (demanding why-why-why root cause analysis) or permissiveness (trusting workers to stop production). Toyota saw these as complementary, not contradictory.

Amy Edmondson explains that Psychological Safety is one axis of a quadrant. High Psychological Safety with low motivation and accountability can be just as unproductive as low Psychological Safety and low motivation and accountability. Toyota leaders acknowledge this dynamic by choosing what they are authoritarian about. They don't dictate solutions. That would be Taylorism. Instead, they enforce problem-solving discipline: you must investigate root causes, you must validate assumptions through experimentation, you must involve people closest to the work. The standards are about *how* to think, not *what* to think.

Most Western implementations of "Toyota-style leadership" miss this. They copy the visible behaviors of asking "why" five times, conducting gemba walks, and holding daily standups without understanding the underlying respect for people that makes those behaviors productive rather than performative. The why-why-why becomes irritating at best and an interrogation at worst, missing learning altogether. The gemba walk becomes "*look busy for the boss.*" The standup becomes status reporting rather than alignment and impediment removal.

The practice without the principle becomes theater.

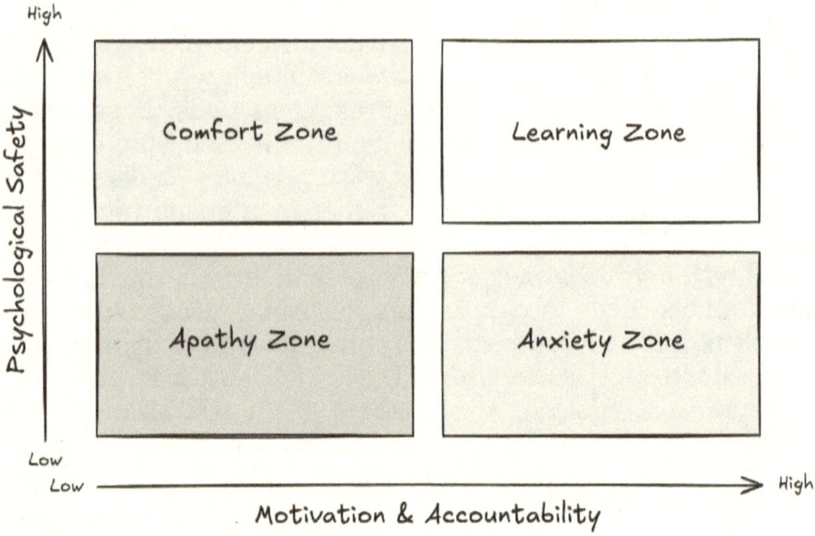

Figure 10.1 - Safety Quadrant

Psychological Safety has been a common theme throughout this book. While the concept may feel intuitive, it warrants more explicit attention. Amy Edmondson defines Psychological Safety as the belief that one won't be punished or humiliated for speaking up with ideas, questions, concerns, or mistakes. However, it is fundamentally a property of culture, not of individuals.

Ron Westrum's research on organizational culture identified three types of cultures: pathological (power-oriented), bureaucratic (rule-oriented), and generative (performance-oriented). Pathological cultures suppress information, shoot messengers, shirk responsibilities, discourage bridging between teams, cover up failure, and crush new ideas. Bureaucratic cultures tolerate information, neglect messengers, compartmentalize responsibilities, allow but discourage bridging, investigate failure to assign blame, and treat new ideas as problems. Generative cultures actively seek information, train messengers, share responsibilities, reward bridging, inquire into systemic causes of failure, and welcome new ideas.

When systems suppress information, the cost isn't inefficiency—it's catastrophe. In pathological cultures, those consequences are often measured in lives.

On January 28, 1986, NASA launched the Space Shuttle Challenger despite concerns raised by engineers at Morton Thiokol, the contractor responsible for the solid rocket boosters. The engineers had identified a critical flaw: the O-rings sealing joints in the rocket boosters became brittle in cold temperatures. The forecast for launch day predicted temperatures well below the O-rings' safe operating range.

The night before launch, engineers recommended postponing. Management overruled them. NASA faced intense pressure to maintain the launch schedule since Challenger had already been delayed multiple times, and the agency needed to demonstrate reliability to justify its budget. The engineers' warnings traveled up through multiple management layers, losing urgency and specificity at each step. Those closest to the technical reality lacked the authority to stop the launch. Those with authority to stop it were furthest from understanding the risk.

73 seconds after liftoff, the O-ring failed exactly as the engineers predicted. The shuttle broke apart. All seven crew members died.

The Rogers Commission investigating the disaster found that NASA's organizational culture prioritized schedule adherence and political optics over safety concerns. Engineers learned that raising problems created career risk. Speaking up marked you as someone who "wasn't a team player." The path to advancement required demonstrating you could overcome obstacles and maintain schedules, not that you could identify technical risks.

NASA didn't lack smart people or technical competence. It built a system that constrained judgment rather than allowing it to operate where it mattered most. It turns out, it was never about rocket science.

The pattern repeats with depressing consistency. On April 20, 2010, the Deepwater Horizon drilling rig exploded in the Gulf of Mexico. 11 workers died. The subsequent oil spill became one of the worst environmental disasters in U.S. history, releasing an estimated 4.9 million barrels of crude oil over 87 days.

BP workers on the rig had identified safety issues and risky procedures in the months before the disaster. Multiple warning signs surfaced: a failed cement bond test, unexpected pressure readings, drilling mud loss indicating formation integrity problems. Workers close to the operations recognized these signals as dangerous. But the culture prioritized maintaining drilling schedules and minimizing costs. Raising safety concerns meant project delays, budget overruns, and career consequences for whoever slowed things down.

The investigation revealed that workers feared repercussions for speaking up. The company's incentive structure rewarded speed and cost efficiency while treating safety concerns as obstacles to overcome rather than as information to act on. Like NASA, BP didn't lack intelligent people or technical capability, but it did lack the same cultural conditions required for people to voice concerns without fear.

In 2014, General Motors began recalling vehicles for faulty ignition switches that could inadvertently turn off engines while driving. The sudden lack of power disabled power steering, braking assistance, and airbags. The defect had been present in vehicles for over a decade, since at least 2001. GM employees had documented the problem through internal memos and engineering analyses as early as 2004. The switches cost less than $1 to replace. At least 124 deaths were linked to the defect.

Internal investigations revealed that warnings about the ignition switches had been repeatedly dismissed or buried in bureaucratic processes. Engineers who raised concerns found their assessments challenged or ignored by managers focused on avoiding the cost of recalls. The culture punished bad news. People learned to stay quiet.

People stayed silent in all three of these cases because speaking up carried personal cost while remaining silent carried only abstract, distant risk. Raising concerns marked you as ignorant (asking questions others might assume you should already know), incompetent (admitting you couldn't solve problems independently), disruptive (slowing down projects and schedules), or negative (not being a team player). The conclusion was simple: speak up and damage your career now or stay quiet and hope someone else raises it. When everyone has that same response, one begins to doubt if the risks are as severe as they first appeared.

As covered in Chapter 2, stress from hostile work environments triggers cortisol production, which suppresses the cognitive function required to challenge authority or question established procedures. People experiencing chronic workplace stress find themselves lacking critical functions to assess situations appropriately, problem-solve solutions, or communicate concerns clearly.

Google's Project Aristotle reinforces Westrum's findings with modern empirical data. After studying 180 teams across the company over 2 years, researchers expected to find that the best teams were composed of the best individuals. Those with the most degrees, accolades, and strongest resumes. What they found surprised them:

The single most important factor determining team effectiveness was Psychological Safety. Not talent. Not resources. Not experience. Not even the manager's technical competence.

Teams with high Psychological Safety made more mistakes visible because people felt safe reporting them, which meant they fixed problems faster. They experimented more because failure wouldn't be punished. They shared information more freely because asking questions didn't signal incompetence. The data was significant and clear: Psychological Safety mattered more than any other dynamic in predicting team performance.

Creating Psychological Safety requires leaders modeling the behavior they want to see. Alan Mulally's turnaround of Ford Motor Company demonstrates this principle at the highest level of one of the world's most iconic companies, when the stakes couldn't have been higher.

When Mulally arrived as CEO, Ford was hemorrhaging billions annually and headed toward bankruptcy. His first act was implementing a weekly "Business Plan Review" where executives reported status using the tried-and-true color code system: green (on track), yellow/amber (concern), red (serious problem). Every metric, every program, every initiative required a color.

The first several meetings were a sea of green. This was statistically impossible as Ford was weeks from running out of cash, yet everything was being reported as fine. The previous CEO, Jacques Nasser, was a fan of Jack Welch and attempted to pull from that playbook. Executives learned that admitting problems meant *you* were the problem. Over time, this trained leaders to optimize for appearances rather than accuracy. By the time Bill Ford sought outside leadership, the reporting system itself had become unreliable—hence the need for Mulally's intervention.

In subsequent meetings, Mulally changed nothing about the format. He simply waited. When Mark Fields (head of Ford Americas) finally showed the first red status for a critical launch delay, the room went silent. Everyone waited for Mulally to explode, to demand explanations, to start the blame cascade. Instead, Mulally started clapping. He thanked Fields for his honesty, asked what resources Fields needed to address the problem, and mobilized other executives to help.

The following week, the report was full of yellow and red. Once executives learned that surfacing problems led to help rather than punishment, honest reporting followed. Ford became the only member of the Big Three to avoid bankruptcy and government bailout during the 2008 crisis, in part because leadership could see problems early enough to address them.

This isn't a feel-good story about nice leadership. It's a strategic intervention in information flow. Mulally recognized that executives optimizing for appearing successful rather than being honest meant he was flying blind. The color-coded system was useless if everyone gamed it. Changing how bad news was received changed what information was shared, which changed what decisions were possible.

Each response shapes behavior. Pattern recognition is fast and people learn quickly whether speaking honestly brings help or punishment. Once they learn that honesty carries risk, the information you need most evaporates. Behavior as a mechanism for change will be covered more in Chapter 13.

Research consistently shows that culture is a leading indicator of team performance. Culture is not stated values or policies; it is what is tolerated and rewarded through daily actions. Better culture enables better information flow, which leads to better decisions. Teams in generative cultures identify and address problems faster because people are not afraid to surface bad news.

As we explored in the Waste chapter, Toyota operationalized this through the andon cord so any worker could stop production when identifying a problem. The system worked because Toyota's culture supported it. Workers weren't punished for stopping the line; they were expected to stop it when appropriate. Management treated stoppages as opportunities to learn rather than as disruptions to minimize.

Most organizations operate the opposite way, like Ford before Mulally. Problems are hidden until they become catastrophic. Workers learn that surfacing issues brings scrutiny and blame. Managers hear what people think they want to hear rather than what they need to know. Decisions are made with incomplete information because accurate information is too dangerous to share.

Edward Thorndike and B.F. Skinner observed that any motivation we have is a function of our desire to repeat behaviors that make us feel good or avoid stressful situations. The second half is the one most people miss. When we hear the word *incentive*, we picture rewards—bonuses, promotions, recognition. The most powerful incentives in many organizations are not rewards for doing the wrong thing, but consequences for doing the right thing. Every policy, every metric, every celebration, every promotion—all of these shape behavior, whether leaders intend them to or not.

Consider how work gets funded. Organizations that fund projects create incentives aligned with hitting milestones: on time, on budget, on scope. Teams measured against project timelines prioritize anything that moves those metrics, often at the expense of quality or long-term value. Organizations that fund products create different incentives. Teams measured against product outcomes prioritize whatever makes the product better, even unglamorous maintenance work.

What leaders celebrate signals what they value. Do you praise someone who pulled an all-nighter to fix a production incident? That signals that heroics are expected and that prevention isn't as valuable as dramatic rescues. Do you ask teams juggling multiple projects where they are on each one? That signals they should make progress on everything simultaneously rather than completing work sequentially.

These behaviors create heroes—individuals who save the organization from catastrophe. Heroes get promoted, get bonuses, and get recognized publicly. This seems reasonable until you realize it creates perverse incentives. If being a hero requires catastrophes to solve, why would anyone prevent catastrophes?

As Deming observed, a better strategy is focusing not on trying harder within the current system but on changing the system so that success is built into it. Relying on heroic measures is a poor way to manage.

Promotions signal what the organization values. When you promote someone, that person will do more of whatever earned the promotion. Everyone else adjusts their behavior to match. If people get promoted for hitting short-term numbers regardless of how, that's what people optimize for. If people get promoted for developing others, for improving systems, for making the organization more effective, that's what people prioritize.

Performance reviews represent another well-intentioned system that produces outcomes opposite to its stated purpose. In fact, it's where all of these forces collide: measurement, incentives, Psychological Safety, and the illusion of control. Organizations claim reviews improve performance, develop talent, and ensure accountability. What they actually do is corrupt behavior, destroy Psychological Safety, and waste enormous amounts of time on a process nobody values.

In practice, performance reviews tend to say more about the manager doing the reviewing than the person being reviewed, reflecting the evaluator's biases, expectations, and worldview rather than objective performance. The fundamental flaw is that performance reviews deliver feedback when what people actually want is attention. Yet multiple industry surveys report that nearly three-quarters of employees want more feedback, while over two-thirds of managers admit they avoid giving it.

This reveals two fundamental problems. First, there is a skill gap in leaders' ability to communicate effectively with their employees. Second, the issue isn't that employees are hungry for evaluation—it's that feedback has become the only socially acceptable form of managerial attention. An annual review is the organizational equivalent of ignoring your spouse for 364 days, then sitting them down for a formal discussion of their shortcomings. A failure both in frequency and execution.

Marcus Buckingham and Ashley Goodall's research in *Nine Lies About Work* reveals an even deeper dysfunction: people don't develop by understanding their weaknesses. They develop by building on their strengths. The entire premise of traditional performance management—identify gaps, create improvement plans, focus on deficiencies—runs counter to how humans actually grow. Trying to "fix" weaknesses consumes energy while producing minimal improvement. Developing existing strengths creates compounding returns. And a strength isn't necessarily what you're good at—those are just *abilities*. A *strength* is what brings you joy.

They also point out that competency models are flawed because they're too broad of a list of behaviors, and many competencies are impossible to truly measure. In fact, there is little evidence that competency or performance can be reliably measured, nor that increasing scores on such competencies leads to improved performance.

This explains why performance reviews consistently fail to improve performance. They focus attention on what someone can't do well rather than on what they do exceptionally. The employee leaves the conversation demoralized, the manager feels like they've delivered difficult but necessary feedback, and nothing improves. Both parties have performed their roles in a system designed to make development feel like correction.

The gaming behavior is predictable. Employees sandbag goals to ensure they can exceed them. Managers hoard difficult feedback until review time, destroying Psychological Safety in the process. Politics trump performance as people optimize for appearing successful rather than being effective, while recency bias ensures months of work can be erased by a bad quarter.

Netflix explicitly abandoned traditional performance ratings altogether by reframing the evaluation process. Instead of asking how someone performed relative to last year, managers ask whether they would hire this person today for the job they are currently doing. If the answer is yes, then they evaluate what they would have to pay to hire this position on the open market. Compensation is adjusted accordingly.

Netflix argues that this approach only works under a specific condition: high talent density. Their claim is not that any organization can operate without reviews or guardrails, but that when a workforce is composed almost entirely of exceptionally capable people, less structure is required. High judgment replaces process. Context replaces control.

This assumption is rarely examined by organizations eager to copy visible practices without addressing their underlying constraints. Are you operating like Big Tech, selectively hiring from the top tier of the labor market? Or are you competing broadly for talent, optimizing for coverage and cost rather than elite concentration? If your hiring strategy is merely competitive, then expecting Netflix-level autonomy, judgment, and self-management is inconsistent with the incentives you've established. Everyone wants to hire a unicorn, but they budget for a donkey. Donkeys can be hardworking; just don't expect miracles.

Systems must be designed for the people they actually employ, not the people leaders wish they had. When expectations exceed capability, organizations respond by adding controls, reviews, approvals, and oversight. What looks like a failure of discipline is often a mismatch between talent strategy and system design.

The point isn't that Netflix's approach is universally desirable. It trades stability for speed and psychological comfort for candor. But it exposes the contradiction most organizations preserve implicitly. They operate market-based compensation systems in practice while pretending loyalty-based systems exist in principle. A mixed narrative dating to Welch's dismantling of traditional corporate commitment (covered in Chapter 4), a move GE employees dubbed *the campaign against loyalty*. But loyalty goes both ways. Turnover becomes a feature of the system, not a failure of commitment—a dynamic especially pronounced in the technology sector. The result is a quiet but powerful lesson: loyalty is rewarded with stagnation, while exit is rewarded with a promotion, higher compensation, or both. Forbes has reported that employees who remain in the same role for more than 2 years earn significantly less over their lifetime.

Other major companies have abandoned the practice of annual reviews entirely. Adobe eliminated theirs in 2012. Microsoft followed in 2013. Deloitte, Accenture, and eventually even GE—whose rank-and-yank system under Welch epitomized performance review dysfunction—all moved away from formal reviews. The irony of GE abandoning its own signature practice should not be lost on anyone.

What replaced them wasn't chaos. It was the boring management that Sadun's research identified: regular one-on-ones, continuous check-ins, ongoing conversations about development. Not more frequent feedback but more frequent attention. The shift is from "how did you perform?" asked once a year to "what are you working on and how can I help?" asked weekly.

This aligns with both Psychological Safety and intrinsic motivation. When difficult conversations happen in the moment rather than being saved for formal reviews, problems get addressed before they compound. When managers focus on developing strengths rather than fixing weaknesses, competence grows naturally. When attention is continuous rather than episodic, connection deepens.

Bonuses introduce similar dynamics. Organizations design incentive programs to drive performance but discover that people game the metrics, pursue rewards in ways that damage the organization, or focus on measurable activity at the expense of unmeasurable value. Wells Fargo employees opened millions of unauthorized accounts to meet aggressive sales targets. Loan officers maximized volume before the 2008 financial crisis because origination bonuses rewarded it, regardless of creditworthiness. The incentive wasn't the bonus. It was keeping your job. No one was rewarded for committing fraud—they were punished for falling short of targets that couldn't be met honestly.

Deming was especially critical of numerical targets and incentive schemes that divorced performance from understanding. He argued that quotas and arbitrary goals often produce compliance rather than improvement. This encourages people to optimize for the metric instead of the system that generates it.

When rewards are tied to narrow measures, behavior predictably narrows with them. What looks like accountability is often just a redistribution of risk downward, leaving the system itself untouched.

Jordan Cram, CEO of Enstoa, eliminated employee bonuses in 2013 and added them to base salaries instead. Within 4 quarters, revenue per employee grew by 40 percent. Removing the variable incentive eliminated gaming behavior and allowed people to focus on creating value rather than optimizing for bonus criteria.

In the end, as Peter Scholtes argues, improvement efforts should focus on systems, processes, and methods—not on individual workers. Efforts focused on improving individual attentiveness without changing systems constitute a low-yield strategy with negligible short-term results and no lasting impact.

Managers are often told they're responsible for results. Simon Sinek posits this framing is flawed. Managers aren't responsible for results. They're responsible for the people who are responsible for results. And as we have established, the best way to drive performance is to create an environment where information flows freely, mistakes can be highlighted, and help can be offered and received.

This requires letting go of control over how work gets done while maintaining clarity about what needs to be accomplished. It means removing obstacles rather than directing every action. It means asking questions rather than providing answers. Leaders who apply the PDCA cycle to systems themselves: plan interventions, do them, check whether they produced intended effects, act on what you learn.

Leadership, done well, reduces the need for constant intervention by building high-performance into the system. This can cause leaders who are accustomed to being more *hands-on* to feel their role is being devalued. However, they are more critical than ever. Their responsibility is to actively tend and protect the system. Without that stewardship, incentives drift, bad actors exploit gaps, and the conditions that made high-performance possible inevitably erode.

One of the most consequential systems a leader manages determines who gets brought into the organization in the first place. The next chapter examines how organizations approach hiring and team composition, and the inevitable gap between perception and empiricism.

CHAPTER 11
Headcount Is Not Strategy

"Executives spend more time on managing people and making people decisions than on anything else—and they should. No other decisions are so long lasting in their consequences or so difficult to unmake. And yet, by and large, executives make poor promotion and staffing decisions." – Peter Drucker

Hiring and firing may be the least examined strategic levers in modern business. Organizations set hard headcount limits without assessing need. Leaders treat number of direct reports as a success metric. Firing someone requires so much red tape that employees get relegated to a corner where they can do the least damage—at least until layoff season. Mass layoffs then become the default staffing strategy. And there is little formal training on when to hire, how to assess skill gaps, or what hiring strategies actually work.

At first glance this may seem like it would live in the domain of Human Resources, but it doesn't. HR is measured on how hiring happens: time-to-hire, requisitions filled, offer acceptance rate, candidate satisfaction scores. HR is often siloed from the work itself and rarely trained in the roles they recruit for. Managers, meanwhile, aren't trained in HR. The gap is structural.

The result is predictable dysfunction. Managers identify a gap between current capacity and desired outcomes, submit headcount requests, and HR begins sourcing candidates. The assumption that the gap requires additional people goes unexamined. Hiring becomes the reflexive response to constraints.

I've watched this pattern repeat across every organization I've consulted for. A team of six delivers consistent value. Leadership wants more, so the team grows to twelve, then twenty, then thirty. Throughput barely changes. Coordination overhead consumes the gains, and most additional features add little value. We have increased the capacity to produce waste. The original six who understood the system spend most of their time explaining it to newcomers who keep arriving faster than they can absorb context. Eventually leadership diagnoses the problem: we need better people. So, they lay off the original six who have obviously failed, and hire more senior engineers, more experienced product managers, more credentialed candidates who attempt to understand a legacy system they never built. The cycle continues.

The technology industry demonstrated this pattern at scale during the pandemic. As remote work drove demand for digital services, companies hired as many software engineers as they could find, as fast as they could process them. Headcount became a growth signal—proof to investors that the company was capitalizing on the moment. Then demand normalized. The same companies spent years conducting rolling layoffs, often multiple rounds, sometimes quarterly. Even after each layoff, headcount remained higher than before the hiring spree began. They weren't correcting to a sustainable baseline. They were unwinding years of undisciplined growth while punishing employees for decisions those employees never made.

The human cost compounds in ways balance sheets don't capture. Engineers who joined during the boom—often leaving stable positions for equity packages and growth narratives—found themselves unemployed in a market flooded with other laid-off engineers. The companies that over-hired created the surplus that made their own former employees harder to place. This isn't a market correction. It's the predictable consequence of treating headcount as strategy.

Brooks told us in 1975 that adding people to late projects makes them later. Metcalfe's Law explains why: communication overhead grows quadratically while capability grows logarithmically. Brooks calculated that a project requiring twelve person-months of effort cannot be completed in one month by twelve people. The work carries too much sequential dependency, too much context transfer, too much coordination. More people result in more meetings, more handoffs, more misunderstandings, and more rework.

Fifty years later, organizations still treat headcount as the universal solution to capacity problems. All the standard HR metrics measure how efficiently the hiring machine operates. None measure whether hiring was the right intervention.

Before asking who to hire or how to assess them, the first question should be whether to hire at all. Most organizations skip this step entirely. Headcount requests move forward without revisiting whether the original constraint was structural rather than human. But as we explored in Chapter 9, there are many reasons why work struggles to be completed, and rarely are those a headcount issue.

Most open requisitions exist to backfill a role or justify a business case built on assumptions. Then when a manager declares they need another senior engineer, another product manager, another designer, HR translates this into a job description copy-pasted from similar companies. Recruiting begins. Six months later, a new person joins. Nobody revisits whether the original problem was solved, whether it still exists, or whether hiring was the right intervention. The hire becomes a headcount statistic, not a learning opportunity.

This matters more as organizations scale. Early-stage companies can detect hiring mistakes through proximity and rapid feedback. Everyone works closely enough to notice quickly when someone isn't contributing. Correction happens naturally through regular interaction. As companies grow past Dunbar's number, this breaks down. People work in different offices, different time zones, and different functional silos. A poor hire can persist for years, collecting salary while contributing little, because no one has enough visibility to see the pattern.

The cost isn't just salary. It's opportunity cost. Coordination overhead. Morale erosion when underperformance goes unaddressed. And the compounding effect when that person hires others.

Organizations that default to hiring create permanent capacity problems. Each new person adds coordination costs that reduce effective capacity of existing people. As effective capacity declines, pressure to hire increases. The cycle continues until the organization becomes primarily a coordination mechanism rather than a value creation engine. Meetings multiply. Decision-making slows. Simple changes require navigating increasingly complex approval structures. The organization doesn't collapse. It just becomes slower, heavier, and more expensive.

Research on growing professional teams is limited. But extreme environments have studied team composition rigorously: military special forces, surgical teams, and long-duration spaceflight. These results reveal patterns about team composition that corporate hiring ignores almost entirely.

U.S. Army Special Forces organize into twelve-person Operational Detachments (ODAs), commonly called A-Teams. The structure is deliberately redundant: two weapons sergeants, two engineers, two medics, two communications specialists, two operations/intelligence sergeants, plus a captain and warrant officer. This redundancy serves multiple purposes. Teams can split into two independent six-person elements when needed. If one specialist is injured or killed, the team retains capability. Cross-training is built into the structure by enabling engineers to learn medical skills, medics learn communications, communications specialists learn engineering.

Military research analyzing teams found that 5-6 people worked most effectively, with productivity persisting until roughly 9 people. The trade-off is between coordination overhead and specialized capability. Smaller teams communicate faster, make decisions quicker, adapt more easily. Larger teams offer more specialized skills but pay for them in coordination costs.

Surgical teams demonstrate the same pattern from different angles. When nurses turnover frequently, efficiency collapses. In one study, each additional team member added over 15 minutes to procedure length—independent of complexity. Team familiarity matters more than team size: a stable team that's worked together repeatedly performs better than a larger team of individually skilled surgeons who lack shared experience.

NASA's research on long-duration spaceflight teams identified five critical variables for crew composition: cultural and gender differences, personality, abilities and expertise, team size, and familiarity. Like Google's Project Aristotle, traditional selection methods optimize for individual qualifications. But collaborative work under unpredictable conditions requires team skills like communication, conflict resolution, and mutual support. Skills that individual credentials don't predict. You can't swap crew members mid-mission to Mars. The composition has to work from the start, and it has to keep working for years under extreme stress.

The pattern across these domains is consistent: team composition is optimizable, context matters enormously, stability beats turnover, and smaller teams with cross-training outperform larger teams with narrow specialization. Extreme environments have no tolerance for getting this wrong. And while startups usually rely on cross-functional teams out of necessity, none of these patterns appear across business hiring practices.

Team composition is often left to the preferences and biases of the hiring manager. Hiring decisions are based on skills and roles they personally value. And while they may rely on the infamous behavioral questions or cultural fit—questions and approaches that are fundamentally flawed at best—rarely do they truly understand the intricacies of team dynamics.

Job descriptions define roles in isolation: "Looking for a Senior Software Engineer with 5+ years of experience in Java, expertise in microservices architecture, and strong communication skills." Managers rarely evaluate the current strengths and weaknesses of the team. They think, "I lost a senior engineer, so I need to hire another senior to backfill them." They don't ask if they need someone more pragmatic to balance the more creative existing seniors, or has the team grown too comfortable and therefore needs someone who will challenge norms, or could the team use someone that helps level internal tension? The hire is evaluated against abstract requirements, not against how they'd combine with specific existing people doing specific existing work.

This creates predictable pathologies. Teams become functionally homogeneous even when demographically diverse. Everyone shares similar educational backgrounds, similar work experiences, and similar mental models. They agree quickly because they think alike. They miss opportunities because they all have the same blind spots. Groupthink masquerades as high-performing teamwork.

The alternative is to treat teams as systems, not collections of resumes. What capabilities does the system need? What does it already have? What's missing? What's overrepresented? How do combinations interact?

This is harder than filling requisitions one at a time. It requires actually understanding the work, actually observing how current team members collaborate, actually identifying where breakdowns occur and why. It means hiring might take longer because you're searching for specific complementary capability rather than generic "qualified candidates." It means sometimes the answer is "This person is individually excellent but would create imbalance in our current team composition."

Organizations resist this because it requires judgment, and judgment is messy. In fact, they often optimize against this by creating interview processes that ask every candidate the same questions regardless of role or context. It's much easier to define requirements, screen for credentials, conduct standardized interviews, and claim objectivity. The process feels rigorous. It distributes accountability across multiple interviewers so nobody owns the outcome. It generates documentation that protects against legal challenges.

Most organizations skip all of this. They don't analyze composition. They don't examine the gap carefully. They don't train people on how to interview. If they have the headcount, they just hire.

37signals operates on a simple principle: hire when it hurts, not before. Don't hire based on forecasts, growth projections, or what you think you'll need six months from now. Hire when the pain of not having someone becomes acute enough that it's clearly the constraint.

This approach contradicts everything conventional management teaches. Standard advice is to hire proactively by identifying future needs, building the team before you need them, and getting ahead of growth. The logic seems sound: hiring takes time, and if you wait until you're desperate, you'll make poor decisions under pressure.

But hiring proactively means hiring for imagined future needs that may never materialize. It means bringing people on when you can't fully utilize their capability yet, hoping that utilization will arrive. It means creating coordination overhead before you've earned the value that justifies it. It means paying for capacity you don't have work for, which creates pressure to generate work to justify the headcount, which often means building things nobody needs.

The alternative of waiting until it hurts has several advantages. First, the pain makes the constraint obvious. You're not guessing what capability you'll need. You know precisely what's breaking right now. Second, the urgency creates clarity about what actually matters. When you're buried under support tickets, you know you need support capability. The work itself tells you what's missing.

Third, and most importantly, you've exhausted other options first. Before the pain became acute, you tried process improvements, automation, elimination of low-value work, and reorganization of responsibilities. You learned what approaches worked and which didn't. A full backlog is often a prioritization problem, not a staffing problem. Stressed teams don't necessarily need more teammates; they might need fewer meetings, clearer priorities, or elimination of low-value work.

When you finally hire, you understand the context well enough to onboard effectively. The new person isn't joining an abstract future need; they're joining a concrete present problem with defined success criteria.

The question isn't whether people are busy. Everyone is busy. Hiring should be the answer to a more specific question: "How do we understand what our customers need?" Maybe we should start by training our team on User Experience, and then if the gap persists, we can hire a User Experience Researcher. "How do I know that we're building solutions in an effective way?" Are those closest to the work contributing to our solution discussions? Are we giving them the time and training required to know these things? After those are answered, then maybe we should hire a Solution Architect. This isn't pressure to be T-shaped, M-shaped, full-stack, or whatever buzzword is circulating this cycle. It's to eliminate the waste of non-utilized talent first.

The concern is that waiting creates suffering. People burn out covering gaps. Quality suffers. Customers experience degraded service. All true. But waiting to hire doesn't mean distributing the gap across existing people until they break. It might mean the work doesn't get done yet. These costs are visible and immediate. They force the organization to make explicit trade-offs: Is this pain sufficient to justify the coordination costs of another person? Are we sure this is a people problem and not a process problem? Have we actually tried solving this without hiring?

The difference is that these pains are acute. They surface quickly and demand response. Over hiring results in a more subtle, chronic pain that everyone feels but rarely understands what causes it. Instead, they respond to symptoms.

This is not a justification for understaffing. Chronic understaffing destroys organizations through burnout, attrition, and quality degradation. The principle isn't "stay understaffed forever." It's "let the pain be your signal." When the pain becomes acute enough that it's clearly the constraint—when process improvements and eliminations aren't sufficient anymore, when people are consistently overwhelmed rather than just temporarily busy, when customers are experiencing real harm—then hire. Use the pain as information about what capability gap actually matters rather than what you imagine might matter later.

As we explored in Chapter 9, this pattern applies beyond just headcount. Organizations hire ahead of need in other ways: building features for imagined future customers, creating processes for imagined future scale, implementing tools for imagined future complexity. All create costs today for hypothetical benefits tomorrow. The discipline of waiting until it hurts forces validation. Does this problem actually exist? Is it severe enough to justify the solution's cost? Have we exhausted simpler alternatives?

Even if we perfectly identified when hiring is necessary, we would still face a second problem: how to determine who to hire. Most organizations assume their assessment approach is more than adequate, if not outright sophisticated. Yet evidence points to the contrary.

It is common practice that people conducting assessments don't understand the role they're filling. Job descriptions are templates adjusted by HR generalists who don't perform the work. Titles mean different things across companies, sometimes across teams within the same company. "Senior Software Engineer" could signify architectural decision-maker, specialized domain expert, or productive individual contributor with no leadership expectations. These ambiguities show up in the job posting. How are the right candidates going to know to apply if the job title and/or description don't match the work?

Then the application process itself optimizes against finding the right people. Candidates submit resumes, then re-enter the same information into application forms—a redundancy that signals how little the system values their time. Applicant tracking systems parse submissions using keyword algorithms that filter before any human reviews anything. By the time recruiters review applications, the algorithm has already biased their attention toward keyword gamers rather than capability. Open requisitions generate hundreds of applications that no team can meaningfully evaluate, so they don't. HR recruiters skim for keywords without understanding the work those keywords represent. They pattern-match on credentials. They default to the familiar.

One widely circulated experiment illustrates how broken this is.

In 2021, a software engineer grew frustrated with job searching. His real resume earned a 3 percent callback rate despite years of experience. So, he created a fake persona "Angelina Lee" with a resume listing experience at Instagram, LinkedIn, Microsoft, and Zillow. All fabricated. He included absurd claims: setting a fraternity record for vodka consumption, spreading herpes to sixty percent of the intern team at Microsoft, leading a team that mined Ethereum on Instagram's company servers, organizing potato sack races at Zillow. Every hyperlink on the resume redirected to Rick Astley's "Never Gonna Give You Up."

The callback rate was 90 percent.

Companies including AirBnB, Blend, Reddit, and Dropbox responded, some within hours. When recruiters were asked what stood out, they cited prior work experience at major tech companies. When given multiple opportunities to actually read the resume, none did.

The experiment revealed what many suspected, but few wanted to admit: the screening process optimizes for brand recognition, not capability assessment. An applicant tracking system parses for keywords like Instagram, Microsoft, LinkedIn, and human review, when it occurs at all, confirms what the algorithm flagged. The content of the resume barely matters. If it did, "spreading herpes to sixty percent of the intern team at Microsoft" might have raised questions.

If the screening process cannot distinguish between legitimate experience and satire, what exactly is it measuring?

As the engineer put it: "I think everyone knew FAANG [Facebook, Apple, Amazon, Netflix, Google] is a golden ticket, but I literally did not think it would give you diplomatic immunity with recruiters." While the story is anecdotal and the engineer remained anonymous, it echoes cases like Kyle Behm's, whose rejection from a minimum-wage job revealed that automated personality screening tools were asking questions nearly identical to clinical mental health evaluations —a potential ADA violation that prompted an EEOC investigation.

But what does ex-FAANG actually signal? The credential only confirms someone was hired once by a company whose hiring process demonstrably doesn't work. It reveals nothing about why they were hired, how they performed, or why they left. Perhaps they were exceptional and departed for better opportunities. Perhaps they were mediocre and survived by avoiding attention. Perhaps they were terminated for underperformance. The brand name itself provides no information to distinguish between these scenarios.

The assumption that FAANG companies select superior talent deserves examination. These companies optimize hiring for their specific scale, constraints, and risk profile. One structural factor often overlooked is that cost of labor and cost of living are only loosely correlated. The starting salary for entry-to-mid level positions is often very similar, while living costs between the West Coast and the rest of the continental US vary drastically. This makes these opportunities prime for fresh from university, young pre-family engineers who are willing to accept trade-offs that more experienced professionals often reject.

Just like any company that hires based on no-experience or previous experience in similar companies, this creates indoctrination rather than education. Junior engineers learn that Google's approach represents "how software works" rather than "how Google works at Google's specific scale and context." They internalize processes designed for coordinating thousands of engineers across hundreds of services, then export these processes to organizations with entirely different constraints. A practice that makes sense when managing massive scale becomes cargo cult ritual when imported into a fifty-person company.

What worked at Amazon—their leadership principles, their two-pizza team structure, their relentless focus on metrics—may be precisely wrong for your organization. The engineer who thrived in that environment may lack capabilities required elsewhere. They may have never learned to work without enormous infrastructure teams supporting them, to ship features without extensive upfront planning, to make decisions without data pipelines that don't exist yet. The credential predicts little about transferable capability.

Yet recruiters treat these brands as validation, outsourcing judgment to name recognition. This is the same mechanism that gave Angelina Lee a 90 percent callback rate. The system recognizes patterns of prestige rather than capability. Organizations assume someone else has already verified competence through rigorous selection. No one has. Everyone is making the same assumption about everyone else's hiring process, and everyone's hiring process is equally broken.

This extends beyond FAANG to credentials generally. Years of experience explains about 3 percent of performance variance. Educational level explains about 1 percent. These aren't merely weak relationships—they're weak enough that relying on them produces outcomes barely distinguishable from random selection. Yet salary bands, job levels, and interview decisions hinge on these variables because they're easy to verify and create defensible documentation.

Meanwhile, the most qualified candidates often aren't applying at all. They're employed, or consulting, or selective about where they invest effort. The people most likely to submit applications through broken systems are those desperate enough to apply everywhere—which includes talented people in genuinely bad circumstances, but the system can't distinguish them from candidates who've been rejected repeatedly for reasons that would matter if anyone investigated. The open req model assumes talent is waiting in a queue. It isn't. Effective recruiting requires actively searching for specific capability, building relationships before positions open, and moving fast when the right person appears. Almost no organization does this because it doesn't scale, and HR is optimized for scale.

If candidates make it past the submission hurdle, they're then met with the standard toolkit for assessment, including personality tests, behavioral interviews, case studies, technical screens, culture-fit ratings, and credential checks. Organizations invest enormous resources into these processes. Candidates spend hours completing assessments. Hiring committees spend hours reviewing results. HR departments spend hours coordinating schedules and aggregating feedback. The apparatus looks rigorous while disguising the absence of validity.

Start with personality tests. Myers-Briggs, DISC, Belbin Team Roles—all marketed as scientific instruments for understanding human behavior and predicting job performance. All have negligible predictive validity for job performance. The correlations with actual work outcomes range from zero to weakly negative depending on the study and the metric. They persist not because they work but because they feel scientific, they're easy to administer, and they provide a shared language for discussing differences even when those differences aren't meaningfully predictive.

The tests persist because they're "harmless." Taking one wastes thirty minutes and creates a report that says things like "You're analytical and prefer structure" or "You energize by being around people." These statements feel accurate through the Barnum effect—they're vague enough that most people find them personally meaningful (like horoscopes). Organizations interpret these reports as revealing insights about candidates when they're revealing nothing more than the candidates' ability to answer questions in ways that align with culturally approved self-descriptions.

The methods of knowing we explored in Part I appear here in concentrated form. Credentials are authority: trusting that someone else—a university, a previous employer, a certification body—has already verified competence. First impressions are intuition: pattern-matching within seconds based on appearance, confidence, and demographic similarity. Personality tests are failed rationalism: instruments that feel scientific but predict nothing. Work samples approximate empiricism: attempting to test claims against actual performance, though every simulation distorts the conditions it's trying to replicate. Structured interviews, when conducted with genuine rigor, are the strongest single predictor available—but "genuine rigor" requires a level of evaluator competence, discipline, and predetermined scoring that most organizations never achieve. Organizations claim to want evidence-based hiring while systematically failing to implement the methods that would generate evidence.

Interviews suffer from different but equally severe validity problems. Unstructured interviews—the kind where different interviewers ask different questions based on conversation flow—explain about 4 percent of performance variance. This is barely better than random selection. You'd make better hiring decisions by flipping coins than by trusting your gut about whether someone "seemed sharp" in conversation.

Structured interviews perform better, explaining about 18 percent of performance variance when done properly. But "done properly" requires standardizing questions across candidates, defining good and bad answers in advance, scoring responses against predetermined rubrics, and training interviewers on bias mitigation.

Most organizations believe they're already doing this. They have behavioral question banks. They use panel formats. They fill out scorecards. But structure without evaluator competence is theater. When the person asking "tell me about a time you resolved a conflict" has never done the role, can't distinguish between a rehearsed STAR response and genuine experience, and couldn't define what a five-star answer looks like—the format is structured but the evaluation is still gut feel. The research validity of 18 percent assumes trained evaluators with predetermined rubrics grounded in actual job requirements. Strip those away and you're back near the 4 percent, just with better documentation.

As researchers Frank Schmidt and John Hunter put it: "In fact, many employers, both in the United States and throughout the world, are currently using suboptimal selection methods. For example, many organizations in France, Israel, and other countries hire new employees based on handwriting analyses by graphologists. And many organizations in the United States rely solely on unstructured interviews, when they could use more valid methods. In a competitive world, these organizations are unnecessarily creating a competitive disadvantage for themselves."

Schmidt and Hunter wrote that in 1998. Nearly three decades later, the graphologists are mostly gone. But the underlying pattern persists: organizations adopt the visible artifacts of better methods—the standardized questions, the scorecards, the panel formats—without the substance that makes those artifacts meaningful. They've upgraded from unstructured to the appearance of structured while leaving the evaluation just as subjective.

Interview panels expose this confusion. Hiring managers may be years removed from performing the role themselves, having progressed into management through different skills than the role requires. Peer interviewers understand their own work, which may differ substantially from the open position. Cross-functional stakeholders optimize for their needs regardless of what the role actually demands, e.g., the sales VP wants engineers who understand customer requirements, the infrastructure lead wants engineers who understand operational complexity.

Nobody on the panel necessarily knows what good performance looks like because nobody has precisely defined what the job is. So, they default to proxies: educational pedigree, workplace confidence, communication polish, cultural similarity. The candidate who performs interviews well receives the offer. Six months later, when they're struggling, everyone expresses confusion. The role required deep expertise in legacy systems; the interview assessed ability to discuss modern architecture patterns. The role required stakeholder management across hostile organizational functions; the interview assessed technical problem-solving. The role required shipping incremental improvements under ambiguity; the interview assessed ability to present polished case studies.

The fundamental problem is that interviews measure interview performance, not work performance. These are related but distinct capabilities. Some people are exceptional at work but mediocre at performing confidence under examination. Some people are exceptional at projecting competence but mediocre at doing work. The interview selects for the latter.

Research shows that bias forms within a tenth of a second of meeting someone. The rest of the interview is confirmation theater. Interviewers form an impression—usually based on attractiveness, confidence, demographic similarity, and credentials—then spend the remaining time gathering evidence that supports their initial judgment while discounting evidence that contradicts it. The structured questions, the careful note-taking, the post-interview debriefs—all create an appearance of objectivity that masks what's actually happening: intuitive pattern matching disguised as rational assessment.

"Culture fit" compounds the problem by providing language that legitimizes preference as principle. The stated purpose is noble: we want people who will thrive in our environment, who share our values, who will collaborate well with existing team members. The actual function is to filter for demographic and cultural homogeneity. When everyone agrees that someone is "a great culture fit," they usually mean "this person reminds us of ourselves." When someone isn't "a culture fit," they usually mean "this person makes us uncomfortable in ways we can't articulate without revealing our biases."

The interview process doesn't just fail to predict performance—it selects for traits misaligned with the work. Confidence over competence. Polish over substance. Credentials over capability. Cultural similarity over complementary difference. If the goal is building effective teams, this is precisely backwards.

Work sample tests—asking candidates to actually do the work—explain about 11 percent of performance variance. Properly structured interviews explain about 18 percent. Neither sounds impressive in isolation. But in medicine, a treatment that reduced adverse outcomes by a comparable margin would be considered clinically meaningful and worth prescribing to millions. The numbers aren't the problem. The problem is that organizations treat their hiring process as though it explains 80 percent, then act surprised when hires don't work out.

Work samples appeal because they feel like empiricism—testing the actual work rather than talking about it. But every work sample is a simulation, and simulations carry their own distortions. Ask a project manager to draft a recovery plan from a written brief and you're testing whether they'll comply with an artificial constraint, not whether their first instinct would be to talk to the people doing the work—which is what you'd actually want them to do. Ask a software engineer to code on a whiteboard and you're testing performance under observation pressure, not their ability to build systems collaboratively over weeks. The closer the simulation approximates actual working conditions, the better it predicts. But perfect fidelity is impossible, and some of the capabilities that matter most in knowledge work—judgment, navigating organizational complexity, knowing when to push back—are exactly what simulations struggle to capture. You're not going to ask a heart surgeon to perform a two-hour procedure as an audition.

Structured interviews have their own limitations. The 18 percent validity figure assumes evaluators who understand the role deeply enough to score answers against meaningful rubrics. As we've established, most don't. But interviews at least test reasoning and communication in real time, which work samples often miss. The strongest prediction comes from combining methods—pairing structured interviews with work samples produces better results than either alone because they measure different dimensions. Interviews reveal how candidates think through problems. Work samples reveal whether they can execute. Together, they triangulate across perspectives that no single method captures.

Instead, organizations stack methods that measure the same thing. Credential checks, unstructured interviews, and culture fit assessments are three different ways of asking "does this person pattern-match to what we already have?" They're not triangulating. They're confirming the same bias through three different instruments.

Once, as a manager, I was fortunate enough to be able to shape my own hiring process (normally I'm at the mercy of the current system). I approached hiring as a learning system rather than a transaction. I worked closely with my recruiter—not just handing over requirements, but training him on what I was actually looking for. Every resume he sent that didn't fit, I explained why. Not generic feedback, but specific patterns like vocabulary that signaled understanding versus vocabulary that signaled someone had absorbed terminology without grasping substance. In delivery leadership roles, controlling verbs like "managed" and "directed" told a different story than "facilitated" or "enabled." Someone who truly understood collaborative work would describe it differently than someone responding to the job posting or trying to ride industry trends.

Every candidate we interviewed but didn't hire received meaningful feedback. I was explicit that "not a culture fit" was not acceptable—if we couldn't articulate what was missing, we hadn't actually evaluated them. No one interviewed alone. Panels were diverse in how they showed up, and afterward we compared interpretations rather than averaging scores. Every single person had to agree to extend an offer. I was vetoed once myself. Even as the hiring manager, I was held to the same standards.

I rarely asked generic questions. I read resumes and asked pointed questions that someone who understood the work should know to ask. One candidate told me afterward it was the hardest interview he'd ever had—he thought he'd failed. He became one of our highest performers. The interview felt hard because it tested substance rather than polish.

The process was rigorous but not slow. Three interviews total, including the recruiter screen, completed within a month. I wasn't comparing candidates against each other searching for the best one. I entered every interview looking for reasons to accept this candidate. Most interviewers default to reasons for rejection. Anyone who passed got hired. The system defined what good looked like; I trusted it.

Over two years, I hired this way. My team members were consistently in high demand across the organization. What I was doing wasn't complicated. It was evaluating people on what actually mattered rather than what was easy to measure.

I realize my process wasn't perfect. I didn't know this research at the time, and by the research taxonomy, my interviews were technically unstructured—different questions for each candidate and no predetermined scoring rubric written down. If I attempt to assess the difference, it was that the system I built around those interviews incorporated the mechanisms that drive structured interview validity: interviewers chosen for both their ability to perform the role and their own diverse backgrounds, unanimous agreement that forced articulation of reasoning, a ban on vague justifications like "culture fit," and specific written feedback on every rejection that prevented bias from hiding behind comfortable language. I was also, without naming it, combining methods—job descriptions I wrote and had peer reviewed, resume analysis that screened for vocabulary patterns indicating real understanding, and pointed questions catered to each candidate that tested whether they could reason about actual problems rather than recite rehearsed responses.

None of these methods were perfect on their own. No single signal was definitive. Together, they were useful.

This suggests something the research supports but organizations resist: the goal isn't finding the one right assessment method. It's building a system where multiple imperfect signals combine, where evaluators understand the work deeply enough to distinguish substance from polish, and where safeguards prevent the biases that the research identifies from operating unchecked. Likewise, this book has repeatedly warned against adopting practices without understanding the principles behind them. Perhaps my approach was an example of these principles in action, or perhaps it was the kind of survivorship bias this book warns against.

The assessment failures we've examined apply to external hiring. As we explored in the previous chapter, internal promotions—where familiarity replaces evaluation entirely—are often worse.

Organizations face a choice in how they think about hiring: optimize for immediate needs or build adaptive capability. Few organizations recognize this as a choice. Immediate needs command attention; adaptive capability doesn't announce itself until it's missing.

Hiring for immediate needs means defining roles based on current gaps. The product backlog is growing, so we need more engineers. The testing queue is piling up, so we need more testers. Each hire addresses a present constraint.

This approach makes tactical sense. Immediate problems are concrete and measurable. You can specify precisely what someone would do on day one. You can evaluate whether the hire solved the problem within months. But it creates long-term fragility.

First, it assumes current work represents future work. Organizations change. Markets shift. The capability that's scarce today may be oversupplied tomorrow. Second, it selects for people who have done that exact work before—highly effective under current conditions, brittle when conditions shift. Third, it creates dependencies on specific individuals who become bottlenecks and points of failure.

The alternative—hiring for adaptive capability—is harder to assess. It's not about what someone has already done but how they think, how they learn, how they approach unfamiliar problems. The trade-off is between immediate productivity and long-term flexibility. Someone hired for adaptive capability may not check every box on day one. But as the organization's needs change, they will change with it.

The composition question applies here too. A team of all specialists lacks flexibility. A team of all generalists lacks depth. The optimal balance depends on how stable the work is, how quickly the environment changes, and how long people typically remain in their roles. Most organizations face something in between, which means teams need both: specialists who go deep where depth matters and generalists who connect across domains and adapt as needs shift.

None of this appears in job descriptions or interview rubrics. Organizations hire as if all roles have the same time horizon, the same stability requirements, the same trade-offs between depth and breadth. The process treats hiring as a series of independent transactions rather than as composition of a system that must function across time and changing conditions.

Even if organizations conducted truly structured interviews, incorporated work samples, combined methods to triangulate across different dimensions of capability, and thought carefully about long-term team composition, hiring would still involve irreducible uncertainty. The best combinations of predictive tools still leave the majority of performance variance unexplained. The rest comes from factors unknowable at hire time: team dynamics, role evolution, organizational changes, personal circumstances, and the thousand small ways context shapes outcomes.

The conventional response to this uncertainty is making hiring more rigorous. More interview rounds. More approval layers. More committee reviews. More verification of credentials. The result is the notorious day-long interview or an interview cycle that spans months employed by Big Tech. However, as we have explored throughout this book, uncertainty isn't solved by more control up front, but by the ability to adapt.

And yet, the same risk aversion that makes hiring slow makes termination slower. The process is deliberately burdensome to protect against wrongful termination claims, which means it protects underperformers as effectively as it protects the organization. Managers avoid initiating the process because it's exhausting and time-consuming. It becomes easier to work around the person than to work through the bureaucracy of removing them.

People who aren't contributing productively find organizational corners where they can persist indefinitely, largely unnoticed. They deliver just enough to avoid attention. They attend meetings, send emails, and generate activity that resembles work. They might be actively struggling or they might be checked out—it doesn't matter because the cost of removing them exceeds the cost of tolerating them. High-performers watch this and draw conclusions about what the organization actually values regardless of what leadership claims to value.

Layoffs become the primary mechanism for removing underperformers because layoffs bypass individual performance assessment. The organization declares certain roles or teams are no longer needed. Everyone in those categories gets terminated regardless of individual contribution. This protects the organization legally while solving the performance problem indirectly. This is the logical endpoint of the Welch playbook we examined in Chapter 4. Stack ranking and forced attrition were designed to create perpetual internal competition. But the mechanism that was supposed to continuously elevate performance instead became a blunt instrument for avoiding the harder work of genuine assessment and development. Yet layoffs are rarely performance-based. They target recent hires and high-performers in "non-strategic" functions while tenured underperformers in "critical" roles persist.

This is backwards. If hiring involves irreducible uncertainty, the solution isn't making hiring perfect. It's making correction faster. Organizations pour enormous resources into making hiring decisions more rigorous while investing almost nothing in making hiring mistakes cheaper to fix.

Sometimes a "bad hire" is a good person in the wrong role, on the wrong team, or solving the wrong problem. Organizations that allow fluid internal movement—whether through rotation programs, internal transfer markets, or self-selection into projects—treat placement as a hypothesis rather than a permanent assignment. The system corrects mismatches by enabling movement rather than requiring termination. Medicine solved the "you can't audition a surgeon" problem not through better selection tools but through residency—a years-long supervised correction system where competence builds incrementally and people wash out at multiple checkpoints before operating independently.

Most organizations don't have residency programs, instead they have correction mechanisms like a 90-day probationary period. Though rarely have I seen an organization use this probationary period. The same bureaucratic inertia that prevents honest evaluation at month eighteen prevents it at month three. A real probationary period would mean explicit evaluation criteria defined before day one, a genuine decision point at 90 days, and no stigma attached to either party saying, "this isn't working." Instead, the probationary period passes unnoticed and the employee transitions into the same protected status as everyone else with their fit unexamined.

The contract-to-hire model attempts to solve this differently by shifting risk entirely onto the candidate. The organization gets a trial period with no commitment. The contractor gets no benefits, no job security, and no guarantee that performance will lead to an offer. The asymmetry reveals the intent: it's not a mutual evaluation period. It's a way for organizations to defer commitment while extracting full-time work at reduced cost and obligation. The principle of correcting mistakes quickly is sound. Implementing it by making one party bear all the risk is not.

Netflix approaches correction from the manager's side with what they call the keeper test: would I fight to keep this person? If the answer is no, generous severance and a respectful exit. The mechanism forces regular honest assessment rather than allowing ambiguity to persist. It also surfaces patterns—if a manager consistently loses people, that signals something about the manager, not just the hires.

But what if we took that concept one step further? What if severance was always available? Not as punishment, not as a last resort, but as a standing offer. Anyone could opt out at any time with a few months of compensation and benefits. No performance improvement plan. No extensive documentation. No termination meetings. Just mutual acknowledgment: this isn't working.

This removes three problems simultaneously. First, people in bad fits can leave faster. They don't endure months of stress hoping to survive the next performance review. They can depart with dignity and runway to find something better. Second, managers receive honest feedback faster. If multiple people leave the same team in short succession, that signals something about the work, the leadership, or the expectations. The pattern becomes visible before it destroys the team. Third, it encourages healthy mobility. On average, people change roles every few years. Interests evolve. Skills compound. Organizations shift direction. Even healthy relationships eventually reach a natural transition point. It doesn't benefit anyone when employees overstay. Stagnation erodes performance more quietly than misalignment.

The objection is likely cost. Providing generous severance to anyone who wants it sounds expensive. But consider what organizations currently pay for bad hires: six months of salary while someone struggles, manager time attempting to coach someone who won't improve, team productivity lost to covering for weak performers, morale damage when productive employees watch dysfunction go unaddressed. A few months of severance is cheaper than a year or even years of underperformance.

The deeper objection is cultural. Organizations treat termination as failure—failure by the employee, failure by the manager, failure by the system. Making exit easy feels wrong, as if we're giving up on people or admitting defeat. This framing assumes perfect prediction was possible and ignores the reality that people change roles every 2-5 years. No one owes the other permanence, and change is not inherently bad.

Some people will take advantage of this. They'll collect a few months of compensation knowing they're underperforming and leave before being pushed out. This is desirable. The alternative is people collecting years of compensation while hiding in organizational complexity which is vastly more expensive.

Organizations that optimize for fast correction spend less time on hiring and more time on feedback. They accept that some hires won't work. They create conditions where non-working hires resolve quickly, and people who have exhausted their commitment can leave before turning toxic—through voluntary departure. They measure hiring success not by initial offer acceptance rates but overall team performance over time.

The scientific method does not eliminate uncertainty. It builds systems that learn from it. Hiring is no different. The goal is not perfect selection. It is rapid learning, thoughtful composition, and the humility to treat every hire as a provisional decision inside a living system.

It's perfectly human to be excited about a new hire. You should be. Belief in someone is a precondition for giving them a real chance to succeed. Just make sure you've built a system that doesn't depend on that belief being right.

CHAPTER 12
Designing Habitats for Humans

"All architecture is shelter, all great architecture is the design of space that contains, cuddles, exalts, or stimulates the persons in that space." – Philip Johnson

In the 1920s, researchers at Western Electric's Hawthorne Works in Cicero, Illinois set out to answer a simple question: does lighting affect worker productivity?

The results confounded expectations. Productivity spiked when lighting improved. It also increased when lighting was dimmed. It temporarily increased regardless of the direction of change. What the researchers eventually discovered wasn't about illumination at all. Workers performed better when they received attention, when they felt their input mattered, and when they were treated as participants in improvement rather than as interchangeable components of a production system.

The Hawthorne Effect has since been cited countless times, often dismissively, as evidence that observation distorts behavior—a concern we examined in Chapter 10 when observation is treated as a mechanism of control.

While that dismissal is technically correct, it misses the point. The so-called "reactivity" wasn't noise in this instance; it *was* the signal. Humans aren't machines that can be optimized through physical adjustments alone. We respond to being treated as thinking, capable people whose input matters.

This connects directly to the intrinsic motivators we explored in

Chapter 2: control, competence, and connection. The Hawthorne workers experienced all three—autonomy over their participation in the studies, the opportunity to develop and apply their judgment about the work, and a sense of inclusion beyond mere task execution.

That was a century ago.

Yet organizations today design environments as if those studies never happened. They optimize for cost and control while systematically eliminating the very conditions the Hawthorne research identified as critical to performance. This chapter examines why the environments organizations create reveal their actual priorities far more accurately than their mission statements do.

Research examining happiness across 40 common activities found that work ranked 39th—just above being sick in bed. Work isn't inherently miserable. It's because most workplaces are designed without regard for human needs, optimized instead for cost minimization, surveillance, or outdated assumptions about what "professional" environments should look like.

Every environmental choice is a values statement. The question is whether organizations recognize what they're communicating.

Consider the open office, which swept through corporate America in the 2000s as a way to increase collaboration, reduce real estate costs, and signal that hierarchies were flattening. The pitch was compelling: tear down walls, create sight lines, and force interaction. Innovation would flourish when people couldn't retreat into private offices.

The reality proved different. Open offices increased distractions, decreased productivity, and reduced face-to-face interactions as people compensated for lack of privacy by using headphones, email, and instant messaging. Sick days increased because illnesses spread more easily. Stress levels rose because constant visibility meant constant performance awareness—the feeling of being watched even when no one was actually watching.

The problem is that knowledge work requires both collaboration and deep focus. Open offices optimize for neither. What they actually optimize for is cost. Half-cubicles are expensive, but not as expensive as full ones, and surely not as much as actual walls.

Fluorescent lighting tells the same story. It's inexpensive, provides consistent illumination, and became the default despite evidence that it contributes to headaches, eye strain, and disrupted circadian rhythms. Hawthorne's studies may have been inconclusive regarding the levels of lighting, but contemporary findings have found a clear correlation between the type of lighting and well-being. Natural light improves mood, energy, and sleep quality, supporting circadian regulation and serotonin activity. Yet windows are treated as premium amenities reserved for seniority rather than as basic requirements for human well-being. The corner office isn't just a status symbol; it's access to the sunlight everyone needs but only executives receive.

Temperature affects productivity differently for different tasks and individuals, but most offices maintain uniform temperatures regardless of the work being done or who's doing it. When organizations optimize for the comfort of executives in suits rather than for the diverse needs of their workforce, they're making a choice about whose comfort matters. The thermostat is a values statement.

Conference rooms are cognitive death traps. Studies show that CO2 levels in poorly ventilated meeting rooms measurably impair decision-making. By the end of a two-hour meeting, participants are literally dumber than when they walked in. The solution is embarrassingly simple: open windows, better ventilation, shorter meetings, or just stepping outside. I invested in air quality monitors during the pandemic and discovered what should have been obvious: indoor air is often more polluted than outdoor air, and the fix is frequently free.

These aren't minor inconveniences. They're systemic degradations that accumulate over hours and days, creating baseline discomfort that people adapt to but never fully overcome. The impact is measurable: decreased cognitive performance, increased error rates, higher turnover, and more sick days. Organizations accept these costs because they're diffuse and hard to attribute to specific causes. Nobody tracks productivity lost to bad lighting. The connection between environmental degradation and performance remains abstract until someone explicitly measures it—and measuring it feels ridiculous, which is why it doesn't happen.

If you want to know what an organization actually values, don't read its mission statement. Check its bathrooms.

This sounds trivial until you recognize that most office workers use the bathroom 6 to 8 times per workday. Over a year, that's roughly 1,500 to 2,000 interactions with facilities the organization decided were adequate.

Single-ply toilet paper saves perhaps a few hundred dollars annually per floor, if it saves anything at all, since people just use more. The message it sends—that employee comfort during a basic biological function isn't worth a marginal cost—costs far more in morale than the savings delivered in budget relief. The same calculation applies to soap dispensers that require three pumps to get enough soap, paper towel dispensers calibrated to dispense one inadequate sheet at a time, bathroom stalls where the doors don't latch properly, and facilities that require walking across the building because space planners optimized for desk density rather than human needs.

Standard office environments are also designed for a body that is rare: average height, average weight, neurotypical sensory processing, no chronic conditions, no mobility constraints. Everyone who deviates adapts. The 5'2" woman and the 6'7" man both contort themselves to use the same "standard" desk, and neither complains because who can actually change it. Meanwhile, both perform below their potential because the environment fights their bodies 8 hours a day.

The economics are absurd. A $1,000 ergonomic chair amortized over 5 years costs $200 per year or roughly $0.80 cents per workday. A height-adjustable desk costs slightly more. The ROI against back pain, neck strain, reduced focus, and accumulated discomfort is overwhelming. The sitcom *Better Off Ted* satirized this with Veridian Dynamics testing uncomfortable chairs to boost productivity, which works in the show until employees reach their breaking point (depicted as screaming and running from the frame). Satire only lands when it exaggerates something real. Organizations cheap out because furniture is a visible line item while the productivity costs remain invisible. Nobody tracks output lost to physical discomfort. The connection between the cheap chair and the afternoon slump never gets measured, so it never gets addressed.

More importantly, control over one's immediate environment matters independently of the specific adjustments available. Can employees change their desk height, adjust the lighting, put up a calendar or leave materials in progress? The degree of environmental control correlates directly with autonomy, which we've already established is fundamental to motivation and performance. Hoteling arrangements and clean-desk policies signal that your presence is temporary, your work is interruptible, and your continuity doesn't matter. You can't think in day-to-day arcs when you have to reconstruct your workspace every morning. It's the spatial equivalent of the WIP problem: everything is always being set up, nothing is ever optimized for sustained effort.

Meanwhile, executive floors typically feature upgraded fixtures, softer paper, and properly stocked supplies. The discrepancy isn't accidental. It reflects actual organizational priorities made visible through purchasing decisions. Every employee who walks from the standard bathroom to the executive one for a functional toilet understands exactly what their company thinks of them.

The same pattern appears in break rooms. Coffee that tastes like it was brewed in a shoe. Refrigerators too small for the number of people who need to store lunch. One microwave that creates lines to rival bathroom queues at a concert. These are solvable problems with trivial costs, yet they persist because nobody with decision-making authority experiences them daily.

This extends to water fountains that produce a pathetic trickle, conference room chairs that destroy your back after 30 minutes, and laptops without enough external monitors that guarantee neck pain. Each one is individually defensible as a minor issue. Collectively, they create environments that actively fight the people working in them.

The cost to fix these problems is usually negligible. Upgrading toilet paper costs less than one employee's daily salary. Adding a second microwave costs less than the productivity lost to people leaving the building for food. Installing proper bathroom facilities costs less than the recruiting fees to replace someone who left because a thousand small signals told them they weren't valued.

Riot Games offers free lunch not as a cultural perk, but as an economic decision. Los Angeles traffic made lunch breaks unpredictable. People left the office, got stuck, returned late, and meetings slipped. Productivity suffered. So, Riot did the math and realized it was cheaper to feed people than to absorb the downstream cost of delay. The free food wasn't generosity. It was removing friction from the system. It also eliminated time pressure, resulting in people no longer feeling rushed—which further improved performance.

At Toyota Motor Corporation, clean and orderly work environments aren't about aesthetics or discipline. They're about information. Tools have designated locations so that missing tools become obvious immediately. Clear floors make leaks, defects, and hazards visible at a glance. In these environments, disorder isn't tolerated because disorder hides learning. When everything has a place, deviations stand out. When deviations stand out, people can respond quickly. The environment does the cognitive work that policies and reminders usually fail to accomplish.

The contrast with most Western offices couldn't be sharper. In typical workplaces, cleaning happens invisibly. Someone else empties your trash, wipes your surfaces, vacuums around your desk. The arrangement teaches learned helplessness: you stop noticing messes because noticing them isn't your job. I once asked where I could find a vacuum to clean up dust bunnies that had accumulated for weeks along a row of equipment. They looked at me like I'd just asked to borrow their toothbrush. The boundaries were clear, even if unspoken: people like you don't clean.

The economic waste compounds. A custodian I know points out that most companies pay for spot cleaning like emptying trash, surface wiping, and creating the appearance of tidiness. Items that workers could handle themselves with minimal training and supplies. This would free custodians to do actual deep cleaning: the skilled work that prevents mold, eliminates allergens, and maintains facilities long-term. Instead, companies pay professional rates for amateur tasks while the professional work never happens. The office looks clean when executives walk through, so long as they keep walking.

Hoteling arrangements amplify this dysfunction. If it's not your desk, why would you care for it? The transience breeds neglect, which creates more work for invisible cleaners, which reinforces the separation between those who use spaces and those who maintain them. The cycle continues until everyone has adapted to an environment that's nobody's responsibility.

A work environment isn't just physical space. It's also how time is structured for work hours, meeting schedules, project timelines, and the rhythm of organizational life.

Many "modern" workplace practices are recent inventions mistaken for fundamental truths. The 5-day, 40-hour workweek is a twentieth-century construct popularized by Henry Ford, who recognized not only that better work happened when people were rested, but that paying a daily wage required a legible, bounded workday with standardized shift lengths. These structures were later negotiated through labor movements rather than discovered as some optimal human rhythm.

Organizations inherit these structures and treat them as immutable, even when they clearly don't serve current needs. The 40-hour week made sense for manufacturing, where production required bodies present at machines. Ford himself speculated that as machines became more efficient, the need for human labor time would decline; by the late 1920s and early 1930s, he was publicly discussing the possibility of shorter workweeks, including a four-day model.

Nearly a century later, large-scale trials across the UK, Iceland, and other countries validated that intuition: organizations that moved to shorter work weeks saw productivity hold steady or improve, while burnout, absenteeism, and turnover dropped. The data exists. The structures remain.

Knowledge work, however, operates differently than physical labor. Value comes from thinking, not from occupying space for prescribed durations. Yet most organizations still measure presence rather than output, conflating visibility with productivity. And when they do try to measure output, the way they do it usually produces the adverse effects we explored in Chapter 7.

Organizations make choices about temporal structure constantly, usually without recognizing them as choices. They create artificial urgency through arbitrary deadlines, generating stress without corresponding increases in value. They schedule 8 hours of back-to-back meetings, leaving no time for the work those meetings supposedly coordinate.

The white space principle applies here. Calendars packed with consecutive obligations leave no room for thinking, no space for unplanned interactions, no buffer for dealing with unexpected problems. A calendar that appears fully utilized is actually fully constrained, unable to absorb anything new. I once audited an executive's calendar for a quarter: if you didn't count weekends, holidays, or PTO, he was at 140 percent utilization from meetings alone. The number would be comical if it weren't so common.

Organizations need slack. Not waste, but intentional excess capacity that enables adaptation and innovation. Think of it like a WIP limit for your calendar. As we explored in Chapter 9 on waste, when every hour is spoken for, when every resource is fully utilized, when every team member is allocated to multiple concurrent efforts, the system becomes brittle. It's similar to a computer processor running at 100 percent capacity—everything slows to a crawl, programs start crashing, and eventually it overheats. You're then met with everyone's favorite Blue Screen of Death (unless you're a Mac user, in which case it's the spinning beach ball of existential dread).

Building white space into schedules means accepting that utilization won't hit 100 percent, but that "unutilized" time is productive because it enables time to think, to learn, and to respond to the unexpected. The organization that can't absorb a surprise is the organization that collapses when one arrives.

The pandemic forced a natural experiment on work environments: could knowledge work happen effectively when everyone worked remotely? For many organizations, the answer was yes. Sometimes, even more effectively than before.

This actually wasn't unprecedented. Long before the pandemic, many organizations had already demonstrated that fully remote knowledge work could function effectively when it was deliberately designed that way. Companies such as 37signals, Automattic, GitLab, and Zapier operated this way by default, not as an exception.

Then executives started demanding returns to the office. The rationale varied: collaboration suffers remotely, culture requires presence, junior employees need mentoring, real estate investments shouldn't sit empty, and so on. Some concerns were genuine. Some were thinly veiled preference for the familiar or due to a discomfort with reduced managerial visibility.

The data on remote work effectiveness is clear: when organizations design for it, working from home can increase happiness, improve productivity, and reduce burnout. This reinforces a fundamental need we've consistently explored throughout this book: remote work provides autonomy over environment and schedule. People can structure their days around peak cognitive hours, eliminate commutes that consume time without creating value, and design physical environments matching their preferences.

This doesn't mean everyone should work remotely or that offices serve no purpose. It means that mandating presence for its own sake wastes human potential. That waste compounds when environments are not optimized for the kind of work they are meant to support, as we've been exploring throughout this chapter.

Remote work also revealed something uncomfortable about accommodation. For decades, disabled workers requested flexible hours, work-from-home arrangements, adjusted environments—accommodations companies deemed unreasonable or too expensive. Then the pandemic proved those accommodations were entirely feasible. Organizations did in 2 weeks what they'd refused to do for 20 years.

Remote work didn't just accommodate disability; it bypassed the accommodation process. The paperwork, the disclosure, the stigma of being marked as requiring special treatment, all vanished. No one had to explain their body to HR. Return-to-office mandates disproportionately push disabled workers out (or those that care for disabled family members), and that's rarely part of the conversation. The environments we're demanding people return to were never designed for them in the first place.

Hybrid models attempt to split the difference but often combine the worst of both approaches: people commute to offices to sit on video calls, teams struggle to coordinate schedules, and proximity to a building determines who gets flexibility. Offices become crowded on mandatory days and empty on others. The arrangement satisfies nobody while claiming to satisfy everyone.

Effective hybrid work requires clarity about what should happen in person versus remotely. It also means limiting the talent pool to local markets. "Collaboration" often means "we paid for this building." "Culture" often means "I prefer managing people I can see." If the actual goal is mentoring, create structured programs. If the actual goal is culture, recognize that culture is created through behavior and values, not geographic proximity. If the actual goal is justifying real estate costs, at least design them for productivity.

Some organizations succeeded with remote work because they already had strong cultures, clear documentation, and trust between teams and leadership. Others struggled because dysfunction hidden by in-person coordination became visible when that coordination disappeared. Return-to-office mandates in those cases treated symptoms rather than causes—attempting to restore the illusion of productivity rather than addressing underlying problems.

Remote work should not be treated as a perk. Instead, the question should be asked: "what does this work require, and how do we create conditions where that work can happen effectively?"

When we confuse structural design with perks, the pattern repeats. Many organizations now advertise mental health benefits as evidence of care. On paper, this looks like progress. In practice, it often becomes another source of friction.

The benefit exists, but buried inside a vendor portal, restricted to a limited number of sessions, routed through unfamiliar providers, and rarely discussed openly. Usage is technically available but socially invisible. Employees are left to discover it on their own, navigate it alone, and decide whether it's "worth" the effort during an already depleted moment. Availability is not the same as accessibility.

The same pattern shows up across modern perk catalogs. Companies accumulate subscriptions, discounts, apps, and platforms—each one defensible in isolation. Taken together, they create a scavenger hunt that wastes employee time with rarely any gain. The benefits exist to be listed on job postings, not to be used by employees.

This reflects a deeper confusion between *providing resources* and *creating conditions*. An Employee Assistance Program doesn't address the workload causing burnout. A meditation app doesn't fix the meeting culture that fragments attention. A gym subsidy doesn't compensate for the stress that makes exercise feel impossible. These offerings treat symptoms while leaving causes untouched—and often serve primarily as liability shields. *We offered support; they didn't use it.*

Health insurance provides a particularly clear example of how organizations shift complexity while framing it as empowerment. Many companies now favor high-deductible plans paired with Health Savings Accounts, often arguing that employees are intelligent enough to manage their own health decisions and that, on paper, individuals can spend roughly the same amount as they would under traditional coverage.

What this framing omits is the work required to navigate the U.S. healthcare system itself. Comparing plans, estimating future medical needs, negotiating opaque pricing, contesting bills, delaying care to preserve cash, and absorbing the anxiety of getting those decisions wrong all consume time and cognitive energy. That effort does not disappear simply because it happens outside the office. Since work and life are not cleanly separable systems, the stress and distraction created by this complexity inevitably bleed back into the workday—reducing focus, increasing burnout, and quietly degrading performance.

I experienced this firsthand. Under my consultancy's traditional plan, I paid roughly $5,000 annually for full coverage for my family. When the company was acquired, the new owners switched us to an HSA model. Subsequent years, even with the extra work of shopping around and holding off on certain treatments, my household health-related expenses regularly exceeded $20,000.

In most developed nations, this isn't a concern at all. Health coverage is decoupled from employment, which means organizations don't bear the administrative burden and employees don't face financial catastrophe because their employer chose a different plan structure. Employer-provided health insurance is an American invention, not an economic inevitability.

What most people actually want isn't another benefit to manage. They want flexibility—the ability to step away without penalty, the freedom to structure their day around energy rather than optics, the trust to handle their work without proving they're handling it through constant visibility. In other words, they want an environment that reduces pressure, not a menu of services designed to help them survive it.

The distinction matters because it determines where organizations invest. Adding benefits is easy. You sign a contract with a vendor and update the employee handbook. Changing conditions is hard. It requires examining why people are burning out, which often leads back to decisions leadership would rather not revisit: the number of initiatives, the constant priority shifts, the understaffing, the unrealistic deadlines, and the culture that treats exhaustion as commitment.

Performative care is worse than no care because it creates the appearance of having addressed the problem while leaving the problem intact. It shifts responsibility to the individual: *we gave you tools, why aren't you using them?* Meanwhile, the conditions producing the need for those tools remain unexamined.

Genuine support looks different. It looks like managers who notice when someone is struggling and adjust workload before being asked. It looks like policies that actually get used because using them doesn't carry career risk. It looks like senior leaders modeling sustainable behavior rather than glorifying their own overwork. It looks like asking why people need mental health support in the first place. Much of what gets labeled as individual well-being is actually relational.

Loneliness is one of the clearest examples. It isn't a mental illness, but it is a powerful risk factor for mental health deterioration when it becomes chronic, and it's increasingly common in modern work arrangements. People can be surrounded by coworkers, buried in Slack notifications, and still feel socially isolated because the environment produces interaction without producing connection. When the system is optimized for throughput, surveillance, and constant coordination, relationships become transactional. Employees don't just lose camaraderie; they lose a basic buffer against stress.

That may seem to contradict the case for remote work, until you recognize that connection doesn't require constant physical proximity. What it requires is shared purpose, mutual respect, and opportunities for interaction that matter. Physical proximity can help create those conditions—but proximity without intent rarely does.

Another consideration is that environments either reinforce or counter homophily—the tendency of organizations to hire and promote people similar to existing members. When all informal gathering spaces are designed around certain assumptions, like alcohol at social events, sports on break room televisions, and conversation topics assuming shared cultural references, people who don't share those assumptions learn they don't fully belong. The research on diversity's impact is extensive: varied perspectives foster innovation, broader idea generation improves problem-solving, and the financial performance data is clear. Once again, this is not simply a humanitarian, feel-good effort. It's an advantage.

Shared environments require constant negotiation over temperature, noise, scents, and space. Some people get migraines from perfume. Others find certain food smells intolerable. These aren't preferences; they're physiological responses that affect whether someone can function. But can you actually tell a coworker their fragrance is making you sick without it becoming an HR incident? Can you ask someone not to microwave fish without it feeling like a cultural judgment? Most people can't, so they suffer silently or seethe quietly, and the shared environment degrades for everyone.

This connects back to Psychological Safety. If your culture can't handle "hey, that smell is making it hard for me to focus," it definitely can't handle "hey, that architectural decision is creating technical debt" or "hey, that strategy isn't working." The small negotiations are diagnostic. Those who can't have a conversation about microwaved fish probably can't facilitate a conversation about anything harder.

This extends to digital environments. Slack channels that tolerate constant off-topic chatter become noise people mute. Email threads that balloon with everyone copied become information overload. Notification systems that interrupt work for every update train people to disable them entirely, causing them to miss information that actually matters. Organizations often confuse more communication with better communication. Sometimes less is more.

If environment shapes behavior and environments are choices, then experimenting with environmental changes becomes a legitimate way to discover what works. As we established in previous chapters, experiments don't all succeed, that's the point. It is a huge red flag if they do.

Four-day workweeks have succeeded in some organizations and failed in others, revealing that success depends on context rather than on the structure itself. Unlimited vacation policies sometimes increase vacation usage and sometimes decrease it, depending on whether the culture actually supports taking time off or whether "unlimited" becomes a test of commitment where taking vacation signals lack of dedication.

This suggests that copying practices from other organizations rarely works as intended. The practice is visible; the environment that makes it work isn't. Google's famous perks of free food, on-site services, and playful office design worked at Google because they aligned with its culture, hiring practices, and business model—including expectations about how much of employees' time and attention work would occupy. Transplanting those perks into a different organization without the supporting context produces cargo cult management: the appearance of Google's environment without the substance.

What does transfer is the principle: intentionality about one's environment as a factor of performance. Asking what environmental factors enable or obstruct the work. Testing changes. Measuring impact. Adjusting based on what you learn.

Most environmental factors operate below conscious awareness. You notice them when they're egregiously bad, but subtle degradations accumulate without triggering conscious attention. Making the environment visible means asking questions that usually go unasked.

This connects back to Chapter 10's discussion of gemba walks.

Leaders should observe work environments directly rather than assuming they know what those environments feel like based on brief visits or reports from those who benefit most from current arrangements.

Ask people to describe their ideal work environment. Not as a wish list for impossible luxuries, but as a serious inquiry into what would actually help. Some answers will be impractical, but patterns will emerge. If everyone mentions noise as a problem, that's actionable information. If people consistently describe feeling watched or unable to focus, that's environmental dysfunction that can be addressed.

Changes don't need to be expensive. Rearranging furniture can create different interaction patterns. Adjusting schedules can provide uninterrupted time. Clarifying which meetings are mandatory reduces calendar pressure. Providing variety in workspaces costs less than forcing everyone into identical conditions. Upgrading the toilet paper costs almost nothing.

The goal is progress over perfection. Moving from environments that fight people to environments that support them. Creating conditions where it's easier to succeed than fail.

Joe Krebs, in *Agile Kata*, points out that *habit* and *habitat* share the same etymological root—both derive from the Latin *habere*, meaning to have or hold, and *habitare*, meaning to dwell or inhabit. This isn't linguistic coincidence. It reflects something fundamental about how humans operate.

We become what we repeatedly do. What we repeatedly do is shaped by where we dwell. The spaces we inhabit—physical, temporal, digital—create affordances that make certain behaviors easier and others harder. Over time, the easier behaviors become automatic. They become habits. The habitat produces the habit.

This explains why individual willpower fails as a lever for organizational change. Telling people to collaborate more while housing them in open offices fights psychology. Encouraging innovation while scheduling every hour with status meetings creates friction that willpower cannot overcome. The environment wins. It always wins.

Adaptation is humanity's defining trait. We survived ice ages, deserts, and built civilizations in climates that should have killed us. This flexibility is our greatest evolutionary advantage.

This same capacity allows us to normalize dysfunction, but it also allows us to embrace better conditions when they appear. Change the environment, and people don't just tolerate the new reality—they adapt to it, often faster than anyone expects. What felt impossible under the old conditions becomes obvious under the new ones.

This is the lever the next chapter examines: not convincing people to change their minds but changing the conditions they're adapting to. Belief follows behavior. Behavior follows environment. Start there.

CHAPTER 13

Behavior Before Belief

"I did then what I knew how to do. Now that I know better, I do better." – Maya Angelou

By this point in the book, the pattern should be clear.

You understand that systems drive behavior more powerfully than intention, that incentives shape outcomes regardless of mission statements, and that environments enable or obstruct performance. The formula seems obvious: apply scientific thinking to the organization itself. Observe dysfunction, test small, learn fast, and iterate.

And yet.

You also already know, from Chapter 2, that knowing something is good for you has never been enough to make you do it—otherwise there would be no smokers, soda companies wouldn't exist, and we'd never skip the gym. Knowledge is necessary but insufficient. That tension has threaded through every chapter. Now it arrives in your hands.

Change is big business. Organizations spend billions every year on consultants who promise transformation. They launch initiatives with compelling names like Horizon, Accelerate, Elevate, Polaris, Apollo, Everest—or the perpetually doomed *Phoenix Project*. They form steering committees and publish roadmaps. Then, months or years later, they discover that little has actually changed. The same dysfunctions persist. The same frustrations repeat.

The usual diagnosis is simple but uninspired: people resist change.

Yet humans adopt new smartphones, try the new restaurant everyone is raving about, and watch their bodies change so gradually that a new wrinkle blindsides them in the mirror one morning. Change comes naturally to most of us outside work. So, the question sharpens: why is organizational change so hard?

The answer isn't resistance. Change fails because it is imposed rather than cultivated, mandated rather than enabled, and treated as an event instead of a process requiring patient, persistent work.

Change isn't about convincing people to behave differently. It's about altering the systems, incentives, and environments that produce the current behavior. If you hold executive authority, then that is where you start: perform a non-accusatory root-cause analysis of the behaviors you dislike. But since many of us do not hold executive authority, this chapter explores how to do that without relying on authority, mandates, or belief.

Some of the most effective behavior change doesn't rely on visibility or persuasion at all. It comes from designing environments that quietly embraces predictable human behavior instead of fighting it. Hotels figured this out years ago. Many place a runner at the foot of the bed, not to decorate the room, but because guests reliably drop bags or clothes on the nearest horizontal surface when they arrive. The runner protects the comforter without a sign, a policy, or a lecture. Nothing about the guest changes. The environment does.

I've seen the same principle work in team spaces. In one shared room, I brought in a container of wet wipes and left it on a table. I didn't announce it or make it a policy, even though that would have produced immediate compliance—and likely only once. Within a week, people were wiping down laptops and desks. Over time, some teams began ending each two-week iteration with a quick cleanup. No one was persuaded. The visible presence of the wipes provided the prompt, their availability reduced effort, and the behavior became habit.

This is the difference between trying to pull a plant taller and tending a garden.

A gardener doesn't create growth directly. They choose what to plant, where to place it, how to space it, when to prune, and how to prepare the soil. They can improve the odds and remove obstacles. But they cannot command the weather, eliminate pests, or force a seed to sprout on a schedule.

Good gardening is an act of both care and restraint. You intervene locally, observe patiently, and adjust based on what the environment reveals—not based on what you hoped would happen. Growth follows conditions, not intention.

Organizational change works the same way. When change is imposed, it fights the system. When it is cultivated, behavior shifts first—and belief follows later, once the results become undeniable.

In software development, this often shows up as things like configuring WIP limits in a work management system so new work can't be started when capacity is full. But an even stronger intervention happens upstream. When planning only provides enough work for engineers to focus on one thing at a time, the temptation to multitask disappears entirely. No one needs to be convinced to focus. The environment makes focus the default.

The same pattern appears when work is intentionally sliced smaller, delivered vertically, and prioritized narrowly. These changes don't rely on discipline or agreement. They change what is possible in the system, and behavior follows.

Many change efforts fail not because their ideas are wrong, but because they're introduced in the wrong order.

I see this struggle constantly in people tasked with improving how teams work. They begin by correcting people instead of redesigning the systems those people are responding to. They encounter teams that won't limit work in progress, won't attend retrospectives consistently, or won't keep their boards updated. When confronted about these behaviors, the teams ignore, justify, or disengage from the person entirely. This is often interpreted as resistance.

It isn't.

The team isn't resisting change. They're protecting themselves from a system that punishes the behaviors this new change champion is trying to introduce. A system that has trained them, through experience, that speaking up is risky, slowing down is dangerous, and change initiatives can be safely waited out.

What's actually happening is rational behavior.

If performance reviews reward visible busyness across multiple projects, limiting work in progress feels unsafe. If retrospectives consistently fail to result in real change, attending them feels like wasted time. If leadership adds priorities without removing any, focusing on one objective means disappointing someone whose displeasure carries consequences.

The basis of cognitive behavioral therapy (CBT) is often illustrated as a triangle: thoughts influence feelings, which drive behaviors, which reinforce the original thoughts. The biology we explored in Chapter 2 explains why this loop is so difficult to break. Stress triggers cortisol, which suppresses the cognitive function required to question the thought that created the stress in the first place.

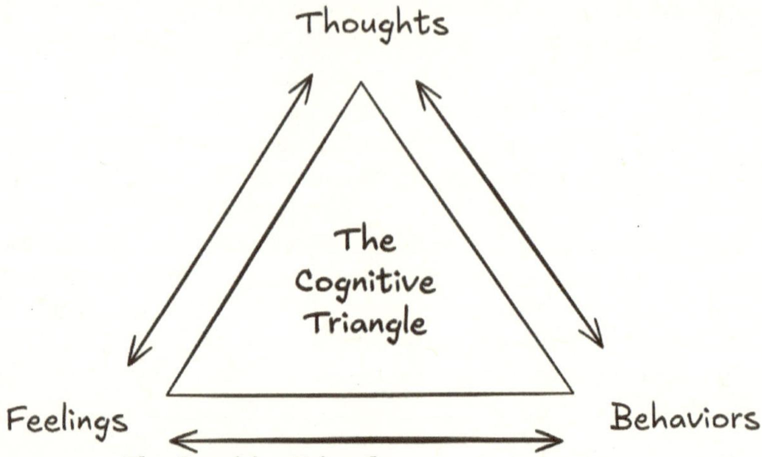

Figure 13.1 - The Cognitive Triangle

The result is a self-reinforcing cycle that cannot be interrupted through rational argument alone. Just as you can't will yourself into feeling happier, the feeling precedes the evidence. Only sustained behavioral change eventually shifts belief by compounding evidence that challenges the other two sides of the triangle.

Dysfunction is cyclical. So is learning. The difference is which loop you practice.

As Richard Pascale, Mark Millemann, and Linda Gioja observed in their study of organizational change, it's easier to act your way to a new way of thinking than to think your way to a new way of acting—a point John Shook later popularized through his experience at NUMMI. Most change initiatives get this backwards. They try to change minds first and assume behavior will follow. It works better to change behavior first and let belief catch up once results become undeniable.

To change behavior, you must first understand the system producing it.

People operate on autopilot most of the time. This isn't laziness—it's efficiency. The brain conserves energy by automating repeated actions. As we briefly discussed in Chapter 2, while automatic behavior is efficient, it comes at a cost: it suppresses feedback. When actions are executed without conscious attention, the brain is no longer evaluating alternatives. It is simply executing a script.

Learning requires a temporary interruption of that automation. Novelty does this reliably. When something changes—when a routine is disrupted, even slightly—the brain re-engages. Attention returns and feedback becomes visible again. This is not because novelty is inherently motivating, but because it signals uncertainty. The brain shifts from execution mode back into evaluation. However, this re-engagement can feel uncomfortable, and the brain is content to continue running its regularly scheduled program.

It's important to remember that people are just trying to do their jobs. Philosophical arguments for change and detailed process explanations may be interesting, but they're often experienced as noise by people who are already overwhelmed. Teams are frustrated by bottlenecks, confused by contradictory priorities, stressed by unrealistic deadlines, and demoralized by waste they can see but can't address. They don't care why those things are bad. They care that they hurt.

Behavior design shows that actions become more automatic when they're paired with positive emotion or relief from negative emotion. The antidote to resistance isn't persuasion. It's relief. This also means timing matters. A team buried under a release deadline is neurologically incapable of the openness that change requires. Cortisol is acting as a bouncer, and learning is not on the guest list.

Relief restores attention—and attention is what makes learning possible. So, start by treating the pain, and when a small change reduces friction or frustration, it creates immediate evidence that an alternative is possible. That evidence matters more than explanation ever will. People don't need to be convinced to change when they can feel the system working differently.

One of the most reliable ways to create that relief is to make work visible. Visibility turns frustration into shared evidence. It replaces opinion with something people can point to together. When work, queues, dependencies, and delays are visible, problems stop being personal and start becoming solvable. This can look like visual management boards, radiators, and tiered diagrams.

An everyday example of this can be found on the road. Those radar speed signs that scan your approach and flash your actual speed back at you in real time have been shown to consistently reduce speeding, even though the data isn't recorded and carries no enforcement consequences. The interesting thing is that every driver already has a speedometer. The information isn't new. But there's a difference between private data you can ignore and external feedback that confronts you publicly with your own behavior. That shift from internal awareness to external visibility changes behavior without changing anything else. No tickets, no cameras, no consequences. Just a radiator.

Data is one of the best ways to create visibility. Used well, it creates awareness while removing you from the argument. You're no longer saying something is wrong; the data is. That distinction matters more than it sounds. People are far less defensive when they can disagree with a chart instead of a colleague. Empiricism creates distance between identity and outcome, which is often the only space where change can begin. This only works when data is treated as evidence to investigate, not a verdict to defend. And if they argue the data or method is flawed, then that is the first improvement item.

As the Hawthorne Study demonstrated, trust forms when people feel listened to, involved, and cared for. And as Cialdini's principle of reciprocity shows, people feel an obligation—often subconscious—to return value to those who help them. Influence is earned by removing obstacles, not by delivering speeches.

The first step is building awareness by asking questions that make the invisible visible. Vague frustration doesn't produce change. Diagnosis does. "Everything is broken" invites argument. "We're optimizing for velocity, which Goodhart's Law predicts will distort the metric without improving throughput" creates a specific problem that can be tested.

Ask what's preventing people from finishing their work—not "why aren't you working faster," but what systemic factors create delays? Unclear requirements? External dependencies? Environment access? Approval bottlenecks?

Then ask what single change would make their job easier. That question often surfaces pain people have stopped articulating because they assume nothing will change. Sometimes the answer is small and immediately fixable. Sometimes it exposes deeper constraints you didn't know existed.

Making dysfunction visible requires honesty most organizations struggle to tolerate. Domino's Pizza demonstrated what this looks like in 2009 when it publicly acknowledged that customers hated its product. The campaign showed unfiltered feedback—"boring," "mass-produced," "like cardboard"—and showed executives visibly reacting to it in real time.

This was more than a great marketing campaign; it was strategically disarming.

By naming the problem themselves, Domino's created permission to make the necessary changes. As Robert Cialdini has shown, transparency and ownership strengthen influence by activating multiple principles at once: authority through accountability, liking through humility, and commitment through public acknowledgment.

Domino's rebuilt its recipe, invested heavily in delivery technology, and reframed itself as a delivery company that happens to bake pizza. The admission of dysfunction wasn't the risk. Defending the indefensible would have been.

This reflects the kind of horizontal innovation we discussed earlier—progress driven not by perfecting the product, but by integrating other domains, in this case logistics. Like Little Caesars, Domino's gained advantage by redesigning the system around the product rather than endlessly optimizing the product itself.

Most organizations avoid this level of transparent honesty. Admitting dysfunction feels like career suicide. But dysfunction exists whether acknowledged or not. Naming it doesn't create the problem—it creates the conditions to solve it.

The key is follow-through. If people tell you what's blocking them and nothing changes, they learn that their voice doesn't matter. People who speak up repeatedly are often labeled "negative" or "disruptive," and quickly learn that silence is safer. But if obstacles are actually removed, they learn you're someone who helps them succeed.

This compounds over time. Trust forms through repeated experience, not isolated effort.

Eliyahu Goldratt taught that systems have a single constraint at a time. But not all constraints are physical. Sometimes the bottleneck is a team's willingness to try again after multiple failed initiatives. That constraint isn't removed through arguments—it's removed through evidence.

Esther Derby's work on organizational change addresses this directly. Rather than pursuing dramatic transformations, she advocates for small, safe-to-fail shifts—changes modest enough to try without triggering organizational antibodies. The goal isn't to convince people change will work, but to let them experience it working. Each small improvement replaces a bit of accumulated skepticism with evidence.

This is where change itself must become empirical.

Jason Little formalized this approach through Lean Change Management. He later deliberately dropped "management" from the name because attempting to *manage* change is precisely the problem. Traditional change management assumes change can be designed upfront: define the end state, create a plan, execute the plan, manage resistance. This treats change as something done *to* people.

Lean Change inverts that assumption. It applies scientific thinking to change itself. You form hypotheses about interventions, run small experiments, observe results, and adjust. Instead of prescribing practices, it builds the capability to experiment, learn, and adapt.

Mike Rother's research at Toyota revealed how this capability is developed. The Improvement Kata isn't an improvement methodology to implement—it's a teaching methodology with practice routines to help build scientific thinking as a habit. Teams describe current conditions precisely, articulate target conditions clearly, identify obstacles specifically, and run experiments that test one variable at a time.

Lean Change creates the conditions for experimentation. Kata builds the muscle to do it well. Neither relies on belief nor buy-in upfront. Both rely on behavior first.

Most organizations treat the plan as a north star. When reality deviates, the question becomes how to get back on plan. Scientific thinkers operate differently. They understand the plan isn't truth—it's a hypothesis. When reality diverges, they don't correct reality to match the plan; they correct the plan to better reflect reality.

This distinction determines whether organizations learn or are destined to repeat the same mistakes indefinitely.

Mandated change produces compliance, not commitment. People do what they're told while preserving the underlying system by gaming metrics, adoption performance, and reverting back once oversight fades. Sustainable change accumulates through small wins, visible relief of pain, and repeated proof that speaking up leads to improvement rather than punishment. Culture doesn't change on executive timelines or consulting roadmaps. It changes at the speed of trust—slower than leaders want and faster than cynics expect when done properly.

Success isn't transformation or an idealized end state where no further change is required. It's a long-term strategy for long-term stakes—one without a finish line.

Success is building the capability to notice dysfunction, experiment with alternatives, and adjust based on results. It's creating conditions where people can identify waste and address it without requiring permission from six layers of management. It's developing cultures where failure becomes data rather than something to be hidden or punished.

These capabilities compound. Organizations that build them get better at getting better. They adapt faster because they've practiced adapting. They waste less because they've learned to question whether work creates value before committing resources to it.

This brings us back to habitat and habit. Where people dwell determines what they repeatedly do. You don't change culture by convincing people to think differently. You change culture by changing the systems and environments that shape behavior. New behavior, sustained long enough, produces new belief.

Belief doesn't lead to change.

Behavior does.

Epilogue

This book began with a gap—between what organizations say they want and what they actually reward, between methods that work and methods that get approved, between the conference talk and Monday morning.

That gap doesn't close because you've read thirteen chapters.

Andrew Clay Shafer once said, "You are either building a learning organization, or you will be losing to someone who is." He later explained on my podcast that organizations collect vocabulary and data easily, but nothing has been learned until behavior changes.

Causality in complex systems is nonlinear, indirect, and cumulative. Change spreads through demonstrated results, not arguments. Over time, better outcomes exert more influence than confidence ever could.

That's why the work happens at a local scale. Not because your ambition is small, but because this is where evidence can form. Small teams. Limited experiments. Observable results. Accumulated over time. Until the new becomes normal.

If all of this feels hard, it is. Hard things are hard. But showing up day after day in a broken system—one that quietly extracts value and saps motivation—is also hard. Choose your hard.

The thinking is yours now. So is the work.

So, what is your first experiment?

Notes

"I Think, Therefore I Know"

Chapter 1 – What We Think We Know

1. Encyclopaedia Britannica. "Information theory: Physiology." *Encyclopaedia Britannica*. Accessed February 23, 2026.
2. Princeton Neuroscience Institute. "New Research Sheds Light on How the Brain Learns to Control Attention." February 23, 2024.
3. Arguinchona, J.H., & Tadi, P. "Neuroanatomy, Reticular Activating System." *StatPearls* [Internet]. Treasure Island (FL): StatPearls Publishing; updated July 24, 2023. Available via NCBI Bookshelf.
4. Wiseman, Richard. *The Luck Factor*. Miramax Books, 2003.

Chapter 2 – What Drives Us

1. Maguire, E.A., Gadian, D.G., Johnsrude, I.S., Good, C.D., Ashburner, J., Frackowiak, R.S., & Frith, C.D. "Navigation-Related Structural Change in the Hippocampi of Taxi Drivers." *Proceedings of the National Academy of Sciences* 97, no. 8 (2000): 4398–4403.
2. Kanthamalee, S., & Sripankaew, K. "Effect of Neurobic Exercise on Memory Enhancement in the Elderly With Dementia." *Journal of Nursing Education and Practice* 4, no. 3 (2014): 69–76. https://doi.org/10.5430/jnep.v4n3p69
3. Buckingham, Marcus, & Ashley Goodall. "Reinventing Performance Management." *Harvard Business Review*, April 2015.
4. Accenture. "Goodbye, Annual Performance Appraisals." Accenture Newsroom, August 2015.
5. Economist Intelligence Unit (EIU) / Brightline Initiative. *Closing the Gap Between Strategy and Execution*. Brightline Initiative / EIU, 2017.
6. Achor, Shawn. *The Happiness Advantage*. Crown Business, 2010.
7. Mani, A., Mullainathan, S., Shafir, E., & Zhao, J. "Poverty Impedes Cognitive Function." *Science* 341, no. 6149 (2013): 976–980.
8. Deci, Edward L., & Richard M. Ryan. *Intrinsic Motivation and Self-Determination in Human Behavior*. Plenum, 1985.
9. Karasek, Robert A. "Job Demands, Job Decision Latitude,

and Mental Strain: Implications for Job Redesign." *Administrative Science Quarterly* 24, no. 2 (1979): 285–308.
10. Korb, Alex. *The Upward Spiral: Using Neuroscience to Reverse the Course of Depression, One Small Change at a Time*. New Harbinger Publications, 2015.
11. Maté, Gabor. *When the Body Says No: The Cost of Hidden Stress*. Vintage Canada, 2003. Audiobook ed., Audible, 2021.
12. Laffan, J., et al. "Day-of-Week Variation in STEMI Incidence." *Heart* (BMJ), British Cardiovascular Society Annual Conference supplement (2023).
13. Senge, Peter M. *The Fifth Discipline: The Art & Practice of the Learning Organization*. Doubleday, 1990. Revised ed., 2006.
14. Zak, Paul J. "The Neuroscience of Trust." *Harvard Business Review*, January–February 2017.
15. Buettner, Dan. *The Blue Zones: Lessons for Living Longer From the People Who've Lived the Longest*. National Geographic, 2008.
16. Harter, J.K., Schmidt, F.L., Agrawal, S., Plowman, S.K., & Blue, A. "The Relationship Between Engagement at Work and Organizational Outcomes." Gallup, 2016. (Q12 Meta-Analysis, 9th edition.)
17. Kuvaas, Bård, Robert Buch, Antoinette Weibel, Anders Dysvik, & Christina G.L. Nerstad. "Do Intrinsic and Extrinsic Motivation Relate Differently to Employee Outcomes?" *Journal of Economic Psychology* 61 (2017): 244–258. https://doi.org/10.1016/j.joep.2017.05.004

Chapter 3 – The Science of Good Enough

1. Waber, Rebecca L., Baba Shiv, Ziv Carmon, and Dan Ariely. "Commercial Features of Placebo and Therapeutic Efficacy." *JAMA* 299, no. 9 (2008): 1016–1017. https://doi.org/10.1001/jama.299.9.1016
2. Chernev, Alexander. "Customers Will Pay More for Less." *Harvard Business Review*, June 2012. https://hbr.org/2012/06/customers-will-pay-more-for-less
3. University of Michigan Institute for Healthcare Policy & Innovation. "Pay Less, Take More: Success in Getting Patients to Take Their Medicine." July 9, 2018. https://ihpi.umich.edu/news/pay-less-take-more-success-getting-patients-take-their-medicine
4. University of Connecticut (UConn Today). "Cognitive Biases and Brain Biology Help Explain Why Facts Don't Change

Minds." August 16, 2022.
https://today.uconn.edu/2022/08/cognitive-biases-and-brain-biology-help-explain-why-facts-dont-change-minds/

5. Rozenblit, Leonid, and Frank Keil. "The Misunderstood Limits of Folk Science: An Illusion of Explanatory Depth." *Cognitive Science* 26, no. 5 (2002): 521–562. https://doi.org/10.1207/s15516709cog2605_1
6. Anderson, Cameron, et al. "A Status-Enhancement Account of Overconfidence." *Journal of Personality and Social Psychology* 103, no. 4 (2012): 718–735. https://doi.org/10.1037/a0029395
7. Kruger, Justin, and David Dunning. "Unskilled and Unaware of It: How Difficulties in Recognizing One's Own Incompetence Lead to Inflated Self-Assessments." *Journal of Personality and Social Psychology* 77, no. 6 (1999): 1121–1134. https://doi.org/10.1037/0022-3514.77.6.1121
8. Dewey, John. *How We Think*. D.C. Heath, 1910.
9. Moen, Ronald. "Foundation and History of the PDSA Cycle." W. Edwards Deming Institute. https://deming.org/wp-content/uploads/2020/06/PDSA_History_Ron_Moen.pdf
10. Ford Motor Company. "The Moving Assembly Line and the Five-Dollar Workday." (n.d.). https://corporate.ford.com/articles/history/moving-assembly-line.html
11. Liker, Jeffrey K. *The Toyota Way: 14 Management Principles from the World's Greatest Manufacturer*. McGraw-Hill, 2004.
12. Rother, Mike. *Toyota Kata: Managing People for Improvement, Adaptiveness, and Superior Results*. McGraw-Hill, 2009.
13. Epstein, David. *Range: Why Generalists Triumph in a Specialized World*. Riverhead Books, 2019.
14. Simon, Herbert A. Nobel Prize Lecture. Stockholm, December 8, 1978. https://www.nobelprize.org/uploads/2018/06/simon-lecture.pdf
15. Savage, Sam L. *The Flaw of Averages: Why We Underestimate Risk in the Face of Uncertainty*. Wiley, 2009.

Chapter 4 – Incentives Without Intent

1. Sinek, Simon. *The Infinite Game*. Portfolio/Penguin, 2019.
2. World Inequality Lab (WID.world). Somanchi, A., Yang, L., Zucman, G., et al. "Equality and Development: A

Comparative & Historical Perspective 1800–2025." *World Inequality Lab Working Paper* 2025/25. October 27, 2025. https://wid.world/document/equality-and-development-a-comparative-historical-perspective-1800-2025-world-inequality-lab-working-paper-2025-25/

3. American Society of Pension Professionals & Actuaries (ASPPA). "The 'Real' 401(k) Day." November 14, 2025. https://www.asppa-net.org/news/2025/11/the-real-401k-day/
4. Lazonick, William. "Profits Without Prosperity: How Stock Buybacks Manipulate the Market and Leave Most Americans Worse Off." Institute for New Economic Thinking (INET) Working Paper, 2014. https://www.ineteconomics.org/uploads/papers/LAZONICK_William_Profits-without-Prosperity-20140406.pdf
5. Epstein, Gerald A. "Financialization and the World Economy." *Review of Radical Political Economics*, 2005.
6. IBM Annual Reports (1995–2019).
7. Gutiérrez, Germán, & Philippon, Thomas. "Investment-Less Growth: An Empirical Investigation." *NBER Working Paper* No. 22897, 2016 (revised 2017). https://www.nber.org/papers/w22897
8. Citigroup Global Markets. Kapur, Ajay; Macleod, Niall; & Singh, Narendra. "Plutonomy: Buying Luxury, Explaining Global Imbalances." October 16, 2005.
9. "Revisiting Plutonomy: The Rich Getting Richer." Citigroup Global Markets, March 5, 2006. https://www.sourcewatch.org/images/8/86/CITIGROUP-OCTOBER-16-2005-PLUTONOMY-MEMO.pdf
10. ProxyPulse / Broadridge Financial Solutions. Institutional ownership data; reported in CNBC, October 12, 2021.
11. *Fortune*. Fortune 500 Rankings (annual). https://fortune.com/fortune500/
12. Gelles, David. *The Man Who Broke Capitalism: How Jack Welch Gutted the Heartland and Crushed the Soul of Corporate America*. Simon & Schuster, 2022.
13. *Fortune*. "Of the thousands of firms that have come and gone in the Fortune 500 since 1955, only 49 have been on every list." June 4, 2024. https://fortune.com/2024/06/04/companies-on-every-fortune-500-list-since-1955/
14. Harvard Business School Online. "Innovation in Business: What It Is & Why It's So Important." March 8, 2022.

https://online.hbs.edu/blog/post/importance-of-innovation-in-business

15. Dartmouth Tuck School of Business. "Where Did All the Public Companies Go?" September 26, 2024. https://tuck.dartmouth.edu/news/articles/where-did-all-the-public-companies-go
16. National Academies of Sciences, Engineering, and Medicine. *The Role of NIH in Drug Development Innovation and Its Impact on Patient Access: Proceedings of a Workshop*. 2019. https://www.ncbi.nlm.nih.gov/books/NBK553542/
17. Bonvillian, William B., Van Atta, Richard, & Windham, Patrick (eds.). "The DARPA Model for Transformative Technologies." In *The DARPA Model for Transformative Technologies: Perspectives on the U.S. Defense Advanced Research Projects Agency*. Open Book Publishers, 2019. https://books.openedition.org/obp/12212?lang=en
18. Congressional Research Service (CRS). Labonte, Marc. "Systemically Important or 'Too Big to Fail' Financial Institutions." CRS Report R42150. 2013. https://sgp.fas.org/crs/misc/R42150.pdf
19. GAO. "Fiscal Exposures: Federal Insurance and Other Activities That Transfer Risk or Losses to the Government." GAO-19-353. March 27, 2019. https://www.gao.gov/products/gao-19-353
20. Colbert, Alyson. "How Unilever Won Over Shareholders with Its Long-Term Approach." *The Globe and Mail*, October 13, 2017.
21. ICMR (IBS Center for Management Research). "Unilever Under Alan Jope: The Connected 4 Growth (C4G) Strategy." IBS Case Studies. https://www.icmrindia.org/casestudies/catalogue/Business%20Strategy/restructuring-unilever-excerpts.htm
22. Business Roundtable. "Business Roundtable Redefines the Purpose of a Corporation." August 19, 2019. https://www.businessroundtable.org/business-roundtable-redefines-the-purpose-of-a-corporation

Chapter 5 – The Physics of Growth

1. Brooks, Frederick P., Jr. *The Mythical Man-Month: Essays on Software Engineering*. Addison-Wesley, 1975.
2. Gelles, David. *The Man Who Broke Capitalism: How Jack Welch Gutted the Heartland and Crushed the Soul of Corporate America*. Simon & Schuster, 2022.

3. The Henry Ford (museum). "Henry Ford Quotations." thehenryford.org.
4. The Verge. "Here's how much Valve pays its staff." July 13, 2024.
5. Financial Times (Alphaville). "Valve conquered PC gaming. What comes next?" July 3, 2025.
6. Craigslist (Wikipedia). "Craigslist — Operations."
7. Guinness World Records. "Best-Selling Video Game." guinnessworldrecords.com.
8. Mojang Studios (Wikipedia). "Mojang Studios – History."
9. Dunbar, R.I.M. "Neocortex Size as a Constraint on Group Size in Primates." *Journal of Human Evolution* 22, no. 6 (1992): 469–493.
10. Gladwell, Malcolm. *The Tipping Point: How Little Things Can Make a Big Difference*. Little, Brown, 2000.
11. Fried, Jason, & Heinemeier Hansson, David. *ReWork*. Crown Business, 2010.
12. Amazon. "Our Workforce." aboutamazon.com.
13. Statista. "Number of Spotify Employees from 2016 to 2023." statista.com.

Chapter 6 – Why Outcomes Lie

1. Taleb, Nassim Nicholas. *Fooled by Randomness*. Random House, 2001.
2. Spotify Engineering. "Shuffle: Making Random Feel More Human." *Spotify Engineering Blog*. November 13, 2025.
3. Sun, Yaniv, et al. "Latent Structure in Random Sequences Drives Neural and Behavioral Responses." *Proceedings of the National Academy of Sciences* 112, no.11 (2015): 3545–3550.
4. American Mathematical Society. "The Legend of Abraham Wald." *AMS Feature Column*. June 2016.
5. Housel, Morgan. *The Psychology of Money*. Harriman House, 2020.
6. Epstein, David. *Range: Why Generalists Triumph in a Specialized World*. Riverhead Books, 2019.
7. Rother, Mike. *Toyota Kata: Managing People for Improvement, Adaptiveness, and Superior Results*. McGraw-Hill, 2009.
8. Reuters. "Penney Ex-CEO Johnson Losing a Fortune on His Failed Experiment." April 9, 2013.
9. Sutherland, Rory. *Alchemy*. William Morrow, 2019.
10. Grandin, Greg. *Fordlandia: The Rise and Fall of Henry Ford's Forgotten Jungle City*. Metropolitan Books, 2009.

11. Goldgar, Anne. *Tulipmania: Money, Honor, and Knowledge in the Dutch Golden Age*. University of Chicago Press, 2007.
12. Flynn, James R. *What Is Intelligence? Beyond the Flynn Effect*. Cambridge University Press, 2007.
13. Tetlock, Philip E. *Expert Political Judgment: How Good Is It? How Can We Know?* Princeton University Press, 2005.

Chapter 7 – When Metrics Replace Learning

1. Goldratt, Eliyahu M. *The Goal: A Process of Ongoing Improvement*. North River Press, 1984.
2. Huff, Darrell. *How to Lie with Statistics*. W.W. Norton, 1954.
3. Goodhart, Charles A.E. "Problems of Monetary Management: The U.K. Experience." In *Papers in Monetary Economics*. Reserve Bank of Australia, 1975.
4. Lamberg, Juha-Antti, et al. "The Curse of Agility: The Nokia Corporation and the Loss of Market Dominance in Mobile Phones, 2003–2013." *Business History* 63, no. 4 (2021): 574–605. https://doi.org/10.1080/00076791.2019.1593964
5. *The Transformers: The Movie* 20th Anniversary Special Edition DVD. Directed by Nelson Shin. Shout! Factory, 2006.
6. The New York Times. "Shaping a Sears Financial Empire." February 12, 1984.
7. Kimes, Mina. "At Sears, Eddie Lampert's Warring Divisions Model Adds to the Troubles." *Bloomberg Businessweek*. July 11, 2013.
8. Meriam Library, California State University, Chico. "Evaluating Information – Applying the CRAAP Test." September 17, 2010. https://library.csuchico.edu/sites/default/files/craap-test.pdf
9. Kearns, Cristin E., Laura A. Schmidt, and Stanton A. Glantz. "Sugar Industry and Coronary Heart Disease Research: A Historical Analysis of Internal Industry Documents." *JAMA Internal Medicine* 176, no. 11 (2016): 1680–1685. https://doi.org/10.1001/jamainternmed.2016.5394
10. Open Science Collaboration. "Estimating the Reproducibility of Psychological Science." *Science* 349, no. 6251 (2015): aac4716. https://doi.org/10.1126/science.aac4716
11. Bowman, Douglas. "Goodbye, Google." *Stopdesign*. March 20, 2009. https://stopdesign.com/archive/2009/03/20/goodbye-google.html
12. Vacanti, Daniel. *Actionable Agile Metrics for Predictability:*

An Introduction. ActionableAgile Press, 2015.
13. Forsgren, Nicole, Jez Humble, and Gene Kim. *Accelerate: The Science of Lean Software and DevOps*. IT Revolution, 2018.
14. Savage, Sam L. *The Flaw of Averages: Why We Underestimate Risk in the Face of Uncertainty*. Wiley, 2009.
15. Lyor Cohen, Dr. Dre, et al. *The Defiant Ones*, Episode 4. HBO, July 12, 2017.

Chapter 8 – What Gets Used

1. Ross, Lee, David Greene, and Pamela House. "The 'False Consensus Effect': An Egocentric Bias in Social Perception and Attribution Processes." *Journal of Experimental Social Psychology* 13, no. 3 (1977): 279–301. https://doi.org/10.1016/0022-1031(77)90049-X
2. Nielsen Norman Group. "You Are Not the User: The False-Consensus Effect." October 22, 2017.
3. Pendo. *The 2019 Feature Adoption Report*. February 5, 2019.
4. The Standish Group. "Modernization: Clearing a Pathway to Success." 2012.
5. Kohavi, Ron, et al. "Online Randomized Controlled Experiments at Scale." *Nature Human Behaviour*, 2020.
6. Kaiwar, Shikha. Interview. "Saying NO Without Losing Your Job." *Agile Mentors Podcast*, Episode 57.
7. Perri, Melissa. *Escaping the Build Trap: How Effective Product Management Creates Real Value*. O'Reilly Media, 2018.
8. Conway, Melvin E. "How Do Committees Invent?" *Datamation* 14, no. 4 (1968): 28–31.
9. Kniberg, Henrik. *Making Sense of MVP*. Crisp, 2016. Licensed under CC BY-SA 3.0.
10. Cagan, Marty. *INSPIRED: How to Create Tech Products Customers Love*. 2nd ed. Wiley, 2017.
11. Adžić, Gojko. *Impact Mapping: Making a Big Impact with Software Products and Projects*. Provoking Thoughts, 2012.
12. Ogilvy, David. *Confessions of an Advertising Man*. Atheneum, 1963.
13. Rother, Mike. *Toyota Kata: Managing People for Improvement, Adaptiveness, and Superior Results*. McGraw-Hill, 2009.

Chapter 9 – The Cost of Not Knowing

1. Office of Strategic Services. *Simple Sabotage Field Manual:*

Strategic Services (Provisional). Strategic Services Field Manual No. 3. Washington, D.C.: OSS, January 17, 1944. https://www.cia.gov/static/5c875f3ec660e092cf893f60b4a288df/SimpleSabotage.pdf

2. LIFE Magazine. "Throwaway Living: Disposable Items Cut Down Household Chores." August 1, 1955.
3. Watts, Steven. *The People's Tycoon: Henry Ford and the American Century*. Knopf, 2005.
4. Ford Motor Company. "Moving Assembly Line." Ford corporate history. https://corporate.ford.com/articles/history/moving-assembly-line.html
5. Liker, Jeffrey K. *The Toyota Way: 14 Management Principles from the World's Greatest Manufacturer*. McGraw-Hill, 2004.
6. Rother, Mike. *Toyota Kata: Managing People for Improvement, Adaptiveness, and Superior Results*. McGraw-Hill, 2009.
7. Derby, Esther. *7 Rules for Positive, Productive Change: Micro Shifts, Macro Results*. Berrett-Koehler, 2019.
8. Shaxson, Nicholas. *The Finance Curse: How Global Finance Is Making Us All Poorer*. Grove Press, 2018.
9. Tidelift and The New Stack. "How Much Time Do Developers Spend Actually Writing Code?" October 2019. https://www.sonarsource.com/blog/how-much-time-do-developers-spend-actually-writing-code/
10. Harbour Consulting. *The Harbour Report North America 2004*. Troy, MI: Harbour Consulting, 2004.
11. Wayland, Michael. "Toyota's Per-Car Profits Lap Detroit's Big 3 Automakers." *The Detroit News*, February 22, 2015. http://www.detroitnews.com/story/business/autos/2015/02/22/toyotas-per-car-profits-lap-detroit-big-3/23852189/
12. Forsgren, Nicole, Jez Humble, and Gene Kim. *Accelerate: The Science of Lean Software and DevOps*. IT Revolution, 2018.
13. Goldratt, Eliyahu M. *The Goal: A Process of Ongoing Improvement*. North River Press, 1984.

Chapter 10 – Systems, Not People

1. Appelo, Jurgen. *Management 3.0: Leading Agile Developers, Developing Agile Leaders*. Addison-Wesley, 2011.
2. Taylor, Frederick Winslow. *The Principles of Scientific*

Management. Harper & Brothers, 1911.

3. Soper, Spencer. "Fired by Bot at Amazon: 'It's You Against the Machine.'" *Bloomberg*. June 28, 2021.
4. Center for Democracy & Technology. *Warning: Bossware May Be Hazardous to Your Health*. July 29, 2021.
5. Glavin, Paul, Alex Bierman, and Scott Schieman. "Private Eyes, They See Your Every Move: Workplace Surveillance and Worker Well-Being." *Social Currents* 11, no. 4 (2024): 327–345. https://doi.org/10.1177/23294965241228874
6. Conway, Earl, and Paul Batalden. "Like Magic? ('Every System Is Perfectly Designed to Get the Results It Gets.')" Institute for Healthcare Improvement. August 21, 2015.
7. Shook, John. "How to Change a Culture: Lessons from NUMMI." *MIT Sloan Management Review* 51, no. 2 (2010): 63–68.
8. Peter, Laurence J., and Raymond Hull. *The Peter Principle: Why Things Always Go Wrong*. William Morrow, 1969.
9. Cialdini, Robert B. *Influence: The Psychology of Persuasion*. Harper Business, 1984.
10. Beer, Michael, Magnus Finnström, and Derek Schrader. "Why Leadership Training Fails — and What to Do About It." *Harvard Business Review*. October 2016.
11. Harvard Business Publishing. *State of Leadership Development*. 2019.
12. Hogan, Robert, Robert Raskin, and Dan Fazzini. "The Dark Side of Charisma." In *Measures of Leadership*, ed. Kenneth Clark and Miriam Clark. Leadership Library of America, 1990.
13. Keltner, Dacher. *The Power Paradox: How We Gain and Lose Influence*. Penguin Press, 2016.
14. Deloitte. "The Millennial Survey." 2022.
15. SHRM. Meinert, Dori. "Leadership Development Spending Is Up." 2014.
16. SHRM. "Retaining Talent: A Guide to Analyzing and Managing Employee Turnover." 2008.
17. Gallup. "Employee Engagement Sinks to 10-Year Low." January 2025.
18. Harter, J.K., Schmidt, F.L., et al. "The Relationship Between Engagement at Work and Organizational Outcomes." Gallup, 2020. (Q12 Meta-Analysis, 10th edition.)
19. Karasek, Robert A. "Job Demands, Job Decision Latitude, and Mental Strain: Implications for Job Redesign." *Administrative Science Quarterly* 24, no. 2 (1979): 285–308.

20. Ganster, D.C., Fox, M.L., and Dwyer, D.J. "Explaining Employees' Health Care Costs: A Prospective Examination of Stressful Job Demands, Personal Control, and Physiological Reactivity." *Journal of Applied Psychology* 86, no. 5 (2001): 954–964.
21. Rafferty, Alannah E., and Mark A. Griffin. "Dimensions of Transformational Leadership: Conceptual and Empirical Extensions." *The Leadership Quarterly* 15, no. 3 (2004): 329–354. https://doi.org/10.1016/j.leaqua.2004.02.009
22. Forsgren, Nicole, Jez Humble, and Gene Kim. *Accelerate: The Science of Lean Software and DevOps*. IT Revolution, 2018.
23. Sadun, Raffaella. "The C-Suite Skills That Matter Most." *Harvard Business Review*. July–August 2022.
24. Rozovsky, Julia. "The Five Keys to a Successful Google Team." *Google re:Work*. 2015. https://rework.withgoogle.com/intl/en/guides/understanding-team-effectiveness
25. Westrum, Ron. "A Typology of Organisational Cultures." *Quality & Safety in Health Care* 13, suppl. 2 (2004): ii22–ii27.
26. Presidential Commission on the Space Shuttle Challenger Accident. *Report of the Presidential Commission on the Space Shuttle Challenger Accident*. June 6, 1986.
27. National Commission on the BP Deepwater Horizon Oil Spill and Offshore Drilling. *Deep Water: The Gulf Oil Disaster and the Future of Offshore Drilling*. Report to the President. January 2011.
28. Valukas, Anton R. *Report to the Board of Directors of General Motors Company Regarding Ignition Switch Recalls*. Jenner & Block. May 29, 2014.
29. Edmondson, Amy C. *The Fearless Organization: Creating Psychological Safety in the Workplace for Learning, Innovation, and Growth*. Wiley, 2018.
30. Hoffman, Bryce G. *American Icon: Alan Mulally and the Fight to Save Ford Motor Company*. Crown Business, 2012.
31. Deming, W. Edwards. *Out of the Crisis*. MIT Press, 1986.
32. Thorndike, Edward L. *Animal Intelligence: Experimental Studies*. Macmillan, 1911.
33. Skinner, B.F. *The Behavior of Organisms: An Experimental Analysis*. Appleton-Century, 1938.
34. Liker, Jeffrey K. *The Toyota Way: 14 Management Principles from the World's Greatest Manufacturer*.

McGraw-Hill, 2004.
35. Rother, Mike. *Toyota Kata: Managing People for Improvement, Adaptiveness, and Superior Results.* McGraw-Hill, 2009.
36. Stanford Graduate School of Business. "Adobe: Building Momentum by Abandoning Annual Performance Reviews." Case study. 2012.
37. SHRM. "Stack Ranking Ends at Microsoft." November 20, 2013.
38. Buckingham, Marcus, and Ashley Goodall. *Nine Lies About Work: A Freethinking Leader's Guide to the Real World.* Harvard Business Review Press, 2019.
39. Hastings, Reed, and Erin Meyer. *No Rules Rules: Netflix and the Culture of Reinvention.* Penguin Press, 2020.
40. Keng, Cameron. "Employees That Stay in Companies Longer Than 2 Years Get Paid 50% Less." *Forbes.* June 22, 2014.
41. Stumpf, John G. Testimony before the U.S. Senate Committee on Banking, Housing, and Urban Affairs. September 20, 2016.
42. Cram, Jordan. "Scrapped Bonuses, Grew 40%." *Enstoa.* October 15, 2015.
43. Scholtes, Peter R. "Total Quality or Performance Appraisal: Choose One." *National Productivity Review.* 1993.
44. Sinek, Simon. *Leaders Eat Last: Why Some Teams Pull Together and Others Don't.* Portfolio/Penguin, 2014.
45. Costco Wholesale Corporation. Annual Reports / SEC Filings. 2003 and 2024.
46. Kowitt, Beth. "Inside the Secret World of Trader Joe's." *Fortune.* August 23, 2010.
47. Briceño, Eduardo. *The Performance Paradox: How the Best Get Better Without Burnout.* Ballantine Books, 2023.
48. Ford, Henry. *My Life and Work.* Garden City Publishing, 1922.
49. Whitmore, Paul G., and John P. Fry. *Soft Skills: Definition, Behavioral Model Analysis, Training Procedures.* Professional Paper 3-74. U.S. Army Research Institute / Human Resources Research Organization, 1974.

Chapter 11 – Headcount Is Not Strategy

1. Brooks, Frederick P., Jr. *The Mythical Man-Month: Essays on Software Engineering.* Addison-Wesley, 1975.
2. Dunbar, R.I.M. "Neocortex Size as a Constraint on Group Size in Primates." *Journal of Human Evolution*, 1992.

3. Hammerstrom, Michael L. "Size Matters: How Big Should a Military Design Team Be?" Monograph, School of Advanced Military Studies, U.S. Army Command and General Staff College, Fort Leavenworth, KS, 2010.
4. Cassera, Maria A., et al. "Surgical Time Independently Affected by Surgical Team Size." *American Journal of Surgery* 198, no. 2 (2009): 216–222. https://doi.org/10.1016/j.amjsurg.2008.10.016
5. Zheng, Bin, et al. "Operative Length Independently Affected by Surgical Team Size: Data from 2 Canadian Hospitals." *Canadian Journal of Surgery* 55, no. 6 (2012): 371–376. https://doi.org/10.1503/cjs.011311
6. Xu, Rena, et al. "The Teaming Curve: A Longitudinal Study of the Influence of Surgical Team Familiarity on Operative Time." *Annals of Surgery* 258, no. 6 (2013): 953–957. https://doi.org/10.1097/SLA.0b013e3182864ffe
7. Bell, Suzanne T., Shanique G. Brown, Neal B. Outland, and Daniel R. Abben. *Critical Team Composition Issues for Long-Distance and Long-Duration Space Exploration.* NASA Technical Memorandum NASA/TM–2015-218568. February 2015. https://ntrs.nasa.gov/api/citations/20140016953/downloads/20140016953.pdf
8. Rozovsky, Julia. "The Five Keys to a Successful Google Team." Google re:Work. 2015. https://rework.withgoogle.com/guides/understanding-team-effectiveness/
9. Fried, Jason, and David Heinemeier Hansson. *ReWork*. Crown Business, 2010.
10. O'Neil, Cathy. *Weapons of Math Destruction: How Big Data Increases Inequality and Threatens Democracy*. Crown, 2016.
11. Yahoo Finance Australia. "'Just Incredible': Why This Woman's CV Went Viral." November 3, 2021. https://au.finance.yahoo.com/news/just-incredible-why-this-womans-cv-went-viral-011949733.html
12. Weber, Lauren. "Are Workplace Personality Tests Fair?" *The Wall Street Journal*. September 30, 2014.
13. *Persona: The Dark Truth Behind Personality Tests*. Directed by Tim Travers Hawkins. HBO Max, 2021.
14. Schmidt, Frank L., and John E. Hunter. "The Validity and Utility of Selection Methods in Personnel Psychology: Practical and Theoretical Implications of 85 Years of

Research Findings." *Psychological Bulletin* 124, no. 2 (1998): 262–274.

15. Sackett, P. R., Zhang, C., Berry, C. M., and Lievens, F. "Revisiting Meta-Analytic Estimates of Validity in Personnel Selection: Addressing Systematic Overcorrection for Restriction of Range." *Journal of Applied Psychology* 107, no. 11 (2022): 2040–2068.
16. Roth, P. L., Bobko, P., and McFarland, L. "A Meta-Analysis of Work Sample Test Validity: Updating and Integrating Some Classic Literature." *Personnel Psychology* 58, no. 4 (2005): 1009–1037.
17. Willis, Janine, and Alexander Todorov. "First Impressions: Making Up Your Mind After a 100-Ms Exposure to a Face." *Psychological Science* 17, no. 7 (2006): 592–598. https://doi.org/10.1111/j.1467-9280.2006.01750.x
18. Hastings, Reed, and Meyer, Erin. *No Rules Rules: Netflix and the Culture of Reinvention*. Penguin Press, 2020.

Chapter 12 – Designing Habitats for Humans

1. Roethlisberger, Fritz J., and William J. Dickson. *Management and the Worker*. Harvard University Press, 1939.
2. Bryson, Alex, and George MacKerron. "Are You Happy While You Work?" *The Economic Journal* 127, no. 599 (2017): 106–125.
3. Bernstein, Ethan S., and Stephen Turban. "The Impact of the 'Open' Workspace on Human Collaboration." *Philosophical Transactions of the Royal Society B* 373, no. 1753 (2018): 20170239.
4. Küller, R., and T. Laike. "The Impact of Flicker from Fluorescent Lighting on Well-Being, Performance and Physiological Arousal." *Ergonomics* 41, no. 4 (1998): 433–447.
5. Gooley, Joshua J., et al. "Exposure to Room Light before Bedtime Suppresses Melatonin Onset and Shortens Melatonin Duration in Humans." *The Journal of Clinical Endocrinology & Metabolism*, 2011.
6. Seppänen, Olli, William J. Fisk, and Q.H. Lei. "Room Temperature and Productivity in Office Work." Lawrence Berkeley National Laboratory, 2006.
7. Satish, U., et al. "Is CO2 an Indoor Pollutant? Direct Effects of Low-to-Moderate CO2 Concentrations on Human Decision-Making Performance." *Environmental Health*

Perspectives 120, no. 12 (2012): 1671–1677. https://doi.org/10.1289/ehp.1104789

8. Allen, Joseph G., et al. "Associations of Cognitive Function Scores with Carbon Dioxide, Ventilation, and Volatile Organic Compound Exposures in Office Workers." *Environmental Health Perspectives*, 2016.
9. Haraldsson, Guðmundur D., and Jack Kellam. "Going Public: Iceland's Journey to a Shorter Working Week." Alda and Autonomy, June 2021. https://autonomy.work/wp-content/uploads/2021/06/ICELAND_4DW.pdf
10. Lewis, Kyle, Will Stronge, Jack Kellam, and Lukas Kikuchi. "The Results Are In: The UK's Four-Day Week Pilot." Autonomy, February 2023. https://autonomy.work/wp-content/uploads/2023/02/The-results-are-in-The-UKs-four-day-week-pilot.pdf
11. Bloom, Nicholas, James Liang, John Roberts, and Zhichun Jenny Ying. "Does Working from Home Work? Evidence from a Chinese Experiment." *The Quarterly Journal of Economics* 130, no. 1 (2015): 165–218.
12. DeMarco, Tom. *Slack: Getting Past Burnout, Busywork, and the Myth of Total Efficiency*. Broadway Books, 2001.
13. McPherson, Miller, Lynn Smith-Lovin, and James M. Cook. "Birds of a Feather: Homophily in Social Networks." *Annual Review of Sociology* 27 (2001): 415–444.
14. Krebs, Joe. *Agile Kata: Patterns and Practices for Transformative Organizational Agility*. Addison-Wesley Professional, 2024.

Chapter 13 – Behavior Before Belief

1. Pascale, Richard T., Mark Millemann, and Linda Gioja. *Surfing the Edge of Chaos: The Laws of Nature and the New Laws of Business*. Crown Business, 2000.
2. Shook, John. "How to Change a Culture: Lessons from NUMMI." *MIT Sloan Management Review* 51, no. 2 (2010): 63–68.
3. Gates, Timothy J. *Efficacy of Speed Warning Technologies*. Research Report SPR-1748. Michigan Department of Transportation, May 2025.
4. Cialdini, Robert B. *Influence: The Psychology of Persuasion*. Harper Business, 1984.
5. Avery, Jill, and Renée Mauborgne. *Domino's Pizza*. Harvard Business School Case 812-059. 2011.

6. Little, Jason. *Lean Change Management: Innovative Practices for Managing Organizational Change*. Happy Melly Express, 2014.
7. Derby, Esther. *7 Rules for Positive, Productive Change: Micro Shifts, Macro Results*. Berrett-Koehler, 2019.
8. Goldratt, Eliyahu M. *The Goal: A Process of Ongoing Improvement*. North River Press, 1984.
9. Rother, Mike. *Toyota Kata: Managing People for Improvement, Adaptiveness, and Superior Results*. McGraw-Hill, 2009.

Acknowledgment

No book is written alone, even when only one name is on the cover. These ideas were shaped by years of debate, disagreement, shared mistakes, and hard-won insight. I can't always trace the exact moment something clicked, but I know it rarely happened in isolation. If you recognize your thinking in these pages, that's not an accident.

While many people have shaped my thinking over the years, I want to offer a specific acknowledgment to Mike Rother. Not only is his work on scientific thinking a foundational influence on my own, but he personally reviewed the sections referencing his work for accuracy, provided substantive feedback, and offered overall guidance as I finished the book. Thank you, Mike.

Author

Brad Nelson has led teams in manufacturing, software, product, and consulting—a range wide enough to notice that the same dysfunctions repeat across all of them. His work is motivated less by theory than by frustration: frustration with flavor-of-the-week frameworks, confidence mistaken for competence, and activity mistaken for progress.

He lives in Michigan with his family. More at BradleyN.com.

www.ingramcontent.com/pod-product-compliance
Lightning Source LLC
LaVergne TN
LVHW101613210926
848480LV00008B/373
9798994532102